PRO OR CON?
With America at the threshold of a history-making decision on the future of human rights— which will you choose?

"THE EQUAL RIGHTS HANDBOOK IS SPLENDID. It is beautifully and clearly written and organized, and sets out the case for ERA authoritatively, judiciously, and convincingly. . . . It tells the reader how she or he can do what needs to be done to make the much-to-be-desired passage of ERA a reality."
Ashley Montagu

"RIANE EISLER'S HANDBOOK IS A QUICK AND USEFUL REFERENCE when I am faced with fearful, speculative arguments about the effects of the Equal Rights Amendment. With a lawyer's detailed analysis based on the experience of the State ERA's and the report of the Senate Judiciary Committee as well as other responsible sources, she presents the case for the Equal Rights Amendment as a matter of simple justice."
Jean Stapleton

"THE EQUAL RIGHTS HANDBOOK CLEARS UP THE DISTORTIONS levelled against the Equal Rights Amendment and provides essential information on organizing and fund raising to promote equality for women."
Ruth Hinerfeld
President, League of Women Voters

"THE EQUAL RIGHTS HANDBOOK IS AN IMPORTANT TOOL for reaching all the people who need to get their facts clear about ERA."
Valerie Harper

The Equal Rights Amendment
or ERA

Section 1. Equality of rights under the law shall not be denied or abridged by the United States or by any State on account of sex.

Section 2. The Congress shall have the power to enforce, by appropriate legislation, the provisions of this article.

Section 3. This amendment shall take effect two years after the date of ratification.

THE EQUAL RIGHTS HANDBOOK

Riane Tennenhaus Eisler

AVON
PUBLISHERS OF BARD, CAMELOT AND DISCUS BOOKS

*To my daughters Andrea and Loren
and to Elliot and David*

The Equal Rights Handbook

For information address:
toExcel
165 West 95th Street, Suite B-N
New York, NY 10025
www.toExcel.com

Published by toExcel, a division of Kaleidoscope Software, Inc.
Marca registrada
toExcel
New York, NY

ISBN: 1-58348-025-0

Library of Congress Catalog Card Number: 98-88856

Printed in the United States of America

0 9 8 7 6 5 4 3 2 1

ACKNOWLEDGMENTS

Wherever possible, specific acknowledgments have been made in the text or notes. Here I would like to thank all those who have contributed their time and efforts to this book. These include David Abrams of ERAmerica, Edi Kjos of the American Association of University Women, Winona McGuire of the Business and Professional Womens Club, Anita Miller of the California Commission on the Status of Women, Madeline Mixer of the U.S. Department of Labor Women's Bureau, Geri Sherwood of NOW, and countless others such as Dr. Jessie Bernard, Georgia Franklin, Shirley Heitland, Erica Jong, Fay Kanin, Karen Kaplowitz, Dr. Ashley Montagu, Judge Roberta Ralph, Mark Siegel, Elizabeth Snyder, and Gloria Steinem, all of whose input have contributed to this book. I also want to express my gratitude to Cindy Sprague for her always cheerful and efficient work. Above all, I want to thank two most remarkable men, Elliot Sanders and David Loye, without whom this book could not have been written.

Contents

• CONTENTS

Introduction

This book comes out of three kinds of experience and knowledge. One kind is what I have personally learned as a woman—as a daughter and mother, as a wife and single parent, and, perhaps most forcefully, as an organizer and writer working for women's rights. A second kind of expertise this book offers is what I have learned as a lawyer—for the questions raised by the Equal Rights Amendment are, above all else, questions of *law*. Finally, this book is the outgrowth not only of my own personal and legal experience but of that of colleagues and friends all across the country who have also studied the meaning and implications of ERA—of the knowledge and experience of literally thousands of women and men who have either directly or indirectly contributed their ideas and work.

The Equal Rights Handbook is designed to be useful whether ERA passes or fails by March 22, 1979. While it centers on ERA as a practical and pressing means to an end, this book at all times focuses on the goal of sexual democracy. By this I mean not simply sexual equality in any kind of society, good or bad, and certainly not sexual sameness, or unisex. What I envision is a society that offers real equality of opportunity and meaningful choices for both women and men—a democratic society in the full sense of the word.

One of my major aims is to provide the facts to set at rest the false fears about the Equal Rights Amendment. To this end, in part 1, chapters 1, 2, and 3 examine and clarify the misunderstandings—and lies—about ERA. Chapter 4 probes beneath the surface to unearth the real forces that today so violently and viciously are fighting equality. Chapter 5 answers the question: will ERA deprive women of their privileges? Here, as throughout the book, the emphasis is on ERA's economic implications for women—the dollars and cents realities. In Chapter 6 the charge that sex equality will destroy marriage and the family is examined and exploded. Throughout, the concern

is with the practical implications of the passage—or failure—of ERA in our daily lives.

Part 2 is a strategy guide and action checklist, an arsenal
of information and actions designed to arm women and
men to fight for ratification of ERA by the handful of
still needed states. Chapters 7, 8, and 9 offer political,
economic, and educational strategies and tactics. They coordinate what has been tried and has worked with new and
fresh ideas, combining my own thoughts with the suggestions of hundreds of national leaders and experts
surveyed to this end. Chapter 10 takes a close look at the
anti-ERA backers, as well as the thousands of well-
established and respected national organizations of all types
supporting ERA.

Chapter 11 provides information and expertise for ERA
interpretation and implementation, particularly during the
critical two-year study and adjustment period immediately
following passage. Chapter 12 sets forth ten goals to work
for on the "grass roots" level. Chapter 13 includes recommendations of specific means for reaching these goals,
focusing on how ERA should be properly interpreted and
enforced—and by whom—for the benefit of us all. Chapter
14 projects how to *continue* the fight for equality and
democracy, whether ERA passes or fails this time.

One final personal statement: Lawyers are trained to
write briefs, arguments to convince others of the justice of
a cause. In a sense, this book is such a brief. It is not,
however, a legal brief, because my concerns go far beyond
law to the broader social, political, and economic implications of ERA, and beyond these to its meaning, its immediate and personal impact on all of us—women and
men.

As a lawyer, I have written other briefs, including one
submitted to the Supreme Court of the United States in
1970, before the Reed case was decided.[1] Unsuccessfully,
it urged that, over one hundred years after the Fourteenth
Amendment was passed, women be included under that
amendment's classification of "persons."[2] I consider this
book the most important brief I have ever written or that
I shall ever write, as a lawyer, as a woman, as the mother
of two teenage daughters, as a person who—to para-
phrase Robert Kennedy's words—sees things not only as
they are, but as they can be, as they must be, if we are
to go forward into a better world.[3]

Part 1

The Equal Rights Amendment: Democracy at the Turning Point

1

At the Crossroads

To most Americans today the idea of equality—racial,
religious, political—sounds just and right. But say *sex
equality*, say that men *and women* should have the equal
protection of our laws, say Equal Rights Amendment, and
a lot of these people will squirm. There was a time when
people used to feel the same way if someone challenged
the "divine" right of kings or the "God-given" institution
of slavery. These too were familiar, "normal" facts of life,
and then, as now, people were told that change was
dangerous and wrong—that what *is*, is right. Yet, if these
assumptions had not been challenged—if what *is* had not
been replaced by what is *right*—America would not be a
democracy today.

The history of Western democracy is the record of these
challenges. It is the story of historic crossroads, of crucial
juncture points when the fate of democracy hung in the
balance. Today we are at such a historic juncture point as
we decide the fate of the Equal Rights Amendment to our
constitution, or as it is widely known, ERA. It is a crossroads that is perhaps more critical than any has ever been
in the past, and the issue of sex equality will determine the
direction we take. The analogy is that of a railroad branching switch. If the train is not switched onto the right track,
the result can be disaster.

That is not to say that the passage of ERA will, of itself,
guarantee us a bright future. The Equal Rights Amendment
is, after all, only intended to insure that "equality of rights
under the law shall not be denied or abridged by the United
States or by any state on account of sex." But the failure
to affirm this principle at this crucial time by incorporating
it in the American Constitution—the document that, even
more than the Magna Carta, has come to stand as a symbol and a bastion of the right of individuals to freedom

3

from unwarranted government controls—can only lead us into a nightmarish future.

This may seem to some an extreme vision. But much of human history is the story of choices leading to consequences that were not generally foreseen. Consider, for example, what would have happened if the Fourteenth Amendment, created to give blacks equal rights, had not passed. The Fourteenth was adopted in 1868 as a response to the so-called "Black Codes," which were passed by Southern states after the Civil War in an attempt to reduce freed blacks again to virtual slavery. The Fourteenth Amendment was designed to prohibit state governments from enacting such laws, and its specific intent was to protect blacks. But out of the prohibition that no state shall "deprive any person of life, liberty, or property without due process of law; nor deny to any person within its jurisdiction the equal protection of the laws" have come some of the most important decisions in American legal history, decisions that have profoundly affected us all, regardless of race.

The Power of the Constitution

Under the Fourteenth Amendment, courts have had to grant poor people the right to be represented by attorneys. It has prevented gerrymandering and poll taxes. It has extended our right not to have to testify against ourselves in state courts. Government administrative agencies—those mushrooming bureaucracies that today poke and pry into every aspect of our lives—have been held at bay by the "due process" and "equal protection" mandate of the Fourteenth Amendment. Perhaps most important has been this amendment's protection against unwarranted state and police interference with our rights to freedom of expression and assembly—rights without which no democratic society can survive.

In short—and this was certainly not foreseen at the time of its passage—the Fourteenth Amendment has become synonymous with protection from government tyranny and discrimination for both blacks and whites.

And yet, even with all the benefits that American society has derived from the Fourteenth Amendment, it was not until 1971 and the case of *Reed v. Reed*[1] that the United

States Supreme Court finally extended its protection to women. Not until this decade—and then only halfheartedly, in a situation in which the sexual discrimination was blatant and wholly arbitrary—did the men who sit on the highest court of our land extend the definition of "persons" protected by this amendment to include women. It took over one hundred years for them to do this. And in later cases these justices have demonstrated—and actually stated[2]—that they will *not* vigorously prohibit sexual discrimination until there is a political mandate for equal rights. Hence, the urgent constitutional need for the Equal Rights Amendment!

But the political and social impact of the passage—or failure—of ERA is not "just" a woman's issue. The American dream, and parts of the American reality, are founded on the principle that the power of the government, the state, must be monitored and defined. Our war of independence was fought to resist taxation without representation because the king, the government, was passing arbitrary laws in which we had no voice. Our constitution, our system of checks and balances, our Bill of Rights, establish this principle, and throughout our history this constitutional protection has been expanded and adapted to meet changing conditions and needs. We cannot afford to interrupt this expansion, to halt this progress at this critical moment in time. We cannot and we must not, but that is precisely what will happen if the Equal Rights Amendment is not passed before the crucial 1980s set in. If this tradition of individual rights and their constitutional protection is not now reaffirmed and reinforced, these rights will shrink and dwindle until they no longer exist.

Fear and Future Shock

It is the recognition of this fact by the extreme right and— less openly—by the extreme left that lies behind the organized opposition to ERA. The campaign that has been mounted against the Equal Rights Amendment is based not on real issues but on skillfully merchandized falsehoods, on half-truths and deliberate lies. It is a campaign to whip up and exploit people's hatreds and fears, as did McCarthy in the fifties before he was exposed and rejected by the American people, as did Hitler, who was not exposed or rejected in time. It is a campaign that appeals not to reason but to emotionality, and it has been successful in diverting us from the real—and urgent—issues we must face as we move into what futurologists call the postindustrial age.

We are in a period of future shock, in the throes of a massive technological, economic, and social shift that is potentially even more disruptive than the transformation of the basically religious, agrarian, Jeffersonian country we once were into the secular, industrial, urbanized America we are today. Naturally, we are concerned and frightened, and this is particularly so for women who are literally being forced out of their traditional place in the home into the "man's world" from which they have for so long been barred. The opponents of ERA are fanning these fears with misinformation and deliberate lies. But it is not ERA that will harm women. It is its failure, at a time when we are inexorably moving toward a redefinition of male and female roles—a redefinition that has already started, that we are all experiencing already in our lives.

The Real Issue

The spurious controversy about ERA is diverting our attention from the real issue, which is how to facilitate this transition of women and men into postindustrial society and make sure that it moves in the right direction. This false controversy blinds us so that we do not even see what is actually happening to women as they are moving, en masse, from their jobs as workers in the home to workers in the labor force. Most women are entering the labor market only on its lower rungs. And, contrary to both our expectations and a lot of poor information, the percentage of women in high-prestige and highly paid jobs has *not* increased. In most occupations it has remained constant—and in some it is *shrinking*. Women, like blacks, are still last to be hired, and first to be fired. Further, and most significantly, a close look at the labor market reveals that, despite all our laws prohibiting sex-based employment discrimination, women are still everywhere being "kept in their place" by the simple, time-tested device of segregating women and men into "separate but equal" "men's" and "women's" jobs. It is a labor market in which men earn 75 percent more than women.[8] On top of all this, it is a labor market beset by unprecedented and seemingly chronic problems, by unemployment and underemployment, by inflation, by scarcities and stagnation, by a growing depersonalization and dehumanization.[4]

Not only the American economy but also the American family and the institution of marriage are undergoing fundamental changes. With the divorce rate now seemingly "stabilized" at one million families per year[5] and sequential marriage rapidly becoming the norm, a new family form is gaining wide currency. Some, living under this new system, call it "the man." Others, observing it, have called it the government's new patriarchal family. It is a family system composed largely of displaced homemakers, many of them former middle-class women for whom there is just *no* place in the labor market. They are a new class of poor, these divorced women and their children, forced by inadequate spousal and child support awards into the Kafkaesque world of the welfare recipient, a world administered by armies of bureaucrats enforcing complex, rigorous, and depersonalized rules.

Before us—and to some extent already with us—is the spectre of expanding governments and corporations, technological mind controls, overpopulation, shrinking natural resources and mounting ecological problems. But at the same time, the new world we are entering offers opportunities unprecedented in human history. We are living in an age of scientific and technological miracles, of proliferating knowledge, of expanding consciousness, of exploding creativity. It is a moment in history, when, no matter how desperately we may want to cling to them, our traditional institutions and values are in a state of flux. It is a frightening time. But it is also a hopeful time, when fundamental social change is still possible.

The Crucial Choice

It is also a very confusing time, in which it is all too easy to get lost in the hurly-burly of events and contradictory "expertise." But underlying the desire for ERA is a very basic historical equation which we should never for a minute fail to keep in mind.

We are today at a branching point. To return to the analogy of history as a train moving forward in time, on one side of that branching is the old track, the patriarchal track that has for so long limited and constrained us all—both women and men. This is the track *we choose* if ERA and all it represents should fail. At the end of this track, with its premise that we are evil and that we must be controlled, lies the society predicted by futurologists unless we change our course: the authoritarian nightmares foreseen by Orwell in *1984* and by Huxley in *Brave New World.*[6]

The other track leads to the humanistic vision in which Eve is no longer the cause of the Fall, a society in which women and men are no longer embattled in dominant-dominated roles. This is the track *we choose* if ERA passes and is properly implemented. At the end of this track lies the better, more hopeful world which, at this point in history, we can still create.

2

Sex Equality:
Facts and Fancies

According to its opponents, the Equal Rights Amendment is a radically dangerous, highly complex, and sinisterly un-American piece of legislation. Actually, the proposed Twenty-seventh amendment to the Constitution would only prohibit our state and federal governments—through their laws, ordinances, court decisions, and administrative rulings—from discriminating against people on the basis of sex. If that is un-American, so is the Declaration of Independence, the Constitution, and the Bill of Rights.

Nevertheless, ERA has run into fierce opposition. Though many Americans are aware of this fact, dangerously few realize what is at stake if ERA fails or why its progress has been blocked. After a fifty-year struggle for an equal rights amendment, by 1972 everything seemed at last clear sailing ahead. In that year, the U.S. Congress approved ERA. In the following year, thirty states ratified. Who could ask for more? But then ERA began to run into one roadblock after another as states failed to ratify—and even tried to rescind earlier ratification.

The Stop ERA drive began in the Southern states. For a while, few took it seriously, for the charges leveled against ERA were obviously false and often patently ridiculous. *But gradually it has become apparent that the Equal Rights Amendment may not be ratified by the necessary thirty-eight American states by the deadline of March 22, 1979.*

This is the reality we have to deal with today, and, to understand it, we have to examine the opposition to ERA: what it is, where it comes from, and why it exists.

The thirteen "fancies" that follow cover the charges most commonly leveled against ERA and give the facts to set them straight.

Fancy 1
ERA Is a Radically Dangerous New Thing

In fact, the Equal Rights Amendment was first introduced before Congress in 1923. Perhaps no other proposed constitutional amendment has been studied so thoroughly. In the forty-nine years prior to congressional approval, ERA was the subject of extensive congressional hearings. It was debated before the House Judiciary Committee in 1948 and before the Senate Judiciary Committee in 1956. It was reported on favorably by the Senate Judiciary Committee in the Eightieth, Eighty-first, Eighty-second, Eighty-third, Eighty-fourth, Eighty-sixth, Eighty-seventh, and Eighty-eighth Congresses. In the Senate Judiciary Committee hearings of May 1970, forty-two witnesses were heard, and the hearing record was eight hundred pages long.[1] When further hearings were conducted in September of that year, another twenty-five witnesses appeared, and the record was 430 pages long.[2]

In 1971, the Senate Judiciary Subcommittee on Constitutional Amendments held three days of hearings during which some of the nation's leading constitutional law experts testified at length. Afterward ERA was again extensively debated on the floor of both Houses, before its final passage on March 22, 1972.[3]

The *Congressional Record* including these hearings and debates as well as the majority report of the Senate Judiciary Committee of the Ninety-second Congress contain what is known as the "legislative history" of the ERA.[4] Here, in great detail, can be found its sponsors' and proponents' statements about how the proposed amendment is intended to affect family, employment, military, criminal, and other areas of existing law. Under our rules of judicial interpretation, courts may not substitute their judgment regarding desirable social policies for that of our elected representatives, so it is to this very detailed expression of legislative intent that the courts will look in deciding how ERA is to be interpreted. Nevertheless, opponents of ERA continue to make irresponsible statements about the consequences of its ratification, resulting in confusion and apprehension about the amendment's impact.

Fancy 2
ERA Will Unleash the Homosexual Menace, Wreak Havoc with Rape and Adultery Laws, and Force American Mothers into Combat Duty

"Who will profit from ERA?" asks the *Phyllis Schlafly Report*. "The homosexuals and the lesbians," answers the *Phyllis Schlafly Report*. "Women will lose, families will lose, society will lose—but certain militant minority pressure groups will profit, and that is where the money and the push come from."[5]

It sounds—and is—ridiculous. But it seems to work. In Florida, ERA had finally mustered the necessary 21 senators for passage. But when it came to vote in April 1977, ERA lost, 21 to 19. Two longtime supporters announced that they had changed their minds. One of these, Senator Ralph Poston of Miami, cited "the homosexual issue" as a reason for his last-minute switch.[6]

When ERA came up for a vote in Georgia, another legislator, Representative Dorsey Matthews, said ERA would "lower our ladies down to the level of men, legalize homosexual marriages, and create havoc in the prisons by preventing segregation of the sexes." Representative N.W. Larsen asked, "If a mother's draft number comes up, can you imagine the men staying home, scrubbing floors, and watching the war news while the child learns a new version of 'When Momma Comes Marching Home Again'?" And former governor Marvin Griffin related the yarn of a man who supposedly said, "Let the women who want to be in the Army go down and join, but don't take my Effie—she's all I got. If they draft Effie, who the hell will cut the stovewood?"[7]

It all sounds like a high school parody, but in Georgia, too, ERA did not pass.

"Co-ed Wards Tied to Rapes at Psychiatric Unit" and "Woman Cabby Raped," headlines the *Schlafly Report* in January 1977.[8] The message—by innuendo—is that ERA and rape go hand in hand. Not only that, but, as quoted by Senator Ervin, "According to the *Yale Law Journal*, adultery laws also contain sex discriminatory provisions which would be impermissible under the Equal Rights Amendment." The message—here achieved by Ervin through the simple expedient of removing the important qualifying phrase "*a few*" from the beginning of the actual *Yale Law Journal* statement—is that ERA and adultery go hand in hand [9]

There is, of course, nothing in ERA that would promote adultery or deprive women from legal protection against rape. Neither is there any merit to the contention that ERA will legalize homosexual marriage. Or to the Schlafly claim that ERA would "interfere with the right of parents to have their children taught by teachers who respect the moral law."

"Surely," writes Schlafly, "the right of parents to control the education of their children is a right of a higher order than any alleged right of, say, the two college-educated lesbian members of the Symbionese Liberation Army to teach our young people "[10]

In fact, whether homosexuals have a legal right to be hired in our schools is an issue that will be adjudicated under the Fourteenth Amendment, *not* the ERA. The same holds true for the legitimization of homosexual marriages. The only legislative intent of ERA is to right legal inequities that discriminate against persons of different—*not* the same—sex. Whether laws discriminate against homosexuals and lesbians is therefore *not* within the purview of ERA, a point which was explicitly made by Senator Birch Bayh about homosexual marriage during the congressional debates of March 21, 1972.

The Equal Rights Amendment would not prohibit a state from saying that the institution of marriage would be prohibited to men partners. It would not prohibit a state from saying the institution of marriage would be prohibited from two women partners. All it says is that if a state legislature makes a judgement that it is wrong for a man to marry a man, then it must say it is wrong for a woman to marry a woman —or if a state says it is wrong for a woman to marry a woman, then it must say that it is wrong for a man to marry a man[11] (emphasis added).

But homosexual marriage, rape, and adultery are sensational issues. They get publicity and media coverage. And they also touch people's prejudices, anxieties, and fears. As we so painfully learned from Watergate, people will fall for the lies of those in positions of authority—at least for a time. The great advantage of lies is that they can be catchy, cute, and oversimplified—and they are often much more "easily understandable" than the truth.

A case in point is the issue of ERA and the military, which anti-ERA propagandists have distorted with a few catch phrases designed to give the impression that, should ERA pass, not only will every woman be drafted, but she will also be forced to fight.

The real and much more complex situation is, first, that we do not have a draft anymore: Our armed forces are now entirely voluntary. In the second place, should there ever again be a draft, the ERA legislative history makes it crystal clear that the anti-ERA propaganda is completely unfounded.

"The ERA will not require that all women serve in the military any more than all men are now required to serve," the Senate Judiciary Committee Report states unequivocally.

> Those women who are physically or mentally unqualified, or who are exempt because of their responsibilities (e.g., certain public officials; or those with dependents) will not have to serve, just as men who are unqualified or exempt do not serve today. *Thus the fear that mothers will be conscripted from their children into military service if the Equal Rights Amendment is ratified is totally and completely unfounded*[12] (emphasis added).

The legislative intent pertaining to women and combat duty is equally explicit. In the debate of March 21, 1972, Senator Birch Bayh went to great pains to show just how farfetched that fear really is. He pointed out that in 1971, the year of the last draft, "5 percent of the eligible males in the country were inducted," and that "less than 1 percent of the eligible males in the whole country were ever assigned to a combat unit. It might be fair to say that this is about the same risk women would be subjected to," he went on, "except it would be fairer to assume that the sex-neutral standards that would be established in the Armed Forces on the basis of physical competence would exclude an even greater percentage of women because of the ordinary physical standards required, such as pushups, chins, running, and other physical and combat characteristics that are necessary for any member of the armed services." Senator Bayh also pointed out, that "just as 85 percent of those who are now in the armed services and who are men are not assigned to combat duties, so the commander would not need to send a woman into the front trenches if he felt that it would not be in the best interest of the combat unit to make such an assignment."[13]

All this is part of the *Congressional Record*, accessible to anyone interested in ERA. Nevertheless, anti-ERA propagandists continue to cite only such "official" pronouncements as former Senator Ervin's statements, purportedly (more about this later) from the *Yale Law Journal*. The Equal Rights Amendment "will require a radical restructuring of the military's view of women" and "will require the military to see women as it sees men," claims Ervin in his statement.[14]

Again, the Senator left out the qualifying phrases that in the original source give the passages *an entirely different meaning!* The *Yale Law Journal* article goes on to characterize the military's view of women as "a narrow and stereotypical one" which the ERA will change by requiring it to "see women as it sees men—as a diverse group of individuals, married and unmarried, with and without children, possessing or desiring to acquire many different skills, and performing many varied kinds of jobs."[15]

From Ervin's half-truths, anti-ERA propagandists like Schlafly then make an astonishing but nevertheless effective quantum leap. "ERA," they assert, "will require a 50-50 coed army and navy," which is why it is backed by "those who want to weaken our military defenses."[16]

By such means ERA is effectively associated with irrelevant fears. Even if the facts are later corrected, the impression that has been made—and remains in the unconscious mind—is that ERA is synonymous with some kind of national disaster.

To those with memories longer than the day before yesterday, this may seem reminiscent of the big lie tactics of Hitler and his rightist American progeny. The similarity between then and now, as we shall see, is no coincidence.

Fancy 3
ERA Will Force Everybody to Treat
Men and Women the Same

Either unknown or unclear to many people is the fact that the Equal Rights Amendment will affect only what is known as governmental action—that is, federal, state, or municipal interference with constitutional rights. It will *not* directly regulate personal or social relationships or even relationships between individuals and private businesses.

The American Constitution, and particularly our Bill of Rights, was specifically designed to protect us from unreasonable and arbitrary governmental interference. The basis for this protection is the principle that there are inalienable human rights which are not and cannot be surrendered by "free men" when they enter into the social contract implied in our system of government—a system which is to be "for and by the people." It is only because the equal protection clauses of the Fifth and Fourteenth Amendments have *not* been judicially construed to include women that we still have so many laws, regulations, and other governmental practices that arbitrarily differentiate between people on the basis of sexual stereotypes.

What ERA would do is to require that the legal rights, opportunities, and obligations of both men and women be based on individual characteristics, circumstances, and needs. It would *not*, as ERA critics claim, "make men and women all the same." For example, special restrictions on the property rights of married women would be unconstitutional. So would criminal penalties that are the heavier for female offenders than for male offenders committing the same crime (and vice versa). Inheritance rights of widows would be the same as those for widowers, and state laws that now require more complex and costly probate procedures for widows would also have to be changed.[17]

In the words of the majority report on ERA of the Senate Judiciary Committee: "The general principles on which the Equal Rights Amendment rests are simple and well understood. Essentially, the amendment requires that the federal government treat each person, male and female, as an individual."[18]

This majority report of the Senate Judiciary Committee contains the views and arguments of the ERA's congressional sponsors and proponents during the session of Congress when the proposed amendment was passed. As such, it is the most important and definitive statement of the ERA's legislative history, on which the courts must rely in interpreting it.[19]

Fancy 4
ERA Will Nullify All Existing
Laws Protecting Women

The majority report of the Senate Judiciary Committee is very explicit on this point: "It is expected that those laws which are discriminatory and restrictive will be stricken entirely. . . . On the other hand, *it is expected that those laws which provide a meaningful protection would be expanded to include both men and women*"[20] (emphasis added).

"There can be no question that the courts, upon holding a statute unconstitutional, can expand the scope of the statute to cure its legal infirmity," the majority report goes on. "The Supreme Court has applied this principle in many cases. In 1880, for example, the court extended a state statute limiting jury service to 'electors' to include blacks enfranchised by the Fourteenth and Fifteenth Amendments rather than striking it down. . . . In 1950, the court held that state laws restricting access to state institutions of higher education on the basis of sex were unconstitutional; it expanded the laws so that black students had equal access."[21]

Despite this clear statement of legislative intent, ERA opponents continue to misinform—and terrorize—women with warnings that if ERA is ratified they will lose what legal protection they have.

Fancy 5
ERA Will Destroy State Labor
Laws Protecting Women

There has been much publicity given to the contention that passage of ERA will deprive employed women of protection from state laws regulating their hours, wages, and working conditions.

A great deal of attention was devoted to this issue during the congressional hearings and debates. Professor Norman Dorsen, one of the leading pro-ERA witnesses, presented a complete analysis of what he called the "crazy quilt of existing state protective laws."[22] He also clearly stated his legal opinion of how the ERA would affect the situation: namely, that *"the ERA would result in the general extension of certain benefits to men that now are available only to women"*[23] (emphasis added).

The following testimony is worth quoting at length because it debunks so much of the anti-ERA propaganda:

First, there is no consensus (among the states) on what is needed protection for either men or women, and much of the legislation, instead of providing solutions to the real problems of women workers, actually "protects" them out of jobs they are perfectly capable of fulfilling. Second, under Title VII of the Civil Rights Act of 1964, much state legislation of this type is being invalidated and will be of no long-term importance. Third, such laws that confer genuine benefits can and should be extended to men under the Equal Rights Amendment.

For instance, while women are allowed chairs for rest periods in forty-five states, they are given job security for maternity leaves of absence in *no* state and maternity benefits under temporary disability insurance in only two states. . . . In the benefit areas most people would consider most important—a minimum wage and a day of rest—men do receive substantial protection already. Only seven states have minimum wage laws for women only, but twenty-nine states, plus the District of Columbia and Puerto Rico, cover both men and women. More important, the federal minimum wage law covers both men and women at *higher* rates than all state laws except one (Alaska).

In contrast, maximum hour laws are a major area where men are not covered. Thirty-eight states cover women only, and three states cover men and women. Since the Supreme Court has upheld the validity of maximum hour legislation for both sexes since 1941, one can only suspect that unions have not pushed for

maximum hour legislation, given their success in obtaining nationwide minimum wage laws for both sexes.
This analysis would give credence to the EEOC and
federal court decisions which have concluded that hour
laws have been used as an excuse to keep women out
of better-paying jobs.[24]

Professor Dorsen then analyzed the laws of eighteen
states prohibiting employees from assigning night work to
women and those of six states prohibiting women from
working for certain periods before and after childbirth.

Women in fact do night work all the time. Nurses,
telephone operators, airline reservationists, and scrub
women have not been protected from night work.
Pregnant women, too, often choose to work right up
to the birth date. Who ever heard of a housewife
being allowed time off from her housework and small
children just because she was pregnant?
Weight laws also are of doubtful protection for
women. There are only four states with weight limits
applicable to all jobs, and these limits are set so low
that, if literally applied, they would prohibit women
from doing any serious labor, including carrying an
unborn child. In the remaining few states with weight
limits, they apply only to certain industries. In New
York, for instance, women are "protected" from lifting weights only in the foundries. The theory, apparently, is that some mystical essence in foundry
weight lifting will injure women, while lifting the same
weight in other industries will not. Possibly it is the
male workers in foundries who are being protected—
from job competition.
Thus, when all of the state laws applying only to
women are examined closely, it becomes clear that
they do not provide a coherent system of meaningful
protection. Nor do they deal with the real problem
for women—exploitation by being underpaid and
funneled into the lowest-paying, most menial jobs of
our society. State labor laws have never dealt with this
problem. Furthermore, the premise that real protection can be based on legislating by sex is fallacious.
In short, analysis of state laws that apply exclusively

to women does not establish that they protect women in the one area clearly applicable to women only—maternity benefits and job security; they are ineffective in dealing with the exploitation of women through lower pay than men; and they are used to discriminate against women in job, promotion, and higher-pay opportunities. They do not furnish a reliable basis for opposition to the Equal Rights Amendment.[25]

So we see that state protective laws have actually *hindered* women in the labor market far more than they have helped. However, for many women confined to the nonunionized bottom layers of our work force, even the most minimal and laxly enforced protective regulations seem better than none at all. It is not surprising, then, that women, so disproportionately represented in the most marginal and least rewarding occupations, should be frightened of an Equal Rights Amendment they have been misled to believe will deprive them of the little protection they have.

But the truth is that, long before the ERA was passed by Congress, and even before the recent women's liberation movement had begun to gather momentum, many of these protective labor laws were already being dismantled. Under Title VII of the Civil Rights Act of 1964, both court decisions and Equal Employment Opportunity Commission rulings have found that most state laws prohibiting night work, employment in particular occupations, overtime, and weight lifting on the basis of sex, in practice discriminated against women.

Even at the time of Professor Dorsen's testimony before Congress in 1971, twenty-two states and the District of Columbia had already repealed or substantially weakened protective labor laws concerning women. "It appears," he noted, "that the opponents of the amendment are trying to erect bridges which were crossed five years ago, when Title VII went into effect."[26] Today, over half a decade later, the opponents of the ERA are still using the same ploy, and the media and some public officials—who either know, or should know, better—are echoing their charges that the ERA must be stopped to protect women in the labor force.

This is being done in the face of the most explicit statements possible of a legislative intent to *protect* women. "The purpose of the Amendment is not to cut down benefits accorded to only one sex, but to extend them to both sexes," testified Senator Birch Bayh, one of the ERA's congressional sponsors.[27] "Where the laws confer a benefit, privilege, or obligation of citizenship," testified Representative Martha Griffiths, another congressional sponsor, "such would be extended to the other sex. . . . Thus, such laws would not be rendered unconstitutional, but would be extended to apply to both sexes by operation of the amendment."[28]

Fancy 6
ERA Will End Alimony, Deprive Wives of Economic Support, and Take Away Little Old Ladies' Social Security

"Wives will lose the right to support and a home!" This drastic charge is made in a snappy little cartoon booklet chockful of such slogans. The publication is issued by Phyllis Schlafly's "Eagle Forum," an organization that claims to be "the alternative to women's lib," formed "so we can work together to preserve religious and family virtues."[29]

As the legislative history definitively indicates, the fact is the ERA will certainly *not* deprive women of the right to support and a home. On the contrary, it is intended to strengthen the position of the American homemaker and to improve the financial position of both married and divorced women.

Senator Bayh flatly stated that "the passage of the Equal Rights Amendment would not make alimony unconstitutional."[30] He pointed out that the statutes of one-third of our states have already extended that right to men and that there is "no reason to not make men eligible for alimony."[31] In his testimony before the Senate Judiciary Committee, Professor Dorsen pointed out that this was the same approach as that taken by the model marriage and divorce legislation proposed by the Commissioners on Uniform State Laws in 1970. "The Uniform Marriage and Divorce Act eliminates definitions based on sex and substitutes those based on function," he said. "This is what the Equal Rights Amendment is intended to do. *By passing it, we will help insure more genuine protection for those who really need it and end the many injustices women still face*"[32] (emphasis added).

The Senate Judiciary Committee's final report on the ERA went further: "Where one spouse is the primary wage earner and the other runs the home, the wage earner would have a duty to support the spouse who stays home in compensation for the performance of his or her duties."[33] Citing this language as clear and unequivocal evidence of legislative intent, Professor Joan M. Krauskopf commented: "The report defines the duty of support under the ERA in functional terms based on factors such as each spouse's earning power, current resources, and nonmonetary contributions to the family's welfare. *Law would have to recognize homemaking tasks as legally a contribution to the family*"[34] (emphasis added).

In January of 1972 the Presidentially appointed Citizens' Advisory Council on the Status of Women prepared a report entitled *The Equal Rights Amendment and Alimony and Child Support Laws.*[35] This publication was specifically designed finally to squelch the claim that the proposed amendment will "weaken men's obligation to support the family and, therefore, weaken the family."

> *Far from resulting in diminution of support rights for women and children, the Equal Rights Amendment could very well result in greater rights.* A case could be made under the Equal Rights Amendment that courts must require divorced spouses to contribute in a fashion that would not leave the spouse with the children in a worse financial situation than the other spouse.
>
> The belief that alimony laws permitting alimony to wives would be invalidated by the courts rather than extended to men is not supported by any legal authority or the legislative history. The legislative history clearly indicates the intent of the proponents in Congress to extend alimony to men in those states now limiting alimony to women. Furthermore, in view of judges' preoccupation with keeping women from becoming public charges, it seems almost certain, should a State Legislature fail to extend to men a law limiting alimony to women, that a judge would extend the law

to men rather than invalidate it. If any judge should invalidate the law, it is clear that legislatures' concern for keeping women from becoming charges would be sufficient to enact a new law applying equally to men and women.

In summary, the Equal Rights Amendment would not deprive women of any enforceable rights of support, and it would not weaken the father's obligation to support the family[36] (emphasis added).

Surely nothing could be clearer or more definite. But we are faced with an opposition that either refuses to read this extensive documentation contrary to its fantasies—or reads and tries to shove the truth under the rug. So on and on, ad nauseam, the anti-ERA propagandists continue to frighten America's homemakers with catchy slogans and cute cartoons, hammering in the same disproved and discredited points: Women will lose not only alimony but support rights during marriage as well!

"Wives and husbands will be *equally* responsible financially for the family," is Eagle Forum's caption over the picture of a distressed homemaker whose dog, husband, and child are all accosting her for money.[37] This, when the majority report of the Senate Judiciary Committee explicitly states: *"It is clear that the Amendment would not require both a husband and wife to contribute identical amounts of money to a marriage"*[38] (emphasis added).

"The support obligation of each spouse would be defined in functional terms based, for example, on each spouse's earning power, current resources, and nonmonetary contributions to the family welfare," continues the majority report on ERA, citing with approval the report of the New York City Bar Association.[39]

Where one spouse is the primary wage earner and the other runs the home, the wage earner would have a duty to support the spouse who stays at home in compensation for the performance of her or his duties. Although courts still probably would be reluctant to interfere in the allocation of support between husband and wife in an ongoing marriage, upon the dissolution of marriage, both husbands and wives would be entitled to fairer treatment on the basis of individual circumstances rather than sex.[40]

Another panel of an Eagle Forum anti-ERA cartoon book shows an old woman crying over her husband's grave. "I can't collect my homemaker's social security benefits because they were special to women only and ERA wiped out all benefits special to one sex,"[41] she wails. Again, this is pure fabrication. In fact, the Equal Rights Amendment would simply require that widowers of covered women workers receive the same social security benefits as those formerly provided only to widows of covered men workers, which is exactly what the United States Supreme Court has already done in the case of *Califano v. Goldfarb!*[42]

When the single poorest segment in our society are widowed, single, and divorced women of over the age of sixty-five, it is unconscionable to fraudulently frighten these women into opposing an amendment which can actually improve, *not* worsen, their situation. Under current social security laws, the homemaker has no protection in her own right. A divorced homemaker gets no coverage if she has been married less than twenty years. These are some of the real issues that old women all over this country have to cry about. The fear that the equal protection principle of ERA will deprive them of widow's social security benefits is unfounded: the United States Supreme Court has already resolved that issue by extending equal social security protection to widowers.[43]

3

More Facts and Fancies

Fancy 7
ERA Is Unnecessary Because the Fourteenth Amendment Already Takes Care of Sex Equality

Some ERA opponents argue that a special amendment dealing with sex-based discrimination is unnecessary because the Fourteenth Amendment already prohibits all discriminatory state laws and practices. This view has been rejected by most of the nation's leading constitutional experts. They point out that although the Fourteenth Amendment has always provided that "any person" shall be guaranteed the equal protection of our laws, it took one hundred years to persuade the Supreme Court to include women in that classification—and then the Court was persuaded only in the case of *Reed v. Reed*, in which the sexual discrimination was so blatant that it was found totally arbitrary and wholly unrelated to the objectives of the state statute involved.[1]

At best, the conclusion of these experts, as Senator Birch Bayh put it, has been that, "if given enough time, the Court would eventually hold that the Equal Protection Clause of the Fourteenth Amendment demands the kind of equality between sexes which the Equal Rights Amendment would guarantee, but that the process would take far too long."[2]

Others like Stanford University's Mary C. Dunlap are less optimistic. They point out that, without the ERA, women may never be given full rights under the law. This conclusion is based on an analysis of constitutional history and—even in those cases where women's rights have been upheld—the underlying paternalism and ambivalence of the men who sit on the Supreme Court. Dunlap's assessment is that the "conflicting state of constitutional law concerning women has now reached a stage of virtual irresolvability which will continue until and unless the Equal Rights Amendment is ratified."[8]

Even after *Reed v. Reed* finally (albeit tenuously) accorded women the protection of the Fourteenth Amendment, the U.S. Supreme Court has continued to vacillate. In *Forbush v. Wallace*, decided a year after *Reed*, the U.S. Supreme Court *refused* to hold that a legal classification based on sex violated the Fourteenth Amendment.[4] The Court held that an Alabama law requiring a woman to give up her own name and assume her husband's had a "rational" basis because it facilitated easy record keeping! Moreover, in this case, the Court refused to apply to legal classifications based on *sex* the stricter test used in civil rights cases in which *race* is involved: namely, that "suspect classifications" receive "strict scrutiny" and require proof of a "compelling state interest" to justify the discrimination.[5]

The kind of legal hairsplitting and fence-straddling this issue faces—unless resolved by ERA—is shown by the 1973 case of *Frontiero v. Richardson*. The Supreme Court's decision struck down an Air Force rule which denied dependent benefits to husbands of female officers while granting them to wives of male officers. Four of the justices based their decision on the grounds that classifications based on sex, like those based on race, are "inherently suspect" and therefore subject to the strict "compelling state interest" test. However, three of the justices—the Nixon appointees, Chief Justice Warren Burger and Justices Lewis Powell and Harry Blackmun—felt that applying the stricter "compelling state interest" test rather than the mild "rational basis" test was a political and not a constitutional issue. And they criticized their fellow judges who had based their decision on the stricter test, arguing that they should have waited to see if the ERA was ratified first![6]

Fancy 8
Justice Will Somehow Prevail in the Supreme Court

Since 1973, the Supreme Court has actually been moving backward. One of the biggest setbacks to any hope that the Supreme Court would act vigorously to prohibit sexual discrimination came in the case of *Kahn v. Shevin*. Justice William O. Douglas wrote the majority opinion holding that a Florida law allowing a property tax exemption to widows, but not to widowers, had a reasonable basis and was therefore not unconstitutional.[7]

Renowned for his contributions to the field of civil rights, Justice Douglas had only the day before written an extensive opinion in a case which involved discrimination based on race. There he applied the strict "compelling state interest" test and asserted that the Fourteenth Amendment required individuals to be judged on the basis of their individual capacities.[8] But the very next day, in the *Kahn* case, Justice Douglas not only applied the permissive "rational-basis test": he further based his decision, not on individual capacities and circumstances, but on stereotypes about sex. He reasoned that, since widows generally have more financial difficulties than widowers, the statutory classification was not arbitrary. Yet, as the dissent pointed out, the desired result of giving poor widows a tax break could have been achieved just as easily and more equitably by granting the exemption to both widows and widowers whose incomes fell below a certain level. There was no real, compelling reason for the statute's sexual discrimination.[9]

To his credit, Justice Douglas apparently later changed his position. In *Geduldig v. Aiello*, which challenged the constitutionality of excluding medical expenses and work loss due to normal pregnancies from state disability insurance systems, Douglas joined Justices William Brennan and Thurgood Marshall in a strong dissent, severely criticizing the majority for "singling out for less favorable treatment a gender-linked disability peculiar to women."[10] The dissenting opinion argued that the majority was in error for applying the rational-basis test and that "classifications based upon sex, like classifications based upon race, alienage, or national origin, are inherently suspect and must therefore be subjected to strict judicial scrutiny."[11] But Douglas is no longer a member of the Court, leaving Brennan and Marshall as an even smaller pro-equality minority. Therefore, for justice to prevail in the Supreme Court, the "political mandate" of ERA is clearly crucial.

Fancy 9
OK, Then Maybe Logic Will Prevail
in the Supreme Court

In *Geduldig v. Aiello*, despite the dissent's charge that the Court was using a "double standard," Justices Stewart, Burger, White, Blackmun, Powell and Rehnquist concluded that economic consideration justified the exclusion of pregnancy from California's disability insurance coverage and that, in any case, there was no real sexual discrimination involved:

> There is no evidence on the record that the selection of the risks insured by the program worked to discriminate against any definable group or class in terms of the aggregate risk protection derived by that group or class from the program. There is no risk from which men are protected and women are not. Likewise, there is no risk from which women are protected and men are not. The appellee simply contends that, although she has received insurance protection equivalent to that provided all other participating employees, she has suffered discrimination because she encountered a risk that was outside the program's protection.[12]

When presented with this kind of reasoning, the constitutional analyst must face some startling questions. Does the Supreme Court really mean to say that, since only those people who can get pregnant ("the risk that was outside the program's protection") are excluded from disability coverage, there is no sexual discrimination involved? Surely, the Supreme Court of the United States is aware that only women can get pregnant. Then what could the Court have had in mind when, in upholding the pregnancy conclusion, it said, "There is no risk from which men are protected and women are not. Likewise, there is no risk from which women are protected and men are not"? And how could the Court conclude that "there is no evidence on the record that the selection of the risks insured by the program worked to discriminate against any definable group or class"?

How can pregnancy constitutionally be singled out for

exclusion under the California statute when, as Justice Brennan points out in the dissent, "voluntary disabilities such as cosmetic surgery or sterilization" are not and "compensation is paid for virtually all disabling conditions without regard to cost, voluntariness, uniqueness, predictability, or normalcy of the disability"?

As *Geduldig v. Aiello* demonstrates, sex-based discrimination is so deeply ingrained in patriarchal society that it is frequently not even perceived as such. The resistance to any fundamental alteration of this reality, not only by our courts but by society at large, is extremely deep-rooted. And, like the criticisms aimed at the ERA, this resistance is grounded in emotion, not in logic or fact.

It is important to note that *Geduldig v. Aiello, Kahn v. Shevin,* and *Frontiero v. Richardson* were all decided by the U.S. Supreme Court *after* Congress had approved the ERA, during a period in which new cases or statutes seeking to correct sex-based discrimination were being reported almost daily in the press. There was no longer any real debate among legal scholars as to whether the ERA should be adopted, and professional journals were already focusing on its legislative history and its potential impact on existing laws. Nevertheless, the majority of the men sitting on the highest court of our land were still wavering and hedging and waiting for a "clear mandate" before granting women and men constitutional protection against sex-based discrimination.

Fancy 10
If Good Old Senator Ervin Is Against ERA, It Must Be Bad

Former Senator Sam Ervin is frequently cited as an authority when attacks on the Equal Rights Amendment are made. His minority views, in which he quotes extensively from an article that appeared in the *Yale Law Journal* in 1971,[13] are also reported in the Ninety-second Congress's *Senate Report on the Equal Rights Amendment*.[14] However, because his views were rejected and the amendment was passed by the Ninety-second Congress, Ervin's arguments in opposition are *not* indicative of Congressional intent and consequently have no real bearing on the ERA's judicial interpretation. This crucial fact is never mentioned by anti-ERA propagandists citing Ervin or in media coverage of their attacks. Neither is the shocking fact—painstakingly documented by the Citizens' Advisory Council on the Status of Women—that the Ervin minority report is full of distortions, misinformation, and misquotations.

> Senator Ervin's minority views, stated in the Senate Report on the Equal Rights Amendment (Report No. 92-689, 92nd Congress 2nd Session), have been widely used to discredit the Amendment by misinterpretation of its meaning. Senator Ervin supports his interpretation by excerpts from the April 1971 *Yale Law Journal* (Vol. 80, No. 5, pp. 871-985), which has been widely used by the proponents of the Amendment. Many of these excerpts mislead the reader by quoting only parts of sentences and sections of paragraphs. . . . He lifts phrases from context, thus distorting, misconstruing, or even inverting their meaning; he omits conditions, specifications, and clarifications that greatly alter the area of significance of the effect under discussion.[15]

These are the words of the Honorable Jacqueline G. Gutwillig, 1972 Chairperson of the Presidentially appointed Citizens' Advisory Council on the Status of Women. They are from the foreword to a report specifically commissioned and published by the council to clarify the confusion about the Equal Rights Amendment created by Senator Ervin.

This report enumerates thirty-one specific instances of distortion and outright misquotation in Senator Ervin's much quoted statements concerning the effect ERA will have on women and the draft, adultery laws, rape, alimony, working conditions, and other major issues affecting women.

For example, Senator Ervin quotes the *Yale Law Journal* as follows: "The ERA would require invalidation of laws specially designed to protect women from being forced into prostitution." The impression that the ERA would be harmful—to women and to society—is created by the stratagem of simply leaving out the following from the *Yale Law Journal* quotation: "Congress could easily bring the Mann Act into conformity with the Equal Rights Amendment by substituting the word 'person' for the words 'woman or girl' in the statute."[16]

On the subject of protective labor laws, the *Yale Law Journal* article cited by the Senator reads as follows: "In general, labor legislation which confers clear benefits upon women would be extended to men. Laws which are plainly exclusionary would be invalidated. Laws which restrict or regulate working conditions would probably be invalidated, leaving the process of general or functional regulation to the legislatures." Senator Ervin's quotation, however, selected only the following half sentence: "Laws which restrict or regulate working conditions would probably be invalidated."[17]

The Citizens' Advisory report on Ervin came out in 1972. Not only has the Ervin ERA analysis been fully discredited: as noted, its views, being the opposition minority report, do *not* reflect the intent of the pro-ERA legislators who passed the ERA and would therefore have no bearing on how the amendment should be interpreted. Notwithstanding all of this, in April 1977 the *Phyllis Schlafly Report* still circulated the former senator's arguments as the authoritative case against ERA.[18]

Fancy 11
ERA Is a Gigantic Grab for Federal Power—and Higher Taxes

"Certain federal payrollers see in ERA a tremendous opportunity to increase their jurisdiction, their control over our lives and activities, the size of their staffs, and the amount of tax money they have available to spend," writes Schlafly. Why and how is this going to happen? "Section 2 of the ERA is a gigantic grab for power in the hands of the government," answers Schlafly in one of her monthly newsletters. She then goes on the explain how "the advocates of more spending and control by the government are desperate to find new sources of revenue. If they can get all the women out of their homes and into paid employment, this will give the government an enormous new source of additional tax revenue."[19]

Here Schlafly's claim is that *both* the state and federal governments are in on this "gigantic grab for power," and "this is why so much federal and state money is now being spent to push passage of ERA before too many people find out about its danger."[20]

In other newsletters, her tack has been that, on the contrary, one of the greatest ERA dangers is that Section 2 of the ERA will let the federal government rob states of their legitimate powers. This "states rights" attack—ironically espoused by both the John Birch Society and the American Communist Party—claims that out of Section 2 of ERA will come federal invasions of privacy, freedom of religion, marriage, divorce, and even recreation.[21]

What is this sinister Section 2? It says that "The Congress shall have the power to enforce, by appropriate legislation, the provisions of this article." The wording is taken from Section 5 of the Fourteenth Amendment. The same types of implementation provisions are found in the Thirteenth, Fifteenth, Nineteenth, Twenty-third, Twenty-fourth, and Twenty-fifth Amendments. *Section 2 is simply the customary enforcement clause of constitutional amendments and does not transfer any authority from the state legislatures to the Congress.*[22]

Much has been made by anti-ERA propagandists of the fact that an earlier ERA version of Section 2 had a different wording: "Congress *and the several States* shall have the power, *within their respective jurisdictions*, to enforce this article by appropriate legislation." But the reason for the deletion of the italized words, as Schlafly's own newsletter reveals, was that they would have created confusion.[23] The change in language was made because of objections to the original unconventional language by constitutional authorities. Their recommendation was that Section 2 be changed to conform to the customary language found in prior constitutional amendments, which is what Congress then did.[24]

The legislative history of the ERA makes this very clear, in both the Senate Judiciary Committee majority report and the Congressional debates.

On October 12, 1971, ERA sponsor Griffiths specifically answered the question of whether the deletion of the word "state" in Section 2 would weaken or deny states the right to legislate in this area. The answer: "ERA does not interfere with the states' right to make laws."[25]

The testimony of Professor Paul A. Freund, the leading constitutional authority in opposition to the original wording of Section 2, is also part of the *Congressional Record*:

Let me point out a serious deficiency in the proposed amendment. Its enforcement clause gives legislative authority to Congress and the States "within their respective jurisdictions." This is a more restrictive authorization to Congress than is to be found in any other amendment, including the Fourteenth. If the new amendment is deemed to supersede the Fourteenth concerning equal rights with respect to sex, Congress will be left with less power than it now possesses to make the guarantee effective.[26]

Some opponents have claimed that the fact that the Sixteenth Amendment has no Section 2 "proves" that Section 2 of the ERA will transfer legislative power from the states to the federal Congress. But no enforcement clause was needed with the Sixteenth Amendment because the amendment itself was a grant of power to Congress, in this case to collect income tax "without apportionment among the several States," the essential point being that no mention of the states was necessary to preserve their power to enact their own income tax laws.[27]

Again, all this is part of the *Congressional Record*, readily available to anyone seriously studying the ERA. Yet anti-ERA propagandists still cite only former Senator Ervin's irrelevant minority report, claiming Section 2 is a dangerous federal power grab. As the Citizens' Advisory Council on the Status of Women points out, although Ervin proposed a number of other amendments to ERA, he never proposed one to Section 2. Further, the two other leading congressional opponents of ERA, Representatives Emanuel Celler and Charles Wiggins, also failed to raise any objections to Section 2 at the time it was debated before its passage by Congress. [28]

Fancy 12
No Real Woman Wants ERA, Only the Misfits, the Militants, and the Freaks

A stock-in-trade of anti-ERA propagandists is the image that the only women who support ERA are sexually frustrated, hysterical, unfeminine creatures: "a handful of militants," "lesbians," "old bags," "a tiny minority of women's libbers," "a handful of misfits and troublemakers."[29]

The fact is that ERA is supported by every major women's organization in the nation, from the YWCA to the American Association of University Women, from the League of Women Voters to the Ladies Auxiliary of Veterans of Foreign Wars, from the B'nai B'rith to the General Federation of Women's Clubs. It is supported by Mrs. Rosalynn Carter and Mrs. Betty Ford as well as by their husbands, President Carter and former President Ford. Lady Bird Johnson has publicly announced her ERA support, and so have the Girl Scouts of America.

The fact is that just about every major political and civic organization endorsed ERA. Both the Democratic Party's and the Republican Party's National Committees have come out in favor of ERA. In 1973, the AFL-CIO, with 116 affiliated unions and about fourteen million members, pledged its support to ERA. So have the United Auto Workers, the United Mine Workers, the International Brotherhood of Teamsters, and the National Education Association, as well as the American Bar Association.

Among religious groups supporting ERA are the United Presbyterian Church, the United Methodist Church Women's Division, the Unitarian-Universalist Association, the National Council of Jewish Women, the California Council of Churches, and the National Coalition of American Nuns.

In short, the ERA has the grass roots support of American women—and men—of all religious, and political persuasions, from every walk of life.

Again, all this information is public and available to anyone seriously interested in ERA. Yet, in the face of all these facts and figures—of which they are surely aware—anti-ERA propagandists persist in caricaturing ERA supporters as a mere handful of radical and mannish weirdos.

Fancy 13
ERA Will Lead Us to Communism

In February 1974, Dr. Fred Schwartz, founder and director of the Christian Anti-Communist Crusade, conducted an "Anti-Subversive Seminar" in Chicago. "The highlight of the weekend," reported *Atlantic Monthly*, "was the Sunday night appearance of Phyllis Schlafly, an apostle of many conservative causes, who is barnstorming the country and urging state legislatures not to ratify the Equal Rights

Amendment to the Constitution. Her argument, shared by Schwartz, was that the amendment represents an attack on the family and therefore fits into the Communist strategy to take over the country!"[30]

This, too, is the claim circulated by the John Birch Society. In urging members to "plunge in and help to relegate this subversive proposal to early and complete oblivion," leader John Welch claimed that "the Communists" were "pouring money into a behind-the-scenes effort to get ERA enacted."[31] And the John Birch Society's HOT DOGs (Humanitarians Opposed to Degrading Our Girls) have actually accused governors' commissions supporting ERA of being under Communist influence.[32]

In fact, the Communist Party USA went on record as early as 1970 against ERA, claiming—as do its rightist opponents—that the amendment would actually harm women, particularly in the area of protective labor legislation.[33] In a 1976 article in the official Communist journal *Political Affairs*, entitled "Why We Oppose ERA," party spokeswoman Carmen Ristorucci was still decrying all kinds of possible dangers to women from ERA, and also this problem for the party: "The danger involved in this oversimplified concept of equality [the ERA's "mandate for equality"] is that it moves away from the reality of women's status under capitalism, and divorces the struggle of women from the basic conflict between the working class and the ruling class."[34] Even as late as 1977—after great pressure from women party members and in the face of ERA support by almost every American labor union—the Communist party position was still at best one of equivocation. Now, under the guise of perhaps finally accepting an ERA that now looked like it might never be ratified, the party was passing leaflets out at the International Women's Year Convention, warning women, in the words of Alva Buxenbaum (Co-chairperson of the Social and Economic Rights Department of the Communist Party USA), of the "dangers of misuse of the ERA and the need for legal protections"[35]—a contradictory, confusing, and actually nonsensical statement, hardly calculated to win the amendment any support.

The Communist Party's position on ERA is a matter of public record of which anti-ERA propagandists are surely aware. But guilt by association is an effective technique.

And red-baiting, as the cases of Nixon, McCarthy, and Hitler demonstrate, brings results. For Nixon "anti-communism" launched his political career in a vicious campaign against Helen Gahagen Douglas. For McCarthy "communist infiltration" meant character assassination and a meteoric rise to national prominence. For Hitler the "dirty bolshevik reds" provided the propaganda fuel that first discredited and finally toppled the democratic Weimar Republic.

These tactics are particularly effective in times of social change and unrest when extremists from the right and left correctly perceive their chance to gain control. This is precisely where the organized opposition to ERA stems from. It has been attacked by such ultra-right-wing organizations as the John Birch Society and the American Independent Party, by a few ultraconservative Catholic groups, by the wealthy Mormon Church, the Ku Klux Klan, and the Daughters of the American Revolution, and by Schlafly's Stop ERA Eagle Forum as well as by the extremist left wing, particularly—as we have noted—the American Communist Party.

The most regressive elements of American society have banded together to stop the ERA. They have mounted an organized campaign based on misinformation and on guilt by association. Their methods may not be new, but this does not make them any less sinister and dangerous. Be it against Jews, blacks, homosexuals, "dirty commies" or "imperialist pigs," prejudice and fear whip up people's emotions and divert them from the real issues.

The question that then arises is why. What is it about an amendment that would give women equal protection under our laws that arouses such violent opposition? And why is it that the opposition comes from both the extreme right and left?

4

Why the Opposition?

Ours is a country based on the principle of legal equality for all. Therefore, there are no logical arguments against ERA. Its opposition is by necessity based on irrationality. Relying on emotion, prejudice, misinformation, and fear, this opposition is buttressed on the patriarchal past, on patriarchal authority, on the "givens" that what is, should be and that was, is not to be changed—certainly not by women, whose "natural" role is to be passive and to let men "take care" not only of them but of all that is important.

In men, this opposition appeals to the reluctance of those who hold power—no matter how illusory or costly that power may be—to give any of it up. In women, it speaks to the fear of those who do not have power: the underlying fear of what will happen if they assert, or even express, their needs.

It is this fear of patriarchal authority that the Stop ERA forces have zeroed in on and exploited with alarming success. They have correctly perceived that their greatest ally is women's fear. It is not only the fear of displeasing the powerful father—whether familial or divine. It is the even more fundamental fear of no longer being valuable if they cannot successfully meet the "feminine expectations," the most basic of which is that they be pretty and good and not cause any trouble.

These expectations we learn from birth, and they are so deeply etched into our unconscious minds that even when we know they are there and realize that they serve to suppress us, they still do not dissappear.

The Voices of Fear

For grown women to listen to grown men tell them that equality is not for their own good would seem ludicrous, if it were not for the power of this fear. It is a fear rooted in the very core of the "feminine" self-image, a fear linked with the very real dependency of every woman born into patriarchal society: the dread that the mere challenge of the existing patriarchal order, no matter how rational or humane that challenge may be, is an act of defiance that will be punished—and, indeed, always is punished, if not by external forces, then by the full force of the patriarchal voices within us.

These patriarchal voices are not only the voices of bearded old men. They are the voices of frightened women who, throughout millennia of patriarchal history, have seen and experienced how powerless they really are.

So if Southern senators orate about the "flowerhood of women" and the protection of all that is "good and pure," the real message behind that pre–Civil War rhetoric is "You better knuckle under or else." If the Mormon Church tells us that the subservience of woman is the will of God, the understood message is "You better not even aspire to equality, or the God of our forefathers will strike you down."

It would be much simpler if the Stop ERA people said this directly. But, of course, they do not. The veiled threat and the implied menace are much more effective. They cannot be directly confronted or challenged, and all one is left with is uncertainty, confusion, and fear. Instead, the Stop ERA people fan these fears, awakening old anxieties and also creating some that are new. In so doing, they use the world's oldest propaganda tactic, which has worked from the time of Nero to Hitler: the telling of lies.

These lies serve other functions as well. They distort and discredit. They appeal to emotion against reason. They ridicule women's human aspirations, and they obscure the real issues. Above all, they undermine confidence because there is in all of us—no matter how "liberated"—that thoroughly socialized part predisposed, indeed preprogrammed, to believe that equality between the sexes is wrong. Rationally, we know better. But, emotionally, the old voices still hold sway. So no matter how preposterous, patently false, and even ridiculous the fabrications about ERA may be, they still do their damage.

The fact it is not easy to exorcise these old, patriarchal voices with reason does not mean it cannot be done. But it is not enough to combat fancy only with current facts. We have to examine the real nature of our society and of our laws. We have to understand how we view maleness and femaleness and how this has been reflected in our pre-ERA laws.

Self-Fulfilling Prophecies

Laws enforce what anthropologists call myths. These social scientists use the word myth not to designate something that is true or false but to describe the value system of a society, what the members of a particular society are told to believe is the truth.[1]

There are three major myths about women in the laws of Western society. The first is the myth of women as property. This view, and the laws that enforce it, define women as the private property of men, usually their fathers' or husbands'. The second myth defines women as incompetent dependents, as relational creatures who have no legal or actual identity except as they relate to men, usually their fathers or husbands. The third and most recent myth—the one the ERA would enforce—is an egalitarian myth. It regards women not as the property of men or as merely relational to them, but as full-fledged human beings in their own right.

Laws and myths interact and form self-fulfilling and self-perpetuating prophecies. Law is, of course, backed up by socialization, the process by which we are taught to conform, to be law-abiding citizens. And law is ultimately backed up by force. But laws not only set the outer limits of what is considered socially acceptable behavior at a particular time and place. They also tell us how we should relate to other people and how we should view ourselves.

How laws and myths form self-fulfilling prophecies is shown by slavery. People who were slaves in this country were legally defined as property.[2] The slave laws enforced the myth that blacks are inferior to whites, not fully human, and therefore incapable of freedom in a civilized society.

As time went on, more and more voices were raised against this myth, and many of them were women's voices, for the abolitionist movement marked the first time in American history when women organized in any numbers. But what happened then? As a response to the argument that blacks were capable of freedom—*if* they were only given the opportunity—new laws were passed in most Southern states making it illegal for anyone, black or white, to teach a slave to read or write![3]

With women, as with blacks, laws have also perpetuated myths of female dependency and inferiority. They have effectively forced women to become in fact dependent and inferior, through the self-fulfilling prophecy of law.

Women as Property

We have in our tradition two cultural strains: the Hebrew and the Greek heritages. They have come together largely thanks to St. Paul (who was a Greek Jew) into what we call the Judeo-Christian tradition. While these two heritages have some very beautiful elements, it is also true that the view of certain people as property was central to both early Hebrew and Greek society.

The Bible illustrates this in many passages, including the Tenth Commandment: "Thou shalt not covet thy neighbor's house, thou shalt not covet thy neighbor's wife, nor his manservant, nor his maidservant, nor his ox, nor his ass, nor anything that is thy neighbor's."[4]

"Maidservant" and "manservant" were euphemisms for slave. Exodus 20 and 21 provide some of the rules for slavery. If the slave was a Hebrew male, he was to be indentured for only seven years. However, no such protection was afforded Hebrew women. On the contrary, if a master gave a woman to a slave and she bore the slave a child, when the male slave was given his freedom, the woman and child had to remain behind with the master.[5]

But women were property whether they were slaves, maidservants, daughters, or wives. When Jacob fell in love with Rachel, wanting to acquire her for his wife, he went to Rachel's father Laban. He said, "I want your daughter for my wife." And the crafty Laban said, "OK, you can have my daughter for your wife if you work for me for seven years." So Jacob worked for seven years. And at the end of seven years Laban gave him a daughter. But he gave him Leah because she was the older, and poor Jacob had to work another seven years to get the woman he had really bargained for. This is not just Jacob's hard luck story. It is a story that again illustrates the Hebraic patriarchal view of women as property.[6]

Women did not fare better in Athenian society, the model for our democratic heritage. An Athenian woman had no legal status or protection except as the ward of her nearest male relative—father, husband, or brother. She could not vote, hold office, own property, or conduct any legal business.[7]

The underlying assumption that women are not capable of freedom in a civilized society was succinctly expressed by Aristotle: "The general law is that there are naturally ruling elements and elements naturally ruled. The rule of free men over slaves is one such rule, and the rule of male over female is another."[8]

Saint Paul then tied the ancient Hebrew and Greek views about women into a hard knot: "Wives, submit yourselves to your own husbands as unto the Lord. For the husband is the head of the wife, even as Christ is the head of the church."[9]

Centuries later, in English common law—which was adopted by most of the colonies in this country—the theme of women as the private property of men was still embodied and perpetuated in marriage. Not only were all women (single or married) denied most of the civil rights accorded men, such as the vote and the right to serve in government: when a woman married she—and her property—came under the husband's full control. A married woman could neither sue or be sued. She could not enter into a binding contract. She could not manage property, even property she had brought into the marriage. She could not work outside the home without her husband's permission, and her husband had the right to her earnings. The husband also had the right to what the prominent legal commentator Sir William Blackstone (1723–1780) called domestic chastisement—which simply meant that, if a wife did not do her husband's bidding, he could legally beat her.[10]

"By marriage," Blackstone said, "the husband and wife are one person in law; that is, the very being or legal existence of the woman is suspended during the marriage, or at least is incorporated and consolidated into that of the husband, under whose wing, protection, and cover she performs everything. . . . and her condition during her marriage is called her coverture."[11]

In nineteenth-century America women were still effectively barred—by law, social convention, and the inaccessibility of the requisite education and skills—from every economically advantageous job and profession. Their situation was like that of commodities: forced to compete with one another in a marriage market in which the luckiest and prettiest got the well-to-do men. If a woman married a man who could not or would not provide for her, she would have to hold down two jobs. She would have to work as a wife and mother inside her home, but she would also have to get a second job on the outside, usually as a domestic servant or a spinner or weaver or sewing machine operator in a sweatshop or factory—or, if she was really fortunate, as a teacher or clerk. If she did not marry, not only was her economic situation (indeed, her survival) precarious: but socially, she was the subject of pity, opprobrium, and shame. So with all its legal disabilities, with its "civil death," marriage was still the best—and often, the only—job opening for women. Hence, the vast majority of American women were governed by laws that clearly and unequivocally placed them under both the physical and financial domination of men.

It was these laws governing the status of married women that Southern states had in earlier years used as models for their slave laws, and it was also during the years before the Civil War, when slavery was under attack, that the first legal reform of the status of married women got under way.

The first feminists saw the similarity between the status of married women and that of slaves, and they fought to gain freedom and equality for both. They fought against the opposition of an entire society, and, ironically—as is the case with the ERA today—often against other women themselves. As Ernestine Rose, an outstanding nineteenth-century orator and proponent of the first petition for a married women's property law in New York State, put it in describing her difficulties collecting signatures: "After a good deal of trouble, I obtained five signatures. Some of the ladies said the gentlemen would laugh at them; others, that they had rights enough; and the men said the women had too many rights already. . . . I continued sending petitions with increased numbers of signatures until 1848 and 49 when the Legislature enacted the law which granted woman the right to keep what was her own. But no sooner did it become legal than all the women said: 'O! that is right! We ought always to have had that!' "[12]

Women as Incompetent Dependents

By the middle of the nineteenth century most American states had passed new laws relieving women from some of their major legal shackles. These Married Women Acts marked a major shift in both American legal and social history. From now on, the main theme or myth enforced and perpetuated by our laws would be that of women not as equals nor as property but as relational creatures who, like children and incompetents, were not to be trusted on their own.

It was this theme that the Supreme Court of the United States voiced when *Muller v. Oregon* was decided in 1908:

> History discloses the fact that woman has always been dependent upon man. He established his control at the outset by superior physical strength, and this control in various forms, with diminishing intensity, has continued to the present. Though limitations upon personal and contractual rights may be removed by legislation, there is that in their disposition (women) and habits of life which will operate against a full assertion of those rights.[18]

While wife beating was now no longer legal, and in most states husbands no longer had the legal right to wages their wives earned outside the home, the property rights of women were still extremely curtailed. In the majority of American states, which had derived their legal system from the English common law, a married man's earnings were —and still are—his own. Even in the few states where the earnings of either spouse were considered the community property of the marriage, the husband legally had the exclusive management and control of the community property.

A woman's very identity was—and still is—defined by law in terms of her relationship to a man. When she was born, she took her father's surname, and when she married, she got to trade it in for that of her husband. Under the law of most states, the husband was—and in many states still is—explicitly defined as the head of the household and as the spouse who had the exclusive right to choose the marital domicile, a decision by which the wife was legally required to abide.

Women as Equal Beings

By the turn of the century the struggle for women's rights became increasingly focused on one central issue: the vote. Suffragist leaders working for the Nineteenth Amendment tried to persuade the American public and its representatives to recognize the inconsistency, indeed the conflict, between the American ideal of equality and freedom for all and the disenfranchisement of one-half of our population. Again, they were met by virulent opposition (often from other women) and by ridicule, opprobrium, and at times even violence.

When the suffragists finally prevailed in 1920—fifty years after the Fifteenth Amendment gave the vote to male former slaves—America adopted its first major piece of legislation embodying the view that women are full-fledged equal beings.

There had been other egalitarian laws before the Nineteenth Amendment to the Constitution. During the First World War when the war emergency required women workers to do "men's work," laws were passed requiring equal pay for equal work. But—just as happened later when these same laws were passed again during the Second World War—as soon as the war emergency was over and women were sent "back to the homes where they belonged," these laws were no longer enforced.[14]

And even, a half century after the Nineteenth Amendment was finally passed, when the prohibition against discrimination on the basis of sex was included in Title VII of the Civil Rights Act of 1964, it was put in as a joke, by a Southern senator who thought such a "ridiculous" provision would ensure the defeat of the whole bill.[15]

The Great Gray Supermyth

Today much of the opposition to ERA, the constitutional amendment that would prohibit government discrimination on the basis of sex, again comes from the South. It does *not* come from the New South of President Carter, but from the Old Southern Guard, the same South that a century earlier fought against the emancipation of slaves. Their allies are the most reactionary political and religious elements of American society: the John Birch Society, the American Independent Party, the Daughters of the American Revolution, the Christian Anticommunism Crusade, the Mormon Church, Stop ERA.[16]

Ironically, while the American Communist Party has also opposed ERA,[17] as we have seen, the proposed amendment's rightist foes would have us believe that its passage will lead to certain "communist state control." Moreover, despite the fact that ERA clearly states as its purpose the protection of individual rights against denial or abridgment by the state, its enemies have coined the canard that passage will "bring an end to our democratic way of life."[18]

These are all false fears deliberately circulated to defeat ERA. There is, however, one fear that, while rarely if ever voiced, is nevertheless real. It is the fear that impels its opponents to try to stop ERA at all costs: the fear that, if the Equal Rights Amendment passes and the principle of equality of opportunity under the law for so many more million Americans becomes entrenched in our Constitution, their basic tenet—the non-democratic premise that all human beings are *not* entitled to equality—will have suffered a major and perhaps irreversible blow.

This is the same gray supermyth that has all along stood in the way of democratic evolution, the myth articulated so long ago by Aristotle that, in the "natural" order of human relations, there are some elements that must "naturally rule," and others that are "naturally to be ruled."[19]

It is against laws enforcing and perpetuating that myth that the great political and legal battles of the West were fought. It is a myth that is the very antithesis of democracy, which is based on the opposite premise: that all the power should belong to the people. While the people may delegate some of their power to their representatives, those who serve in a democratic government are far from being a "naturally" ruling class or group. They hold their power only as a trust, to be exercised for the best interests of the people from whom their powers are derived.

Toward Full Humanity

In the gradual evolution of democracy, every major legal document—from the Magna Carta to the American Constitution and, beyond that, the Thirteenth, Fourteenth, Fifteenth, and Nineteenth Amendments—has represented an arduously won victory against those who seek to maintain their power through undemocratic myths.

But even in this country, where women have been in the forefront of the struggle for the realization of the democratic dream—in the nineteenth-century crusade against slavery and the twentieth-century movement for civil rights —women have until very recently been explicitly excluded from most of its gains. The Declaration of Independence, the Constitution, and even the Thirteenth, Fourteenth, and Fifteenth Amendments were written by and for men. Women's exclusion is so deeply rooted in the old gray myths that one sex must "naturally rule" the other, that this injustice was not even generally perceived until, braving charges that they were "unwomanly" and even "un-Christian," feminists dared to expose it for what it is.[20] When they met for the first women's rights convention in Seneca Falls in 1848, they issued a new declaration of democratic principles in which they rewrote one of the most famous documents of all time. To our Declaration of Independence, they added two words: "We hold these truths to be self evident: that all men *and women* are created equal."[21]

To these early feminists at least it was clear that, on the most fundamental level—politically, economically, and personally—the realization of the democratic dream could never come to pass unless women too were given the equal protection of the law. That issue was brought into the open at Seneca Falls in 1848, and upon its resolution depends the future not only of women but, at this point in history, the future of democracy itself.

5

Will Equality Destroy
Women's Privileges?

Those who oppose the ERA make a two-pronged argument. On the one hand, they tell us that we don't need an amendment because, under existing laws, women already have equal rights. On the other hand, they warn us not to pass ERA because giving women equal rights will deprive them of all their privileges—and in the bargain bring our whole society to certain ruin.

To the student of history, this "now you see it now you don't" sleight of mind has a curiously familiar ring. It has been the official line of the opponents of all egalitarian reforms. It is the same contradictory and confusing illogic that was used against granting women the vote. On the one hand, women were told they had all the rights they needed without suffrage. On the other hand, they were warned that, if they got the vote and began to function in the political sphere, they would lose all their influence on men, threatening the entire moral fiber of our society.

Similarly, in opposing the emancipation of slaves, Southerners contended that "Negroes had all the rights they needed," that to grant them more was not compatible with their nature, and that to give the "contented darkies" their freedom would be the ruination of society. The real situation of slaves was, of course, one of almost complete powerlessness. All blacks, whether they were field hands or house slaves, had few if any rights, and the vast majority of them lived in abject misery.

But some of the house slaves, living as they did in the homes of rich and mighty men, had many privileges. It was the fear of losing these privileges that impelled some of them to actually fight on their masters' side in the Civil War, to help preserve the "security of their homes." Just as many women (impelled by precisely the same dependency psychology) fight ERA today, these misguided slaves fought against their own best interests, for the South. They did this, out of conviction and out of fear, because they had been so thoroughly socialized to identify with their masters and to accept the very value system that defined their own inferior and dependent place as an inevitable, inalienable, and even desirable truth. But their masters' cause was doomed. Despite the South's unquestionably greater dedication, superior generals, and popular support of the war (a support badly lacking in the North), in the end it was the North that won.

Emancipation?

Although many complex factors were involved, ultimately the defeat of the South was part of the industrial revolution, and of the shift of power from the old landed class to the rising mercantile one centered in the North. The Civil War, and with it the legal emancipation of slaves and the partial legal emancipation of women, marked the transition from one phase of the industrial revolution to the next. It was the transition from an economy that was still (particularly in the South) primarily aristocratic and agrarian to the urban, merchant, and industrially dominated mass-production society of the first part of the twentieth century.

This new society required a more mobile work force, a work force that would be free to hire itself out to the factories and the mines. As long as blacks were owned by individual families they would not be available to enter where they were now wanted, on its lower rungs. In the same way, as long as women could not legally work outside their homes without their husbands' permission, their services would also not be directly available to the newly emerging commercial weavers and makers of ready-made clothes.

The Married Women's Acts of the 1800s[1] which legally freed American women from the physical and economic control of their husbands, made possible the spectacular increase of women in the labor force that took place in the middle of the last century. According to the U.S. census, in the twenty years between 1850 and 1870 alone, the number of women working in factories jumped from 225,922 to 323,370.[2] Soon many employers began to hire women in preference to men. One reason was that they seemed more docile, worked for lower wages, and could be required to end the working day by getting down on their hands and knees and scrubbing the factory floor, while the men who usually oversaw their work went home.[3]

This new industrialized America now also required increasing numbers of workers with at least a minimal education. But this, too, could not have been accomplished without at this time giving women further opportunities. For the first time in our history, numbers of women were given access to learning.[4] Until then, only boys and a few daughters of rich men were taught by tutors or sent to universities. As a matter of fact, the education of women had been vigorously opposed by most men on the grounds that it would be bad for their health and their femininity and in general for the moral fiber of the entire nation.[5] Nevertheless, as a response to the new economic and social needs of industrialization, to which were added the voices of the new feminists, the first women's colleges now opened their doors, and women were permitted to become schoolmarms and to work, under a dual pay scale, for less than one half of what a man would get.[6]

Another Kind of Labor

Over one hundred years later, after two world wars during which they made—and then again lost—substantial gains in the labor market, women, like blacks, were still struggling for equal pay and, more significantly, for access to equal work.

However, by the mid-sixties—the decade in which blacks won so many of their most spectacular victories—the situation of women too again seemed to be improving. On the legal front, two very important pieces of legislation were adopted: The Equal Pay Act of 1963 made it unlawful to pay women lower wages for the same work[7] and Title VII of the Civil Rights Act of 1964 made certain types of employment discrimination on the basis of sex a federal offense.[8]

The two decades from 1947 to 1968 had been times of

enormous population increase. The increase was approximately the same for females and males. However, according to the United States Department of Labor, the number of men in the work force during that period increased only 16 percent (from 42.7 to 49.5 million).[9] On the other hand, the number of women in the work force increased in that same period from 16.7 to 29.2 million, a jump of more than 75 percent.[10]

However, when the occupational distribution of these workers was examined in 1971 by the United States Department of Labor in a pamphlet entitled *Underutilization of Women Workers*, a startling disparity was found. Despite the proportional drop of males in the labor force, their share of professional and technical workers had *increased* by almost 10 percent (from 55 percent in 1940 to 63 percent in 1969).[11] Furthermore, in the same period, the proportion of men in the bottom rungs of the labor force—among the lower-paid clerical, service, and sales workers—declined by almost 20 percent. In 1968, men were still 99 percent of all engineers and federal judges, 97 of all attorneys, 93 percent of all physicians, and 91 percent of all scientists.[12]

In the next decade, the 1970s, the numbers of women in the work force swelled even more dramatically. According to the U. S. Department of Labor, they were now the fastest single growing group in the American labor market[18] at the same time that the proportion of men had stabilized and was beginning to decline. But, despite the stories in the media, somehow women were not making such earthshaking strides after all. Men still overwhelmingly dominated all the prestigious professions. The less socially valued work, the less "important" work, was still being performed primarily by women.[14]

As in the past, the pattern seemed to be for women to take over a whole occupation that previously had been exclusively male. In the nineteenth century, it had been teaching. In the twentieth century, it was secretarial and clerical work and such diverse job classifications as telephone operators, social workers, and bank tellers. The results were always the same. As soon as the proportion of women went up, both the prestige and the pay went down.[15]

The Widening Gap in Pay

By 1974 the earnings differential between women and men was actually wider than it was two decades earlier. In comparing the median earnings for year-round, full-time workers, the U.S. Department of Labor found that, whereas in 1955 men's earnings had exceeded women's by 55 percent, by 1974 the $11,835 earned by men was *75 percent* more than the $6,772 earned by women. "When the absolute difference between the earnings of men and women over the 19-year period is expressed in constant dollar terms, to take into account the deflated purchasing power of the dollar, the disparity is even more evident," reported the Labor Bureau. "The difference increased more than 79 percent—from $1,911 in 1955 to $3,433 in 1974."[16]

The same labor market report continued by pointing out that, while in 1950 women accounted for 29.6 percent of the civilian labor force, in 1975 they made up about 40 percent. Nevertheless, in 1974 women accounted for only 5 percent of all year-round, full-time workers earning $15,000 and over. In fact, in 1974, women with four years of college had lower income than men who had completed only the eighth grade.[17]

But with all of that, the women who had jobs were the lucky ones. Unemployed women numbered 3.4 million and accounted for 44 percent of all unemployed persons in 1975. While the unemployment rate of men of all races and ages in 1975 was 7.9 percent, that for women was 9.3. Nearly half a million unemployed women were family heads. Their rate of unemployment was 10 percent, compared with 6 percent for men family heads in husband-wife families.[18]

The Breakdown of Marriage and the Family

But it is not only in the labor market that women find themselves in a terrifying and precarious situation. While marriage is still being presented to women as their ultimate destination in life, it is clearly no longer permanent. Marriages are being terminated by divorce with such frequency that, from a social standpoint, it can be said the phenomenon is not just quantitative, but qualitative. Since the turn of this century, the divorce rate of this country has increased by 700 percent. It actually doubled in the decade between 1964 and 1974, and, while the rate now seems to be stabilizing, it is stabilizing at a point at which more than a million American couples are being divorced every year.[19]

Before the twentieth century, divorce was rare. The rationale behind that fact may have been morality, but the realities were economic. Until the turn of the century, the family home was still the place where clothing, food, and nearly all the other necessities of life were produced: in other words, it was the major unit of economic production. Therefore, a functioning family was essential. It was only after the turn of the century, when first the factory and then the corporation began to take over the former economic function of the family, that the divorce boom began.

Divorce has skyrocketed in urbanized, industrialized Western societies. This development has been attributed to a variety of factors, from the gradual breakdown of religious sanctions and the increased mobility of population, to rising personal expectations for happiness and self-fulfillment, and simply greater affluence. On a more fundamental level, the rising divorce rate is undoubtedly related to underlying technological and ecological developments that are as yet not accurately understood, or even fully perceived.

Social processes do not lend themselves to reversal, nor do they operate in simple cause and effect terms. Throughout history, the structure and form of the family have continually changed and evolved. Recent dramatic changes in the form of the family are reflections of evolving social and economic realities requiring new forms of social organizations. Just as the extended agrarian family was no longer viable in the urbanized industrialized milieu, the "nuclear family" that succeeded it cannot be expected to remain static as vast technological scientific and social changes continue to occur.

The Lie of Equality as Cause

The instability of the nuclear family, the skyrocketing divorce rate, and the changing roles of women and men are *not* the product of women's liberation or the struggle for women's rights. All these tendencies are symptoms of fundamental technological, economic, social, and ecological changes that are deeply affecting all of our lives.

No-fault divorce—the grounds of which are not based on guilt or innocence—and other related trends facilitating the dissolution of marriage are all manifestations of these developments. Far from being a product of the women's liberation movement—or of what some people call the "male backlash"—the first no-fault divorce laws in this country were passed in California early in 1969, by an almost all-male legislature. This was before most people had even heard of the women's liberation movement. In short, the feminist movement is seeing a resurgence in this country, not as the cause but as a *result* of the dislocations that American women are undergoing today.

Inequality as the Real Cause

The great thrust for women's rights today derives precisely from the realization that it is the traditional position of women in our culture—a position of physical, social, and economic dependence on men—that is causing dislocation in the lives of so many American women. The traditional woman—the woman who has been or aspires to be exclusively a homemaker—faces problems comparable to those of workers who in the past were displaced by mechanization, or who are today being replaced by increased automation.

Seen in such economic terms, what is happening is this. As our divorce rate climbs and more and more women become unemployed as wives (that is, no longer supported by husbands), they are forced to find other jobs. For this reason, and because of a whole complex of other social and economic factors, vast numbers of women continue to be admitted, indeed forced, into the ranks of the "gainfully employed." But once so occupied, despite all the new fair employment laws, they still must work for little more than half the earnings of men. Simultaneously, the traditional labor market, particularly the lower segments to which most women are confined, is also shrinking. Consequently, an ever growing number of these divorced women or "unemployed" housewives cannot and will not be absorbed into the general economy. For them—as well as for those who cannot find or hold jobs for reasons of age, demands of child care, or problems with health —the only recourse has been to join the swelling ranks of the nation's poor.

Of these women, the plight of mothers of growing children is particularly deplorable. Finding themselves with insufficient child and spousal support awards (many of which are not paid or even enforced), they are unable to find jobs. And if they do find jobs, proper child care is practically unavailable. A consequence is that, in growing numbers, they have been forced to seek welfare or Aid for Families With Dependent Children (AFDC)—which, in the 1971 case of *Wyman v. James,* the Supreme Court of the United States characterized as a "privilege, not a right."[20]

Fears of the Privileged

There are, of course, some women who are really privileged: the wives of well-to-do, successful men. They are privileged as long as their husbands continue to support them and maintain them in the "standard of life to which they have become accustomed"—in fine homes, costly clothes, expensive jewelry, and all the other trappings popularly associated with the status of a "successful man's wife." So afraid are some of these women of losing these privileges that they are actually fighting on the side of those who would maintain the old order against the passage of the Equal Rights Amendment. Like the black house slaves a century earlier, they are fighting to preserve the "security of their homes." They are fighting out of conviction and out of fear, because they have been so thoroughly socialized to accept the myths of a value system that defines their "proper place" as an inalienable and inevitable truth.

Some of them, like Helen Andelin and Marabel Morgan, are making a tidy profit out of that fight, a fight in which they propagate the gospel (which they, however, do not follow) that the only place for a woman is in her home. Theirs is a business built on fear: fear that to ask for women's rights is tantamount to losing women's privileges, fear that to ignore the dictates that "nothing gives him (man) a more enjoyable sense of power than does his supremacy" or "the husband's word should be law," is to risk the loss of the husband.[21]

If women are frightened, it is because privileges, unlike rights, can also be taken away. As long as women have privileges and not rights, their situation in society will continue to be what it is—precarious, uncertain, and, for the mass of women, socially, politically, and economically second class. It is the perception of this reality that in 1949 led French philosopher Simone de Beauvoir to write the classic study of the underlying situation of women in Western society, which she appropriately called *The Second Sex*.[22] It is the perception of that same reality that in 1973 led economist John Kenneth Galbraith to the conclusion that women constitute what he calls a "crypto-servant" class, or, so to speak, the hidden, underlying proletariat of the home.[23]

Portents of the Crypto-caste

"The convenient social virtue," wrote Galbraith, "ascribes merit to any pattern of behavior, however uncomfortable or unnatural for the individual involved, that serves the comfort or well-being of, or is otherwise advantageous for, the more powerful members of the community. The moral commendation of the community for convenient and therefore virtuous behavior then serves as a substitute for pecuniary compensation. Inconvenient behavior becomes deviant behavior and is subject to the righteous disapproval or sanction of the community. . . . The ultimate success of the convenient social virtue has been in converting women to menial personal service."[24]

But whether they work for free as "crypto-servants" in the home or in the general labor market for only a fraction of the wages of men, the basic situation of women is the same. In the traditional home, women work for men on whom they are dependent for support. If they earn their livelihood outside their home, women work primarily for male bosses, who pay their wages and tell them what to do. *The crux of the problem is the low economic and social valuation of whatever women do in a patriarchal society, be it as "just a housewife" or in occupations which become economically and socially devalued as soon as they are reclassified as "women's work."* For women—whether they work in the labor force or at home—the real issue is whether their status in patriarchal society will finally change.

What is that status? A strong case can be made for characterizing the status of women as that of a lower caste—perhaps, borrowing Dr. Galbraith's use of "crypto" (i.e. hidden, secret), that of a hidden or crypto-caste, underlying our entire social organization. What differentiates a caste from other social groupings is that its members are assigned to it at birth and their membership in it continues for the rest of their lives. In that sense sex, like race, places individuals in a permanent class which they can never leave, no matter what their accomplishments or achievements in life. Sex and race are "large, permanent, unchangeable, natural classes."[25] A caste system is always based on identifiable and immutable physical characteristics. While these characteristics may have no rational relationship to the social status and functions assigned to the members of an upper or lower caste, they are, so to speak, the pegs upon which the myths justifying the "innate and unalterable status of the lower and higher caste" are hung. These myths tend to become so internalized by both the dominated and dominant caste that they are, in effect, invisible: they are no longer seen as social evaluations but simply as "the way things are."

Even major technological, social, and economic changes will not necessarily alter a caste system. This is particularly so for our sexual crypto-caste system, which is all the more insidious and resistant to change because it is so inextricably woven into the whole fabric of our minds and daily lives.

The situation of women is one of great powerlessness. This is evident not only from their inferior economic position, but from the simple fact that if one looks at the places where real power resides—politics, the military, business, and the courts—women are conspicuous only by their absence. While there are, and always have been, some women with privileges, throughout our history, for the vast majority of women this has not been, and still is not, the case.

Even the situation of the few privileged women has been, and still is, fraught with anxieties and fears, since to receive privileges one must please those who have the power to dispense them—or they will be withheld or even withdrawn. This is one reason privileged women fight against their own interests when they oppose the ERA.

But it is not only women, but also men, who act against their own self-interests when they oppose the ERA. Because, as long as women are the lower crypto-caste and men are the upper one, the battle of the sexes will never cease. Only by according each sex full human rights and dignity can men, women, and their children ever achieve happiness and peace. As one of the fathers of modern psychology, Alfred Adler, said: "Two people cannot live together fruitfully if one wishes to rule and force the other to obey."[26]

6

Will Equality Destroy Marriage and the American Family?

Ironically, while the opponents of the Equal Rights Amendment are everywhere generating and spreading the fear that granting women equal rights will destroy the family, in reality, equality between the sexes may be the family's only hope.

There is no question that the family as we have known it, the husband-wife unit that sociologists call the nuclear or conjugal family, is undergoing great stress. Its future—and whether it has one—has become the subject of a growing body of scientific and popular literature about marriage and divorce. Hardly a week goes by without an article or editorial in the Sunday paper about the "crisis" of the family. While psychologists and sociologists are trying to determine what the problem is and how to find a cure, whole armies of social workers and other family counselors are busy trying to help Americans hold their marriages together or, alternatively, make their divorces less painful.

But while there is consensus about the diagnosis—that the nuclear family is in great trouble—there is less agreement about the cure. The approach of most family experts, like sociologist Jessie Bernard and psychologist Carl Rogers, is that the marriage of the future must be centered on a full and equal partnership between the sexes.[1] Others, both in the popular literature and the social sciences, focus on exploring alternative family forms, from open marriages to extended or communal families. Characteristic of both of these approaches is an awareness of present and future social and personal realities and the need to find better ways for humans to relate, both inside and outside the family.

Looking Backward

A third approach is past, rather than present or future, oriented. Its advocates, who oppose ERA, insist that the only way to cure—and preserve—the American family is to go back to the "good old days" when men and women knew and supposedly enjoyed their place. Its popularizers, such as Marabel Morgan, Ingrid Trobisch, and Helen Andelin, have all written "how to" guides for saving unsuccessful and unhappy marriages.[2] Ironically, they simultaneously claim that, although there is nothing wrong with the American family, the only way to hold it together is for women to learn to be more subservient to men.

"It is only when a woman surrenders her life to her husband," writes Morgan, "reveres and worships him, and is willing to serve him that she becomes . . . the glory of femininity. . . ."[3] "God ordained man to be the head of the family. . . . there is no way you can alter or improve this arrangement."[4]

Both Morgan and Andelin, who deplore women's liberation and insist that a woman's proper—and only—place is at home, run profitable classes where women with failing marriages can learn how to be "total women" properly skilled in pleasing, placating, and manipulating men.

But the "total woman" is just one more variant of the myth of the "contented woman." It is an update of what Simone de Beauvoir called the "profitable formula" whereby the inferior position of the lower caste is justified and maintained.[5]

The Contented Woman?

"There are deep similarities," De Beauvoir wrote in *The Second Sex*, "between the situation of woman and that of the Negro. . . . Both are being emancipated today from a like paternalism, and the former master class wishes to 'keep them in their place'—that is, the place chosen for them. In both cases the former masters lavish more or less sincere eulogies on the virtues of 'the good Negro' with his dormant, childish, merry soul—the submissive Negro—or on the merit of the woman who is 'truly feminine'—that is, frivolous, infantile, irresponsible—the submissive woman."[6]

As Gunnar Myrdal observed in *An American Dilemma*, his definitive study of the American black, inferior intelligence, an instinctual and emotional nature, and a great contentment with their own lot have been ascribed to both women and blacks.[7] These myths have been successfully used to keep both in an inferior and powerless position. Both groups have therefore been forced to develop the same accommodational tactics: an ingratiating manner designed to please, an eye for ways to influence or corrupt the dominant group, and a manipulative repertoire, including an assumed air of helplessness and a show of ignorance. These are also the very elements, as Kate Millett points out in *Sexual Politics*, that misogynist literature has for centuries stressed to show how devious, "catty," and generally untrustworthy women really are.[8]

These "feminine traits" are hardly considered desirable in our society, and neither are obedience, servility, or subordination. It is therefore understandable that women themselves learn to think less of themselves than of men. As psychologist Alfred Adler has pointed out, "This type of thinking has become so deeply anchored in our thought processes that in our civilization everything laudable has a 'masculine' color whereas everything less valuable or actually derogatory is designated 'feminine.' "[9]

The inferiority of women is also very subtly perpetuated by the myth of the "contented woman" itself. The stereotype of the obedient, servile, "contented" woman is the image that all women internalize and are taught to strive for. If they feel disatisfied with their inferior position, they are taught to blame not the system, but themselves—for by not being contented, they have failed as women. In the same way, for generations American women have been blaming themselves if their marriages did not work. It is the woman's responsibility, they were told, to hold the marriage together, to accommodate—in short, to make the marriage "happy." If it is not, she has only herself to blame.

How is she to accomplish this? According to the traditional formula, the "total womanhood" formula, she must please, she must placate, and she must ingratiate herself with her husband. She must make him feel superior to her in every way she can. In short, unless she actually works to make herself inferior to him at all costs, she will risk his loss.

Adler, whose great pioneer work in the field led him to coin the term "inferiority complex," summarized the psychological situation of women as follows:

The obvious advantages of being a man have caused severe disturbances in the psychic development of women as a consequence of which there is an almost universal dissatisfaction with the feminine role. The psychic life of woman moves in much the same channels, and under much the same rules, as that of any human beings who find themselves the possessors of a strong feeling of inferiority because of their situation in the scheme of things. . . . An adolescent girl acts very much as though she were inferior, and what we have said concerning the compensation of organic inferiorities holds equally well for her. The difference is this: the belief in her inferiorities is forced upon a girl by her environment. *She is so irrevocably guided into this channel of behavior that even investigators with a great deal of insight have from time to time fallen into the fallacy of believing in her inferiority. The universal result of this fallacy is that both sexes have finally fallen into the hasty pudding of prestige politics, and each tries to play a role for which he is not suited. What happens? Both their lives become complicated, their relationships are robbed of all candor, they become surfeited with fallacies and prejudices, in the face of which all hope of happiness vanishes*[10] (emphasis added).

The net effect of the unhealthy male-female relationship Adler describes is the unhealthy marriage sociologist Jessie Bernard describes. In her book *The Future of Marriage*, an analysis of the research about marriage going back over a period of some forty years, Dr. Bernard not only came to the conclusion that marriage has very different meanings for men and for women, but that "his marriage is far better than hers."[11]

In comparing studies of married and unmarried women, Bernard found that the unmarried woman has more self-confidence, less self-consciousness, and fewer psychological problems than the married one. In contrast, the mental and physical health of married men was statistically superior to that of single men, particularly after middle age. On the other hand, Dr. Bernard found that single women suffer far less than single men from neurotic and antisocial tendencies. But that was not all. While for women marriage and a family were liabilities in the job market, for men they were assets to careers and earning power. Finally, even when Bernard compared *married* men and *unmarried* women, she found that unmarried women seemed to be much better off insofar as psychological distress symptoms are concerned. This suggested to her, as Ashley Montagu had already observed, that women as a sex may start out with an initial advantage, but marriage then reverses it.[12] This seems particularly true for the woman who stays home, as Dr. Bernard reports that being a housewife literally "makes women sick."[13]

The Economics of Marriage

Why then do women marry? This is a complex question, one that involves biological, psychological, economic, sociological, religious, and political factors, not to speak of the entire socialization process through which women and men are channeled into assigned social roles. However, on a very basic level, women as well as men marry primarily for emotional and economic reasons. Emotionally they seek intimacy, companionship, and the reassurance that they are not alone.[14] But they also marry for economic reasons. This is particularly true of the traditional marriage, in which the husband is supposed to go out in the labor market and bring in the money while the wife works only at home.

In this sense, the traditional marriage is basically a private employment contract, the terms of which specify that a woman shall exchange her sexual and homemaking services for her husband's support. This is the contract that women have traditionally been socialized to enter.

In the nineteenth century, marriage was usually the only feasible and acceptable means of survival for middle-class women. Even today, with the partial legal and economic emancipation of women, a "good marriage" is still very often a young woman's best chance for economic security and success. At a time when women earn approximately half as much as men in the labor market, it is this economic reality—not just ignorance and a continued social channeling of girls into conventional roles—that accounts for the persistence of the myth that marriage is still the ambitious woman's most promising and lucrative career. Although this myth (like the Horatio Alger story and the rags-to-riches Cinderella tale) is more motivational than actual, the fact, as one girl put it, is that it is still easier for a woman to marry an executive than to become one herself.

The Politics of Marriage

Even for those women who have achieved economic success through marriage, as we have seen, the emotional and physical cost of their subordinate relationship has all too often been terribly high.

In applying his lifelong work on the nature and dynamics of power in human affairs to the relationship between women and men, Dr. Alfred Adler concluded that the cost of male dominance and female dependency is prohibitively high not only to women but to men and children as well:

> The subordination of one individual to another in sexual relationships is just as unbearable as in the life of nations. Everyone should consider this problem very attentively since the difficulties which may arise for each partner . . . are considerable. This is an aspect of our life which is so widespread and important that every one of us is involved in it. . . . The fallacy of the inferiority of woman, and its corollary, the superiority of man, constantly disturbs the harmony of the sexes. As a result, an unusual tension is introduced into all erotic relationships, thereby threatening, and often entirely annihilating, every chance for happiness between the sexes.[15]

Adler concludes that the subordination of women "explains why one so seldom finds a harmonious marriage, and that this is the reason so many children grow up in the feeling that marriage is something extremely difficult and dangerous."[16] "The distrust which is so universal between the sexes prevents all frankness," writes Adler. "Our whole love life is poisoned, distorted, and corroded by this tension."[17]

Sex and Violence

The ultimate result of this poisoned relationship between men and women is violence. A recent study by Dr. Richard Gelles, *The Violent Home: A Study of Physical Aggression Between Husbands and Wives*, indicates that family violence is much more prevalent than is generally believed. But in trying to pinpoint its causes—other than a high correlation between family violence and alcohol—Dr. Gelles's research was inconclusive. It indicated that while families of low education, occupational status, and income were more likely to experience violence, those with higher education and income did too. While higher stress seemed to lead to violence, in some cases it was low stress or a lack of stress that caused it. In some cases it was too much sex; in others it was not enough. In short, as one reviewer concluded about Dr. Gelles's study, "it appears that just about everything is related to violence."[18]

We have only to look at the explicit accounts of sex and violence, of sadism and masochism on our movie and television screens, in popular literature and in the flood of pornography inundating our lives, to see how tense and unnatural the relationship between the sexes really is. One of the most brutal, increasingly recognized manifestations of this tension is rape.

As Susan Brownmiller points out in her monumental study of the subject, rape is an inherent characteristic of a society based on "men's natural superiority over women." Not only is this evidenced by an analysis of the historical, mythological, and legal annals of rape, but all the research on rapists shows that rape is not the product of sexual desire or lust but of aggression against women. The typical rapist is a hostile man with deep-seated feelings of anger and resentment against women.[19]

Tracing the history of rape through the centuries, Brownmiller demonstrates how woman is often the victim, not only of the individual rapist but also of patriarchal society. Under the renowned Code of Hammurabi, a raped married woman was blamed equally with the rapist, and both participants were bound and thrown into the river. As an interesting indication of the powers and rights of patriarchs over their female dependents, Brownmiller points out that "a husband was permitted to pull his wife from the water if he so desired; the king, if he wished, could let his errant male subject go free."[20] Under Mosaic law a married woman who was raped was stoned to death, and this was often also the fate of a raped virgin.[21] Even in our time, the woman is often afraid to bring her rapist to court for fear that she, and not he, will be put on trial.

Not only do the adult statistics show that rape is far more prevalent than is generally believed, but according to the 1969 report of the Children's Division of the American Humane Association—which analyzes adult sex crimes against children—the sexually abused child is even more prevalent than the physically battered child. Girls are molested ten times more frequently than boys; in 40 percent of the cases sexual abuse is a repeated phenomenon; and 97 percent of the offenders are male, often family friends or relatives—and even fathers.[22]

Brownmiller's study further shows how rape is the male instrument of social control, reprisal, and retaliation. It is inextricably linked with the use of power, with conquest and subjugation. It escalates in time of crisis and social turmoil, particularly during wars when, as Brownmiller concludes from the shockingly endless data on the subject, men's violence against women is given a sanctioned outlet in the form of rape.[23]

This is why, unless men and women cease seeing the sexual relationship as one of male dominance and female submission, there is no hope that rape—and sex murders—will lessen in frequency, much less disappear. As Brownmiller's compendium of data so powerfully demonstrates, rape is inevitable as long as its warped function is to confirm the "masculine mystique" that virility and manhood are based on the superiority and supremacy of men.

Looking Forward

The Stop ERA forces that tell us that we must preserve—even strengthen—this male supremacy to save the family, confuse the illness with the cure. They also ignore the fact that the historical moment for the nuclear family—a by-product of the industrial revolution—has already come and gone.

Throughout history there have been many kinds of

families. The modern nuclear family of mother, father, and children is only a very recent arrival on the scene. Historically and cross-culturally, the larger or extended family is far more prevalent. The extended American family of parents, grandparents, aunts, uncles, brothers and sisters living and working on the land met the economic needs of our earlier agrarian society. It produced not only children, but food, clothing, furniture, housing, and just about everything else its members needed for survival. As industrial society developed, with its requirements for a more urban, mobile work force, the smaller, more isolated nuclear family became economically more functional. As we move into postindustrial society, the family will inevitably change once again.

"New technologies create new environments, and new environments force us to adapt our behavior, our values, and our institutions," write Robert and Anna Francoeur in their recent study of the impact of twentieth-century technology on the changing relationship between men and women. "Human behavior . . . is a response or adaptation of individuals and their societies to a particular environment."[24]

In *The Future of Sexual Relations*, they report on the work of a number of experts who have examined that adaptation in terms of how the future relationship between women and men—and the institution of marriage—can be expected to evolve. While their predictions ranged widely— all the way from "companionate marriages" to "satellite relationships" in addition to marriage, from "specially licensed marriages for parenting" to "female self-reproduction without males" or even "laboratory reproduction without either sex"—the one point of agreement was that the family will inevitably change, and very quickly at that.

The Shifting Bond

One major change that has already taken place is that divorce has risen sharply and sequential marriage—the ability to divorce and remarry ad infinitum—is now sanctioned by our laws. While many factors account for this development—greater population mobility, more affluence, the weakening of religious and moral constraints—an increasingly major cause is that people today expect a higher order of emotional and personal satisfaction out of marriage.

"What has happened is not that our laws have become more indulgent, but rather that our ideas regarding the nature of marriage have changed," explained Dr. Robert Weiss of the Harvard Medical School at a 1970 international symposium on the family and its future. "In the past, our laws held that a marriage must continue so long as each partner properly met the responsibilities of his or her role. Today, more and more, the emotional compatibility of the couple is the issue, and in many jurisdictions a marriage may be dissolved if a court decides it has 'broken down.' "[25]

Or as Dr. Ronald Fletcher, another participant in the same symposium, put it: "The modern family is founded on the basis of free personal choice by partners of equal status, and the expected base of it is that of personal affection (not legal constraint)."[26]

Our new divorce laws—and the changes and experiments we are witnessing in alternative family forms—are manifestations of underlying attitude changes, which are in turn adaptations to new social, economic, and technological trends. There is, therefore, no real basis for any hope that our divorce rate will suddenly reverse itself and shrink away. Neither is there any legitimacy to the claim that only if women return to their "natural" subservient roles, will marriage and the family survive—the claim on which ERA opponents so heavily base their opposition to granting women equal protection under our laws.

There is further nothing in the Equal Rights Amendment that could conceivably be interpreted as a prohibition against marriage. Certainly our high divorce rate cannot be blamed on a constitutional amendment that has not yet become law. If marriage as we have known it is breaking down, it is because it is not properly fulfilling what has become its primary function: the satisfaction of emotional and psychological needs. If these emotional needs are to be met, women can no longer be the second sex. Neither can traditional notions of male dominance and supremacy any longer be condoned—much less reinforced by the defeat of ERA.

As the work of Dr. Adler and contemporary psychologists shows, the patriarchal concept of male supremacy is inimical to, and indeed makes impossible, any real understanding and trust between women and men. "A marriage based on the maintenance of an intimate emotional tie depends on continuing trust between the partners," writes Dr. Weiss in *The Family and Its Future*.[27] "Real trust can be based only on mutuality," writes Dr. Carl Rogers, about what he calls "a full and equal partnership between women and men."[28] Other family sociologists have called it "companionate marriage."[29] Johnson and Masters call it the "pleasure bond."[30] And Dr. Robert Thamm calls it "a relationship based on friendship, love, and involvement": ties which are "democratic" and "egalitarian."[31]

Despite all the prophecies of gloom, these observations by social scientists actually point to some very hopeful family trends. Besides the increasing emergence of companionate marriage, there is also the wider use of individual marriage contracts, in which couples make their commitment, not to a contract that is imposed on them, but to one of their own choice. Another good sign is the large number of college and community courses aimed at helping couples learn better human relations skills, as well as more enlightened parenting. Still another encouraging development is a changing definition of fatherhood, from a primarily economic and disciplinary role to one of greater intimacy, to the kind of nurturing role that was formerly reserved only for women.

The Democratic Family and the Battle for the Future

This greater emphasis on improving the quality of human relations is not an isolated development but part of the democratization of Western society.

"The making of the modern family," writes British family sociologist Dr. Ronald Fletcher, "has been part of the making of a new society . . . On all counts it embodies great improvements. It is not just a convenient arrangement or compromise, but that form of the family which is integrally bound up with . . . the achievement of a new principled democratic, industrialized society. It is in itself a great achievement, and is part of the larger achievement of moving more closely than ever before to a just society."[32]

This modern family (in Dr. Fletcher's words, "founded

on the basis of free personal choice by partners of equal status") is what we have come to speak of as the democratic family. Still imperfect, it is nevertheless one in which increasingly dogmatic patriarchal authority is superseded by reciprocal discussions and sensitivity to family members' individual personalities and needs.[33]

As Dr. Fletcher writes, this democratic family is a "necessary part of the larger process of approximating to the central ideas of social justice in the entire reconstruction of society,"[34] of the historic movement toward democracy that has met such fierce resistance every inch of the way from those with a vested interest in inequalities. It is therefore no accident that the most anti-democratic elements of our society today want to go back to the old patriarchal family based on repression and inequality as the exclusive form. It is also no accident that they oppose ERA, which will shore up and ensure the survival of the democratic family based on trust and equality of relationships.

The battle over ERA is the great contemporary conflict between historic democratic and anti-democratic forces, which are rooted in family life. It is a symbolic battle for control of both the shape of our families and the highest law of our land: the American Constitution. Should the principle of equality and dignity for *both* sexes which ERA embodies now suffer a massive and public defeat, we would be well on our way toward the dehumanized and depersonalized societies foreshadowed in Aldous Huxley's *Brave New World* and George Orwell's *1984*.[35]

These nightmare futures that Huxley and Orwell warned against are notably societies in which close emotional ties between the sexes are absent—in fact, they are prohibited. They are societies in which men—and hard "masculine" power and conflict-oriented value systems—are still in control. They are societies in which the family withers away and is replaced by the state, whose haunting slogan in *1984* is "Big Brother Is Watching You."

This is the great irony and potential tragedy of those who have been duped into opposing ERA in order to "protect the family." They have unwittingly let themselves become tools of authoritarians who would bring on precisely the future feared by everyone who values both liberty and equality. For if the ERA principle of equality and mutuality between the sexes goes down in defeat at this critical time in American—and world—history, with it goes the foundation of the modern democratic family and thereby all hope for a humanistic world based on trust and cooperation between women and men.

Part 2

How to Fight for Sex Equality and ERA, Pass or Fail: Strategy Guide and Action Checklist

Introduction
Political, Economic, and Educational Strategies

ERA can, and must, be ratified.

At this writing thirty-five of the needed thirty-eight states have ratified. Of these, three—Idaho, Nebraska, and Tennessee—subsequently voted to rescind ratification. In the opinion of the United States Department of Justice and the Counsel of the Subcommittee on Constitutional Amendments of the United States Senate, state rescission is not constitutionally binding.[1] This, too, is the opinion of other legal experts who point to favorable congressional and court precedents establishing the rule that, once a state has ratified an amendment, it has "exhausted the only power conferred on it by Article V of the Constitution, and may not, therefore, validly rescind such action."[2]

When a number of states first ratified and then rescinded the Fourteenth and Fifteenth Amendments, Congress accepted *only* the ratification and ignored the rescission. Furthermore, in 1939, in *Coleman v. Miller*, the United States Supreme Court established a judicial policy of nonintervention in the ratification process, declaring that the issue of vote changes is a "political question" to be decided by Congress under its powers to implement Article V (Procedures for Adoption of Constitutional Amendments) of the Constitution.[3] Nevertheless, ERA opponents may bring litigation to challenge these precedents, so the question of rescission remains a loose end.

Another loose end is the question of a ratification deadline extension. Representative Elizabeth Holtzman introduced a joint resolution, cosponsored by eighteen other congressional leaders, to extend that deadline an additional seven years, to March 22, 1986.[4] The Justice Department has expressed the opinion that Congress can vote such an extension, pointing out that the 1979 deadline is *not* part of the Equal Rights Amendment itself and that Article V of the Constitution sets forth no specific time period for the ratification of Constitutional amendments.[5]

Nevertheless, at this writing the question of whether Congress will extend the deadline for ERA ratification is still unsettled. If there is an extension beyond March 22, 1979, we have, in Representative Holtzman's words, "an insurance policy."[6] In that case there is obviously more time, but there is also the danger of becoming too complacent, too slow, and of losing the impetus and thrust required to complete the task. If the time is not extended, we are obviously working under the gun and must move as quickly and as competently as humanly possible. Either way, we've got a big job ahead. But it is a job that can be done with intelligence, determination, and the proper tools.

Chapters 7, 8, 9, and 10 are designed to make these tools handy and easy to use. The contents of these chapters are a combination of my own ideas, methods that have already been used successfully, and the result of a survey of national leaders and experts who have contributed their thoughts and experience (and who are, wherever possible, quoted directly with crediting in the text rather than in chapter notes). The strategies and tactics have been divided into political, economic, and educational. However, these are interrelated, and the division is primarily for convenience of use. Most of the methods can be used whether the deadline is extended or not although there are some that will require more planning and time. While this is not a completely comprehensive list, it is my hope, and the hope of all those who have contributed their thoughts and work, that it will bring results, both directly and by inspiring other and perhaps even better methods and actions.

The primary strategy for ERA passage has to be to apply both direct and indirect persuasion and pressure on the legislators of states that have not yet ratified ERA, in order to ensure their votes. Direct tactics can be from both inside and outside the targeted states. These would include local and national lobbying, letter writing, telephone calls, telegrams, and a variety of other direct contact methods for both individuals and organizations, such as organizationally sponsored legislative breakfasts, all of which will be discussed in detail in the following pages. Indirect pressure and persuasion tactics can also be brought to bear from both inside and outside the targeted states. These include obtaining favorable and intelligent media coverage and, perhaps most important, such economic tactics as the boycotting of targeted states for vacations and conventions.

Although passage of ERA obviously depends on the votes of the legislators themselves, the active help and support of American women and men must be enlisted in order to obtain these votes. Therefore, the second main strategy that must be successfully carried out for ERA passage has to be directed to this end. Most major American organizations have already endorsed ERA, and the polls show that the majority of the American people are in its favor. The task is to turn that into active commitment and support. For this reason, the materials that follow also include tactics designed to educate, motivate, and mobilize every intelligent American to contribute time, money, ideas, and specific actions to persuade their friends and pressure their legislators to pass the Twenty-seventh Amendment to our Constitution.

7
Political Strategies and Tactics

The thrust of the political strategies and tactics that follow—as of the economic and educational ones in the next two chapters—is to obtain ERA ratification by the required thirty-eight states. Nevertheless, most of these approaches will still be useful *after ratification*, to help ensure proper ERA implementation.

The first section of this chapter focuses on how to persuade and pressure state legislators in unratified states to vote for ERA and (where time still permits) to unseat ERA opponents and replace them with candidates who can be counted on for favorable votes. It includes advice from political pros and ERA activists from all over the United States. Entitled "Strategies and Tactics," this section begins with an appraisal of what states should be top targets and includes a variety of political approaches, ranging from methods that have worked in past political and civil-rights campaigns to more innovative tactics specifically tailored to ERA, such as silent vigils and ERA truth squads.

The second section, "Basic Information," provides specific suggestions on letter writing and public-opinion telegrams, as well as politically useful data such as the status of unratified states (including dates of legislative sessions and past voting records).

Strategies and Tactics

Top Target States

It is essential to concentrate our efforts where they will really pay off. To this end, ERA strategists have examined unratified states and concluded that top target states are

Illinois, Florida, North Carolina, South Carolina, and Virginia as well as Oklahoma, Arizona, Missouri, and Nevada.

States with pro-ERA governors who have pledged active support are good possibilities. Florida, where Governor Reubin Askew enjoys great popularity, is one such state. Governor James R. Thompson of Illinois has also expressed his support for ERA, so has Governor James B. Edwards of South Carolina. The particular importance of such states is that here governors can call special legislative sessions to vote on ERA. If we do not have an extension, this may be an essential strategy since in those states where legislatures are not scheduled to meet at that time, friendly governors can call *special legislative sessions for January of 1979.*

To quote Mark A. Siegel, former Special Assistant to President Carter: "Our three states will come from only about a half a dozen where passage is possible. Although we should force a vote by the March 22 deadline in all unratified states, primary attention with respect to money and energy should go to states where a breakthrough is really possible."[1]

National, State, and Local Coordination

There are ERA coalitions in all unratified and in most ratified states. These provide an important focus for political action, both nationally and on a state and local level. (See contacts list at end of chapter 10.) In cities and towns where coalitions do not yet exist, their formation is a top priority. *"Organize ERA coalition chapters in your city or town* by contacting groups such as Business and Professional Women's Clubs, American Association of University Women, and the League of Women Voters," urges Lucy Pierson, Co-coordinator of the Washington State ERA coalition. "All of these organizations have national planks of ERA support. These local ERA coalition chapters can have speakers bureaus, publicity and research committees, etc. And they can sponsor public events that focus on ERA, and provide a united front of political pressure and support."

To avoid duplication and concentrate effort, it is essential that lines of communication be open between all interested organizations and parties in your area and that their primary focus be on ERA. As Anita Miller, Director of the Equal Rights Amendment Project of the California Commission on the Status of Women, points out, the political fight for ERA must take place on the grass roots level as well as in the legislative chambers of unratified states. "ERA ratification plans should be modeled after the successful strategies of other civil right issues . . . strong grass roots campaigns that focus on the well-known political fact that an elected official listens to his own district," she writes. "Established women's organizations have been in charge of ERA ratification efforts. However, some groups who claim ERA as number one priority fail to make it so. Meaningful commitment has not been realized in terms of (a) single-minded *focus* and (b) *resources* of people and money. The first requirement of a successful ratification strategy is to get activists working in the field whose sole purpose is ratification of ERA. An individual's organization ties or other priorities must not be considered in this arena. Resources of people and money must be totally focused on the one issue."

Find, Develop, and Elect Pro-ERA Candidates

If time still permits, we must unseat ERA opponents and elect ERA supporters. Wherever we face anti-ERA candidates—or likely "antis" hiding for a while under the guise of fence-straddling—the first step is finding and, where necessary, developing dependable pro-ERA candidates. The National Women's Political Caucus, Women in Politics, and other groups have been doing just that. A top priority has been the nomination and election of qualified women. Equally important has been the work of women's organizations in obtaining active support and commitment from male political candidates. To win we must have both. Women candidates often have the advantage of being more actively motivated while male candidates have the advantage of more frequently having the ear and confidence of other male legislators. Selecting the right candidate means balancing such considerations, regardless of the sex of the candidate, while giving number one priority to the force, capability, experience—and, of course, commitment and drive—of the candidate.

Where new candidates are being developed, the next step is to help distribute and obtain signatures for the petitions they may need in order to run. Then come the major tasks of fund raising, campaigning—and winning a crucial pro-ERA seat.

A dramatic example of just how effective we can be is the story of what happened in Virginia in 1977. Here a determined, hardworking, and well-organized effort unseated entrenched old-time political figures who opposed ERA. The most prominent of these was the Democratic House Majority Leader James M. Thomson, a longtime power of the General Assembly who was upset in a three-way race. One of the candidates against Thomson, GOP newcomer Gary R. Myers, persistently raised the ERA issue during the campaign, and the fact that Thomson was chairman of the House committee that prevented the measure from reaching the floor.

This elective upset could not have happened without the active and determined support of women and men working for ERA. One of the most important sources of organizational support was the Women's Rights Project of the American Civil Liberties Union Foundation, Southern Project, Richmond, Virginia.

"Well, we did it!" wrote Betsy Brinson, ACLU Southern staff associate. "Jim Thomson was defeated, and Elise Heinz, our chief lobbyist for the last five years, was also elected a House delegate from northern Virginia. Additionally, both the new Lieutenant Governor and the Attorney General are ERA supporters. Our work is cut out for us. The House vote is 46 pro, 38 anti, and 16 swing. The Senate vote is 24 for, 19 against."[2] Ms. Brinson was writing to Elizabeth Snyder of Los Angeles, thanking her and other California women and organizations for their help and support.

One of the most important lessons of the Virginia success story is how effective and essential out-of-state financial help is. Whether we like it or not, it takes money to win political campaigns. The recognition of this political fact of life by seasoned California political workers like Liz Snyder and Maureen Reagan (the daughter of former California Governor Ronald Reagan) paved the way for the raising of money in California to be sent to Virginia for use in that critical 1977 political campaign. A number of women's organizations and pro-ERA coalitions sent money where it was really needed, in an unratified state. Virginia showed that, if we work together toward specific goals, if we send money directly to unratified state ERA coalitions, if we maintain lines of national communication, we are able to do the job.

As Mark Siegel, former Special Assistant to President Carter, points out: "Special targeting should isolate anti-ERA legislators who are defeatable. Recruitment should get superb candidates into these races, and pro-ERA money should pour in to help these candidates. In states like Florida and North Carolina, a few turnarounds would achieve ratification."

Statewide Legislative District Action Corps

The best way to reach already-elected state legislators is to influence them through their units of basic allegiance, their own home districts. This means that delegations and large numbers of letters directed to them must come from these home districts. It also means that attempts to unseat anti-ERA candidates—or to threaten them with pro-ERA candidates in the primaries—must come from their own districts. To carry on such activities effectively, statewide legislative district action corps have been, or are being, formed. Check your key source for information in your state and join this vital activity—or work to form or bolster such organizations if they do not exist or are not working well.

Voter Pledge Cards

Voter pledge cards have proved useful. They consist of cards pledging the signee will vote, work for, and contribute *only* to legislative candidates who support the Equal Rights Amendment. What they accomplish is this. They provide the sponsoring organization with an invaluable file of potential workers. In quantity, they provide the *physical evidence* of commitment that can impress legislators. And they help guarantee that a good intention on the signing person's part becomes more solidified. In other words, it's easy to say, "Oh, how I do want to help." But as church and United Way fund raisers know from old experience, it's also very easy to forget about one's good intention without the bolstering of the card that *pledged* you to really give time and energy. It's a commitment to work and often a first step for women, or men, who would like to do something but don't know where to start.

Political Dinners and Rallies

One of a candidate's vital links with grass roots as well as big money support is the political dinner and rally, which proliferate like mushrooms as elections near. You can make points for ERA by attending, but be *sure* to wear sizable ERA YES buttons. And no matter how shy and retiring you may normally be, sit or manuever yourself into as prominent a place as you can. Work your way in to congratulate and express support for all candidates who support ERA, personally express disfavor with those who don't support ERA, and ask every candidate whose position is unknown to you exactly where he or she stands on it. The time for being a shrinking violet is *after* ERA wins and is implemented. Until then we must all be gracious tigers.

Gallery Sitting

Though legislators will discount this method of influence, don't let them kid you. One way of *continually* reminding them that you mean business is to keep a pro-ERA presence in the gallery. Be sure to wear ERA YES buttons and sit together—don't scatter out. Five people scattered out will hardly be noticed. But five clearly buttoned ERAers sitting together in as prominent a position as possible will be duly noted and fed into the "internal computers" most legislators develop within themselves for filing everything bearing on how they should vote.

Silent Vigil

Few things are more effective in maintaining visibility for the ERA issue than the Silent Vigil. This is a gentle and persistent tactic that applies immediate and constant pressure to the legislators and also has educational value and wins attention from the media. The method is for volunteers to gather in the rotunda or on the steps of state capitols. As with picketing, signs are held bearing pro-ERA messages, and literature may be quietly passed out. An important part of the effectiveness of this strategy is its *silence*. Nothing can be as counterproductive as shouting and stridency here. Silence can speak volumes—if it is *repeated* in the same place, again and again and again, over weeks and months.

ERA Truth Squads

Many ERA supporters in ratified states are frustrated, realizing that their fate depends on actions by legislators in unratified states. There just doesn't seem much they can do about it directly, other than contribute on the financial and educational level. Here's an idea for *direct* action to take. Organize Truth Squads composed of at least *one or two celebrities* accompanied by women who know and are highly motivated by ERA to go into unratified states as a group and spread the word in state capitols, open forums, and at gatherings arranged by pro-ERA supporters within the state. They should take tents and camp out and prepare their own food to make the point that they are refusing to spend a penny in the state until its legislature ratifies ERA. Such Truth Squads, organized, for example, in California and including well-known entertainment figures, could be extremely effective in Nevada. Courageous entertainment figures with name appeal in the South could also be especially effective participants in Truth Squads aimed at melting the ice south of the Mason-Dixon line.

ERA Children's Crusades

As all mothers who have given of their time, money, and energy know, it is not just for ourselves we work for ERA: it is for the future of our children. This can be dramatized by organizing Children's Crusades for ERA. A quick way to do this is to bring up the idea at the next ERA meeting you attend, get participating mothers to fill in cards with names and ages of potential "crusaders" along with the family phone number, and then when you've settled on a date and place, telephone for commitments to march. Ask each child who agrees to participate to bring a friend.

Bring them into play whenever there is a need for some new publicity or pressure on legislators. The children should march to the capitol during weekends and school holidays and, where possible, at times of key voting, bearing signs identifying them as the Children's Crusade for ERA The placards might urge: PLEASE DO NOT DEPRIVE US OF OUR FUTURE RIGHTS. It will add to the impact if the children come equipped with tents and food and camp out on the capitol lawns. Careful adult planning and supervision are mandatory, to be effective and to prevent rightist charges of "irresponsible troublemaking" or vicious rumors of unsupervised sexual hanky-panky. And, of course, the children must be well-behaved, courteous, and aware that what they are doing is of historic importance—because it *is* their future that is at stake.

Legislative Action Breakfasts

The overwhelming majority of state legislators are lawyers by training. Therefore, it can be expected that ERA's potentially strongest legislative proponents, as well as opponents, will be lawyers. For this reason, special breakfasts held to arm ERA legislative supporters with the facts and arguments of this book—and to disarm its opponents—could prove decisive in key states. Interested women's organizations in each key state capital city should cooperate in sponsoring legislative breakfasts. One women's group should initiate action by inviting potential ERA *supporting* legislators to a breakfast designed to *arouse* and *arm* them by a public show of organized support; there would also be briefings based on ERA's legislative history (see, particularly, "Facts and Fancies" in chapters 2 and 3), and these would stress the political necessity for ERA.

Action roles include those of the *inviter*, with responsibility for getting the names and addresses of legislators, drafting and mailing invitations, and making *follow-up phone calls* to guarantee attendance; the *arranger*, with responsibility for selecting the most suitable facility, making food arrangements, etc.; and the *briefer*, who summarizes the case for ERA and the chief fears and lies to be met and overcome. The *briefer* should be bright and articulate, but also—and this is very important—winning and charming, rather than a potentially alienating personality.

Though substantial gains can be expected from the first

breakfast, a series of these breakfasts will maximize impact. After initial contact with legislators, succeeding breakfasts should be sponsored by other women's organizations. However, if the first breakfast produces a good *briefer*, she should be kept involved, no matter who is sponsoring. Also, it is important that the original action team continue contact with legislators to consolidate gains. Further, to build skills and not be wasteful, the experiences of each successive action team—what worked, what didn't—should be shared with other organizations, both locally and in other key states.

Continuing Contact with Leaders and Legislators

A bad mistake to make is to let up on and forget a candidate or leader who has already taken a pro-ERA position. Unfortunately, we have learned the hard way that some do this to get "off the hook" and then switch their vote to the other side under the pressures of political wheeling and dealing. Keep impressing on ostensibly committed leaders— e.g., governors, lieutenant governors, and top state house and senate party leaders—that you're expecting their *continuing* support for ERA as well as continuing action on their part to persuade holdouts and those "on the fence" to get behind ERA on all crucial votes. Don't be turned aside by the claim that leadership cannot do it alone—for they're *not* alone. We're in there pushing in numbers, and they should know it! And we know that leadership *has* moved people and changed events, and it can do so *now* for ERA.

Alice Paul Marches and Rallies

The birthday of Alice Paul (January 11, 1885), author and tireless promoter of the Equal Rights Amendment, should be observed with anniversary marches and/or rallies. Other logical dates for doing this, such as the date when ERA was first introduced in Congress (December 10, 1923), should also be used to focus attention on ERA support. Alice Paul marches or rallies would be preceded by sessions encouraging the reading and discussion of the biography and importance of Alice Paul and the highlights of her forty-nine-year fight to win acceptance of the Equal

Rights Amendment—a human interest story of great appeal. Rallies and marches should feature posters bearing her photograph (or large hand-drawn facsimiles of her portrait). Local ministers should be asked to give sermons or, at the very least, mention this fighter for human rights during services immediately before marches or rallies, and local editorial writers should be asked to devote newspaper space to the story of Alice Paul. Two reasons for the power of this strategy are: (1) one of the most effective ways of enlisting interest in and motivating people to work for an issue is to humanize it in terms of an inspiring personality; and (2) women have for so long been a minority element in politics that they need strong success models showing them how it *can* be done. The story of Alice Paul is tops on both accounts.

She was a remarkable woman, both personally and as a political fighter. As her longtime friend Winona McGuire, of Los Angeles, writes, "Having obtained three law degrees in the space of seven years, Alice Paul was an expert in international law regarding women's rights, The unqualified equal rights pledge in the United Nations Charter resulted largely from her efforts and those of her fledgling World Woman's Party, which she organized in 1938."[8] In this country she organized the National Woman's Party which, in 1923, the year of the seventy-fifth anniversary of the Seneca Falls convention, introduced the Equal Rights Amendment into Congress for the first time.

Her old friend, eighty-seven-year-old suffragist Hazel Hunkins Halliman, came from England to pay Ms. Paul homage at memorial services for her in Washington Cathedral on July 20, 1977. "Her name will go down in history as a woman working for the betterment of all women for all times," said Hazel Halliman, "and in her honor shall we not dedicate ourselves anew to finishing her work?"[4]

Mobilize All Possible Groups

"Leadership must be unified," urges Anita Miller, who is also Director of the Institute for Studies of Equality. "Local community action groups must be mobilized which have not been previously tapped on this issue, e.g., PTAs, unions, farms groups, church groups, service organizations. An assessment of political factors should guide the choice of states for concentrated effort, but the strategy must be directed toward development of effective constituent pressure on the incumbent legislators, regardless of voting record. Polls indicate that ERA supporters are in greater number in every state than those of opposing views. They simply need to be organized for action at the grass roots level."

"Mobilize proponent groups—unions, political parties, church organizations, etc.," advises Nancy Neuman of Philadelphia, ERA Coalition Contact for Pennsylvania. "That means getting their members out to push ERA." You can do this in two ways—from inside or outside. If you are a member of a group with possibilities for action, go to work finding allies within the group to press for action, all the way from another endorsement for ERA (but don't just settle for this alone) to adding ERA speakers to the program schedule and recruiting volunteers for Silent Vigils and other political pressuring moves. From outside, you can influence an organization by asking for the formation of an ERA support committee or volunteer aid. Do this through contacting the organization as a speaker or by requesting, through a friend who happens to be a member (e.g., one's husband), an opportunity to make your needs known very briefly during a regular luncheon meeting. This approach can be very effective with sympathetic men's organizations.

Men for ERA

"Seek the active support of local groups that are predominantly male—e.g., Rotary, Lions, and Junior and Senior Chambers of Commerce. Believe it or not, they are extremely helpful, particularly in the South," writes Attorney Jane Barrett of Beverly Hills, California. Along this line she suggests having local bar association leaders sign impressive petitions for circulation in the state legislatures. Another reason for involving men is that men are the traditional decision makers in most communities; hence, their support will carry weight, particularly with congressmen and senators, when the chips are down in the unratified states.

Fathers for Passage of ERA

"A new organization should be formed—Fathers for the Passage of ERA," writes Mark Siegel, former Special Assistant to President Carter. "I've met so many men who didn't give a damn about the issue. Then suddenly they become the fathers of baby girls, and it hits home. The issue must be personalized."

United We Stand, Divided We Fall

"Don't divide your ERA strength by getting involved in other issues in 1978 and 1979 elections," counsels Liz Snyder of Los Angeles. "Remember, your time and energy are limited—and also the time and energy of those legislators whose eyes and ears you want to reach. So stick to the big issue at hand: ERA!"

The Power of the "Average Woman"

Many women hang back form political involvement not from lack of interest but from a feeling that it calls for "hardened pros" and "superstars." This is simply not true. As Dr. Martha Mednick of Storrs, Connecticut, notes, it is essential that "women at home and in the community and church sponsored pressure groups bombard local legislators." For maximum effect this "has to be seen as coming from 'the average woman.' " In other words, the "superstar" is perceived by many legislators as being *un-*representative of the women who can advance or unseat him. Whereas, when the so-called "average woman" speaks, he tends to think, "If she's aroused, there must be a hell of a lot more like her out there."

Political Research

If you live in an unratified state, check to be sure that there is some really crackerjack group at work researching your legislature. As Martha Pickering of the Pro-ERA Alliance, Louisville, Kentucky, cautions, they should be able to tell you "which votes can be changed to pro, how, and by whom." Generally, this activity will be carried on by state ERA coalitions, the National Women's Political Caucus, or the League of Women Voters, with longtime experience in political research. Should you find it's *not* being done as well as it should, offer to pitch in and help.

The Power of Political Wives

Women who form political caucuses for women in government may overlook a potentially vital extension in membership. "Invite the *wives* of male legislators," advises Shirley Heitland of Brookings, South Dakota and the ERA coalition for that state, "for you may thereby help unleash a new source of power."

Women's Legislative Block

Another suggestion made by Shirley Heitland: "Female legislators should form a 'block' and see if by numbers they can force males to realize they can keep any legislation from passing by refusing to vote with the party." To some, this may seem like idealistic pipe dreaming. Not so. For in South Dakota, as Ms. Heitland points out, "We had enough women to make the difference when they tried to pull off a rescission."

Basic Information

Letter Writing

Letter writing is one of our most important and effective political tools. Politicians *do* respond to their mail, particularly if it comes from their districts. One tip is to write on heavy paper—some politicians actually weigh their mail on issues on which there is more than one viewpoint. Some tips on what to write: to opponents, that we will not stand for a "no" vote on ERA because it is a vote that deprives 51.3 percent of our population of equal participation in American society. To friends, that we expect their continued and vigorous and effective support—in actions, not only in words. To the undecided, both messages and more; that they have a responsibility, a duty, to give us their votes.

Be as specific as possible, using your knowledge and experience in your particular state and district. For example, Jean Maack, president of ERA Illinois, suggested for her area: "Tell them: (1) you know that they are very aware of the economic loss due to conventions not coming to Chicago; (2) you know that they support ERA; (3) with their help, ERA could be ratified—there are enough votes from Chicago to turn the tide."

Public Opinion Telegrams and Mailgrams

Public opinion telegrams, instead of letters, may be sent to the President, governors, senators and representatives. The cost is $2, for a message not exceeding fifteen words, for delivery the same day the message is received by Western Union. The cost for mailgrams is only $2.50 for the first hundred words, $1 for each additional hundred words, for delivery the next day.

Useful Publications

Almanac of American Politics
Information on each state and congressional district as well as census data, information on the economy, and election results for the past four years. Also biographies of each member of Congress, including votes on key bills and ratings by special interest groups. Send your check or money order for $9 to the Fund for Constitutional Government, 121 Constitution Avenue, N.E., Washington, D.C. 20002.

Congressional Record
A daily record of public proceeding of each house of Congress. Cost: 25¢ for a single copy, $3.75 per month, $45 per year. Send your check or money order to the Superintendent of Documents, Government Printing Office, Washington, D.C. 20402.

Congressional Staff Directory
Guide to the U.S. Congress. Lists committees and subcommittee assignments and includes biographies of key members of committees, subcommittees, and congressional staffs. Send your check or money order for $18 to *Con-*

gressional Staff Directory, P.O. Box 63, Mount Vernon, Virginia 22121.

Washington Information Directory
Information on Congress, executive agencies, and private organizations. Available for $18 from *Congressional Quarterly*, Inc., 1414 22nd St., N.W., Washington, D.C. 20037.

U.S. Congressional Directory
Available annually from the U.S. Government Printing Office. Send check or money order for $8.50 to the Superintendent of Documents, Government Printing Office, Washington, D.C. 20402.

State Directories
Each state publishes its own directory of districts, with names, addresses and background information on state legislators. These are usually referred to as the "blue books." They can be used at the local library or obtained at the state capitol.

Selected State Officials in the Legislatures
These directories are published every two years as a supplement to *The Book of the States*, available through the Council of State Governments, Lexington, Ky. 40511.
(See end of chapter 13 for additional useful publications.)

Ratified States

Thirty-five of thirty-eight needed: Alaska, California, Connecticut, Colorado, Delaware, Hawaii, Idaho, Indiana, Iowa, Kansas, Kentucky, Maine, Maryland, Massachusetts, Michigan, Minnesota, Montana, Nebraska, New Hampshire, New Jersey, New Mexico, New York, North Dakota, Ohio, Oregon, Pennsylvania, Rhode Island, South Dakota, Tennessee, Texas, Vermont, Washington, West Virginia, Wisconsin, and Wyoming.

Attempts to Rescind Ratification[5]

Legislatures in Idaho (2/8/77), Tennessee (4/23/74) and Nebraska (3/15/73) have voted to rescind their earlier ratification of ERA. Because legal authorities contend that such action is invalid, these states are counted in the column of ratified states. 1977 rescission resolutions were introduced in Indiana, Iowa, New Hampshire, Ohio, Texas and Wisconsin. Rescission attempts were defeated in 1977 in Connecticut, Kansas, Montana, North Dakota, Oregon, Rhode Island, South Dakota and Wyoming.

Status of Unratified States[6]

Alabama: Legislature convenes May 1, 1979. Length of session: 30 legislative days. Operating under a 3/5 majority rule to ratify. Senate defeated 6–26 in 1973. No floor action in 1977.

Arizona: Legislature convenes Jan. 8, 1979. Length of session: No limit. ERA introduced by opponent in House and defeated in committee Jan. 28, '76, 6–10; passed Senate Committee Feb. 2, '76, 7–2, but lost in floor action Mar. 1 on 15–15 tie. Senate defeated ERA May 5, '77, 11–18.

Arkansas: Legislature convenes Jan. 8, 1979. Length of session: 60 calendar days. Senate tried to amend in 1973. No ERA action in 1975 or 1976. Defeated in House by standing vote in 1977.

Florida: Legislature convenes April 3, 1979. Length of session: 60 calendar days. In 1975, ERA passed House, 62–58; lost in Senate, 18–22. No action in 1976. Senate defeated ERA Apr. 13, '77, 19–21.

Georgia: Legislature convenes Jan. 8, 1979. Length of session: 45 legislative days. No floor action in 1976 or 1977.

Illinois: Legislature convenes Jan. 10, 1979. Length of session: no limit. ERA defeated on House floor June 2, '77, 101–74 (107 votes needed under 3/5 majority rule). House rules permit later reconsideration.

Louisiana: Legislature convenes May 14, 1979. Length of session: 90 calendar days. ERA defeated in House once and passed Senate once. ERA defeated in House Committee June 7, '77, 5–11.

Mississippi: Legislature convenes Jan. 2, 1979. Length of session: 90 calendar days. Defeated in Senate Committee March 9, '76, 3–4. Defeated in Senate Committee Jan. 28, '77, 4–5. ERA has never come to the floor in either house.

Missouri: Legislature convenes Jan. 3, 1979. Length of session: ends June 30. ERA passed in House once, was rejected in House once and in Senate twice. No action in 1976. Senate defeated ERA Mar. 15, '77, 12–22.

Nevada: Legislature convenes Jan. 15, 1979. Length of session: 60 calendar days. No 1976 legislative session. Senate approved ERA Feb. 8, '77, 11–10 on tie-breaking vote of Lt. Gov. House defeated ERA Feb. 11, '77, 15–24.

North Carolina: Legislature convenes Jan. 10, 1979. Length of session: no limit. ERA passed in House once, defeated in House once, defeated twice in Senate. House passed ERA Feb. 9, '77, 61–55; Senate defeated ERA on second reading Mar. 1, '77, 24–26.

Oklahoma: Legislature convenes Jan. 2, 1979. Length of session: 90 legislative days. House rejected ERA in 1975, 45–51. No floor action in 1976 or 1977. Referred back to second House Committee Mar. 15, '77.

South Carolina: Legislature convenes Jan. 4, 1979. Length of session: no limit. In 1975, ERA defeated in House 46–43 on motion to table. No floor action in 1976 or 1977.

Utah: Legislature convenes Jan. 8, 1979. Length of session: 60 calendar days. In 1975, House rejected ERA 21–54; no Senate action. No floor action in 1976 or 1977.

Virginia: Legislature convenes Jan. 18, 1979. Length of session: 30 calendar days. Senate Committee defeated ERA Feb. 5, '76, 7–8. House failed in effort to change rules Jan. 21, '77, 46–62; Senate rejected ERA Jan. 27, '77, 20–18.

8
Economic Strategies and Tactics

Our task is to make our voices heard—and we live in a world where money talks. Economic pressure, both as a carrot and as a stick, is a powerful political tool. We have only begun to use it, and we must develop and use it more fully, both on the local and national level.

The economics of passing ERA can be divided into two main areas: boycotts and fund raising. The section on boycotts focuses on both convention and vacation and travel boycotts and includes background information, organizations now boycotting conventions in nonratified states, and the Chicago, American Psychological Association, and Coors beer boycott case histories. The fund-raising section outlines possibilities for ERA benefit dinners, "ERA is as American as apple pie" sales, fund raising through products boycott or support, unratified sister state funding, and other grass roots ideas and observations.

Boycotts

A General Case History

The ERA boycott idea was born in February 1977 while the Nevada legislature was voting on the amendment. The California branches of the League of Women Voters and NOW took out a small ad in the *San Francisco Chronicle* urging weekend gamblers to stay away from Las Vegas, Lake Tahoe, and other Nevada gambling spots. Recalls Jane Bendorf, chairperson of the political task force: "Nevada Governor Mike O'Callaghan called and screamed at us to stop any further ads. We realized we had hit a pressure point."[1] Later in February the NOW national board set up an economic sanctions committee, and this strategic pressure was off and running.

By late 1977 over forty-five national professional and political groups—including the National Educational Association, the National Association of Social Workers, and the Democratic National Committee—had agreed to boycott nonratified states. Convention sites and targeted states and cities were already beginning to feel the pressure. Miami Beach authorities reckoned that this vulnerable Florida city had lost $9 million in foregone convention business as a result of the boycott. (Warren Erickson, manager of the Miami Beach Convention Bureau, said Florida's failure to ratify ERA "blew us out of the second story. And it will get worse before it gets better.")[2] Chicago admitted its losses were a whopping $15 million (see the separate case history). NOW estimated losses for New Orleans—and Louisiana—at $15 million; for Las Vegas, Nevada, at $30 million; and for Atlanta, Georgia, at $12 million. Said NOW president Eleanor Smeal: "Resolutions are spreading through organizations like wildfire. It wouldn't be happening without tremendous support."[3]

Organizations Boycotting Conventions in Nonratified States[4]

(Monetary figures indicate money customarily spent by these organizations in cities in which their conventions are held)

American Anthropological Association	
American Association of University Women	$500,000
American Federation of Government Employees	$2–3 million
American Federation of Soroptimist Clubs	
American Home Economics Association	$7 million
American Jewish Congress	
American Library Association	$3 million
American Political Science Association	100 exhibits + $900,000
American Presbyterian Council on Women	
American Psychological Association	$5 million
American Public Health Association	$4 million
American Society for Cell Biology	
American Society for Ethnohistory	$4,000
American Society for Public Administration	$50,000
American Studies Association	

American Theater Association	$250,000
American Veterans Committee	$50,000
Americans for Democratic Action	$30,000
B'nai B'rith Women—Mid Atlantic Region	$1,500
Board of Church and Society of the United Methodist Church	
Board of Global Ministries of the United Methodist Church	$400,000
Church of the Brethren	$5,000
Church Women United, National Executive Committee	
Coalition of Labor Union Women	$1 million
Common Cause	
Council of Nurse Researchers of the American Nurses' Association	$11,000
Democratic National Committee	$2,180,000
District of Columbia	$210,000
Division 29 "Psychotherapy" of the American Psychological Association	$2 million
Economists in Business	
Federally Employed Women	
Gray Panthers	
International Personnel Management Association	$50,000
Latin American Studies Association	
Leadership Conference of Women Religious, Board of Directors	
League of Women Voters	$300,000–500,000
National Assembly of Women Religious	
National Association of Social Workers	$120,000
National Community Education Association	
National Council for the Social Studies	$75,000
National Council of Churches	$230,500
National Council of Senior Citizens	
National Council of Teachers of English	
National Education Association	$6–7 million
National Federation of Business and Professional Women's Clubs	$300,000
National Lawyers Guild	
National Organization for Non-Parents	$6,000
National Organization for Women	$420,000
National Woman's Party	
National Women's Political Caucus	$50,000
N-CAP of the American Nurses' Association	$25,000
Organization of American Historians	
Planned Parenthood Federation of America	
Popular Culture Association	

Speech Communication Association	
The General Assembly of the Unitarian Universalist Association	
The General Assembly of the Unitarian Universalist Association: Women's Federation	$7,000
The General Assembly Mission Council of the United Presbyterian Church	
The Los Angeles County Democratic Central Committee	
United Auto Workers	
United Indian Planners Association	$30,000
Western Psychological Association	
Women in Communications	$260,000
Women's Caucus of the National Aid and Defender Association	
Women's Division of the United Methodist Church	
Women's Equity Action League	$10,000– 15,000
Women's Ordination Conference (Catholic)	

Chicago: A Case History

Illinois's decision not to ratify ERA cost its citizens over $15 million during 1977. The target for the boycott has been one of the country's major convention cities, Chicago. Groups which were first to cancel conventions include the League of Women Voters, the National Association of Social Workers, and the Conference on College Composition and Communication. But what hurt the most were the big national organizations that simply prohibited the Chicago Convention and Tourism Bureau from any further bidding on their conventions until ERA was ratified. in Illinois. Frank C. Sain, president of the Chicago Convention and Tourism Bureau, estimated Chicago's losses at $14 million solely from groups like the American Psychological Association, which usually draws fifteen thousand members to a convention city, and the National Education Association, which usually brings in twelve thousand members for six days at a time, worth $3 million in business. Chicago was all but confirmed as the NEA convention site for 1977 or 1978, then ruled out when NEA joined the nationwide boycott.

Positive steps taken by the Chicago Convention and

Tourism Bureau in this case should be carefully noted because this is the kind of economically motivated support which must be encouraged in boycotting pressures. As conventions losses mounted in Chicago, the Convention and Tourism Bureau decided to take affirmative action *for* ERA. On September 27, 1977, the bureau's board of directors passed a resolution supporting ERA and urging state legislatures to ratify it. *A copy was sent to all state legislators.* (A copy of this resolution and covering letter is included in this section so that you can modify it to fit your own boycotting moves.) In this resolution the bureau was usefully specific by noting that the $15 million loss estimate was based on "approximately 75,000 attendees, a conservative 150,000 room nights . . . and $750,000 in state and local tax revenues."

Another noteworthy point, in case you come up against this defense, was this. The bureau contended that Chicago was being unfairly penalized because ERA had been solidly supported by Chicago legislators while being rejected by downstate lawmakers. However, *Chicago Tribune* reporter Michael Hirsley, being on the ball, carefully checked the ERA ratification vote of June 2, 1977, and found that *19* Chicago legislators had voted against the measure—which fell only *6* votes short of the 107 needed for ratification![5]

Copy of Letter to Legislators by President, Chicago Convention and Tourism Bureau

October 7, 1977

Dear Representative:

Writing on behalf of the Board of Directors and membership of the Chicago Convention and Tourism Bureau, Inc., I want to share with you our grave concern over the loss of business to Chicago and other areas of Illinois because our state has failed to pass the Equal Rights Amendment.

An ever increasing number of convention groups are now passing regulations that they will not meet in states which have failed to pass ERA. These groups do not consist of women's associations alone. For example, the American Psychological Association, which has met in Chicago many times, will no longer accept a bid from us until ERA is passed in Illinois.

As you know, convention and trade show revenues are a very important source of income for citizens of the Chicago area and other meeting places throughout this state.

I urge your serious consideration of the enclosed resolution.

Thank you for your attention.

Sincerely,
Frank C. Sain

FCS:rs

Copy of Resolution by Chicago Convention and Tourism Bureau

WHEREAS, the Congress of the United States has passed the 27th Amendment to the Constitution of the United States (Equal Rights Amendment) and, as required by law, has submitted it to the fifty states of the Union for ratification;

WHEREAS, thirty-four States of the Union have considered and voted for ratification of the Amendment;

WHEREAS, the State of Illinois has not yet ratified the Equal Rights Amendment;

WHEREAS, the State of Illinois and the City of Chicago have lost substantial revenues due to the lack of ratification by the Illinois General Assembly;

WHEREAS, the State of Illinois and the City of Chicago will continue to lose revenue as associations and organizations remove from consideration the state as a potential site for conventions and trade shows;

WHEREAS, the State of Illinois has long maintained a pre-eminent position in the convention industry because of the viability of the Chicago Product;

WHEREAS, the lack of ratification by the General Assembly of the Equal Rights Amendment has seriously hindered the ability of the City of Chicago to bid for future business and has caused the State direct financial loss because of the withdrawal of scheduled conferences and conventions;

WHEREAS, over the past year Chicago has lost booked business and has been denied the opportunity to bid on a total of at least fifteen groups; this amounts to approximately 75,000 attendees, a conservative 150,000 room nights and an economic impact of fifteen million dollars ($15,000,000) and $750,000 in state and local tax revenues;

NOW, THEREFORE, BE IT RESOLVED by the Board of Directors of the Chicago Convention and Tourism Bureau, Inc., both collectively and individually, that they support the ratification of the 27th Amendment to the Constitution of the United States; BE IT FURTHER RESOLVED, that the Board of Directors of the Chicago Convention and Tourism Bureau, Inc., contact each member of the General Assembly of the State of Illinois and make known its active and continuing support for ratification of the Equal Rights Amendment.

CERTIFICATION

I, Colgate F. Holmes, do hereby certify that I am the duly elected Secretary and keeper of the corporate records and corporate seal of the Chicago Convention and Tourism Bureau, Inc., a corporation existing under the laws of the State of Illinois, and that the above stated resolution is a true and correct copy of a resolution duly enacted by the Board of Directors of the Chicago Convention and Tourism Bureau, Inc. at its September 27, 1977 meeting, and that the resolution is now in full force and effect.

Note: To this resolution was attached a three-page list of the names of over seventy members of the Board of Directors for the Convention and Tourism Bureau, with their affiliations—including the mayor of Chicago and leading bank, hotel, union, and large corporation presidents.

The American Psychological Association:
A Case History

When you go after your own organization to boycott nonratified states for convention or meeting sites, you will often get an answer like this: "Well, we'd like to do something about it, but we are already committed to Atlanta (or Las Vegas or New Orleans or St. Louis or Chicago) for 1979 (or 1980, 1981, etc.)." Arm yourself—and friends and cause supporters—with the following information and persist until you get them *uncommitted*.

The American Psychological Association, with fifty thousand members, is one of the nation's hottest convention plums. They were seemingly locked in, by preliminary agreements, to hold their national conventions in Atlanta in 1979, in Las Vegas in 1980, and in New Orleans in 1981. Boycott-minded APA members pressured the APA board of directors to withdraw from these tainted sites in nonratified states. Immediately, Atlanta responded with a tearjerking plea to APA not "to punish the present city administration and some eighteen thousand people—both men and women—in our service industry because you are unhappy that the Georgia General Assembly failed to pass the ERA. You are actually punishing the very people who have supported this cause. It is they who will be despondent and unhappy because you are not providing jobs for them because you canceled plans to meet here." They further maintained that this punishment was unfair because "there is nothing they or we can do to alter the present posture of our legislature."[6] *See our Chicago case history for an action rebuttal of what can be done if you are confronted with this or similar pleas.*

It was the Louisiana response, however, that made the APA take pause. For the last paragraph of the New Orleans Tourist and Convention Commission letter read as follows: "The hotels could have booked other business, but a definite agreement was made and agreed upon by all parties. As of this date, the hotels could have turned away business and, if so, it is our feeling that the American Psychological Association could be liable for a $6.5 million dollar lawsuit."[7]

The APA board turned to the association's lawyers, who advised them that it would be safer *not* to withdraw because of "legal risks." So everything was set for the world's largest organization of social scientists, the mighty APA, to knuckle under to a threat from one convention bureau. And it might have if a strong pro-ERA drive had not been so effectively mounted by ERA supporters during the APA annual meeting in San Francisco. Spearheaded by psychologist Jacqueline Goodchilds, they held an emergency meeting and resolved to appeal to the consciences of the APA Council of Representatives, which was meeting the next day. It was too late for them to get another legal opinion since that would have entailed a review of all the correspondence and documents involved.

I explained that to Dr. Goodchilds when she phoned me at the eleventh hour. But we were able to consult on an informal basis, and I helped her prepare the following, as it turned out, persuasive case to help the APA stand firm—and put its principles ahead of its fears.

Since all or most of the hotels involved are national chains, a creative response by APA would be to communicate to these cities that due to changed circumstances—i.e., they are no longer fit states in which to hold conventions because of their position on ERA—our decision is that we will not meet there. However, as soon as alternate states are selected as convention sites, these chains will be given the option of arrangements on the same terms for hotels in the substitute locations.

While it is true that some groups may plan conventions far in advance, some do not. The time allowed is sufficient for them to act to minimize any potential loss. It is the obligation of the complaining party to prove damages. For example, if a tenant breaks a lease, a landlord is obliged to try to remedy the situation. With two to four years notice they would have difficulty proving damages.

It is unlikely that a national hotel chain or city would actually sue in this case. They are risking very bad publicity.

Finally, this matter is one of principle. There is in the land now a clear threat of regressive backlash. It is extremely vital that organizations such as APA stand firm.

I strongly urge you not to let business people—

whose interest is solely the money—use legal process
to intimidate as large and socially significant a professional group as the American Psychological Association.[8]

Products Boycott: The Coors Case History

An economic tactic that is just beginning to gain steam is
the boycott of products whose sales support anti-ERA
forces. One such product is Coors beer, made by the Adolph
Coors Company in Golden, Colorado. Members of the
Coors family—particularly Joseph Coors—are regular major contributors to rightist organizations, many of which
(such as the John Birch Society and Phyllis Schlafly's
Eagle Forum) are now dedicated to the defeat of ERA.
A boycott of Coors beer, in this case launched chiefly by
labor unions and gay rights activists, demonstrates the
specific effects this kind of pressure can have. After only
seven months, Coors sales had slumped 15 percent in the
company's major markets, California and Texas. In July of
1976, for example, 609,400 barrels of Coors were shipped
to California. This dropped to 493,700 for July of 1977.
In 1976, Coors was the biggest seller in California, enjoying 32 percent of total sales for the state, with Anheuser-Busch second with 28.4 percent. By September
1977, the figures were reversed: Anheuser-Busch was running first with 37.5 percent to Coors's 25.5 percent.[9]
  Who is a likely candidate for a product boycott in your
area? Use these facts about the boycott impact on Coors
to discourage them from supporting anti-ERA forces and
to fire up ERA supporters to launch—and publicize—new
product boycotts. And for maximum effect, be sure to
inform other organizations—and governors, legislators,
and state development commissions—about *your* product
boycott.

Vacation and Travel Boycott

You can have an impact on ERA passage by refusing to
vacation or travel in unratified states. Here's a typical case
history from the League of Women Voters of Illinois. They
issued a directive to *all* local leagues to encourage an ERA
Travel Boycott. "If you are now planning a vacation, check

your chosen state's ERA record," they urged. "Avoid those that have not yet ratified. This means forget Florida! But no sacrifice is too big for equality of rights under the law! Once you've readjusted your travel plans to Indiana (a nice gesture of thanks), write the Chamber of Commerce in the Florida city you would have visited and tell them why you canceled. Other states to avoid until . . .: Alabama, Arizona, Arkansas, Georgia, Louisiana, Missouri, Nevada, Oklahoma, South Carolina, Virginia, North Carolina, and Utah. For those places that have no Chamber of Commerce, write to their legislative leaders."[10]

Letters from Ratified States

Jean Maack, president of ERA Illinois, suggests, "For those in ratified states, write letters to Chambers of Commerce and leaders saying that you are joining in boycotting visits and conventions in the state—*and that you resent having your rights taken from you by a few no votes.*"

Business Boycott Honor Roll

"Economic pressure is the only thing that will ever work," maintains Louise Manuel of the Southern California Association of Governments. "Develop and publish a list of businesses which will agree not to hold business conventions in cities whose city councils have not passed resolutions in favor of the ERA."

Selective Political-Economic Boycott

"Organize a selective positive boycott," urges Pat Houseman of Portage, Michigan. "Find out which legislators in unratified states are the most helpful and which are the most obstructionist. Then contact businesses and industries in those areas making a special effort to promote tourism and patronage of businesses in "good" legislators districts and staying away from "bad" legislators districts. For example, the Holiday Inn in Hammond, Indiana, is just across the state line from Illinois within easy driving distance of Chicago. If feminists were to patronize that motel and let Chicago hotels and motels know why, it might be effective. Especially if they stayed there in large numbers."

Boycott Your Own Organization

"Refuse to participate by withdrawing your membership from national organizations that have conferences scheduled in anti-ERA states," counsels Kris Harrison of the Southern California Association of Governments. "Withdrawal of membership should be with as much a fanfare as possible. Pressure for similar symbolic gestures should be put on spouses and employers. Obviously membership withdrawals should only occur if the association's power structure cannot be convinced to cancel the conference. Another strategy is to continue membership, but organize a conference boycott."

Fund Raising

The Basic Fund-Raising Challenge

"First and foremost, the passage of any legislation requires *money*, a tremendous sum of money in this case because our opponents are well financed," writes Edi Kjos of Bismarck, North Dakota, and Chairperson, AAUW. "But unfortunately women traditionally respond with their coin purses, not with their checkbooks. Thus far our campaign has been waged with small donations (i.e., $1 to $10), and that is just not sufficient to combat what the thousands raised by our opposition can buy."

On a national level, the most important single contribution that every American woman and man can make to the ratification of ERA is money. This is the advice of leaders from all over the country:

"Give money, money, and more money to the ERA election fund of the National Women's Political Caucus and to ERA America."——Gloria Steinem

"Contribute money to pro-ERA organizations in unratified states for professional lobbying and media campaigns designed to show the inequities of that state's laws and the need for a national amendment."——Louise Moon, President, Iowa League of Women Voters

"Support the ERA statewide groups in the unratified states with dollars so the people there can concentrate on political action, not on raising enough funds to pay the phone bills, mailings, etc. Become a member of that state group and become informed on how they are doing things."——Joan Maack, President, ERA Illinois

"The first and second and third thing that comes to my mind is to send money to the League of Women Voters ratification fund and urge other people to do the same."——Annabel Kitzhaber, President, League of Women Voters of Oregon

"The first priority right now is to send money to ERA coalitions in key unratified states.——Winona McGuire, Legislative Chairperson, Business and Professional Women's Club of Los Angeles

Sister-State ERA Coalition Funding

Women and men in unratified states are working around the clock to get the needed votes and support for ERA. But we cannot expect them to carry the burden alone. Sister-state ERA coalition funding is an excellent way to provide direct and fast help. On an informal basis, that is what California did with Virginia during the 1977 election. ERA coalitions in Illinois, Florida, South Carolina, North Carolina, and Virginia as well as Oklahoma, Arizona, Missouri, and Nevada have specific budget items with which they need help. Organizations in ratified states can adopt one or more of these states as sister states, establish direct lines of communication, and see how they can best help. This way we can volunteer our time and our contributions and let the women who know their own states and districts best have our active support.

"If you are in an unratified state," Gloria Steinem writes, "work locally. If you are in a ratified state, adopt an unratified state and help *them* work locally."

Neighbor-State Funding

If you live in a state bordering, or near to, an unratified state, raise money for ERA supporters in that key state. For example, women belonging to ERA Wisconsin went to work and presented a check to their sisters in bordering ERA Illinois. Said ERA Wisconsin President Julie Kernahan in making the presentation: "Ratification of the Equal

Rights Amendment in Illinois is important to everyone in Wisconsin and all over the United States."[11] Note also that both ERA Wisconsin and ERA Illinois made the most of this by photographing the presentation ceremony and getting news coverage in an ERA newsletter and local women's pages. This move, in turn, helped build enthusiasm in Wisconsin women to raise *more* money for the Illinois effort and bolstered the spirits and treasury of the Illinois women.

ERA Benefit Dinners

The standard ingredients for a successful fund-raising dinner are some celebrities to draw a crowd and a good dinner to leave good memories. In California, for example, ERA supporters had a successful benefit dinner which charged $57 a plate. How did they do it? Their attraction was a canny choice of "big name" attractions—Maureen Reagan (daughter of Ronald Reagan), to attract Republicans and conservatives, and Judy Carter (President Carter's daughter-in-law), to attract Democrats and liberals. Another California ERA dinner at $125 per plate sponsored by Southern California lawyers and lawmakers included the following names on the program: California Supreme Court Chief Justice Rose Bird, Governor Edmund G. Brown, Jr., and Los Angeles Mayor Tom Bradley as well as Candice Bergen, Barbara Feldon, Valerie Harper, and Marlo Thomas.

You, too, can gain "name" attractions for your ERA benefit dinners. A good way is to look over the calendars of coming attractions for your locality for names of known supporters or potential sympathizers who are being brought in for lectures or other purposes. With their expenses paid by other organizations and purposes, they will be all the more open to helping you out with a fund-raising appearance during your benefit dinner timed to take advantage of their being in your area. Be sure, however, to publicize, publicize, publicize.

Equality Is as American as Apple Pie

Here's a neat idea sparked by the success anti-ERA forces had with loaves of fresh, home-baked bread sent to legislators when ratification was being decided in key states.

Get together your best apple pie bakers or purchase really good bakery pies—but be *sure* they are really good! Affix a big printed slogan to the top of the pie box to this effect: EQUALITY IS AS AMERICAN AS APPLE PIE! Then below this big slogan, in smaller letters, have printed: "Support the passage of the EQUAL RIGHTS AMENDMENT in (your state) with time and dollars." Get churches and all other possible local sponsoring agencies to cosponsor sales of these pies. Be sure, particularly, to set up booths for sales of pies at local, regional, and state festivals and fairs, to which thousands of people are attracted. Be sure to staff these booths with the most attractive "homemaker" types possible, who are also equipped to answer questions intelligently about ERA and direct pie buyers to good sources of information locally and nationally.

Fund Raising through Products Boycott or Support

Fund raising for ERA has been particularly difficult not only because, traditionally, women are not big spenders for causes but because of the lack of *established* vested interest groups relating to the cause of sex equality. One major group with heavy vested interests in the good will of women are the manufacturers and distributors of products aimed primarily at women consumers.

Examples of such manufacturers include the cosmetics group (e.g., Avon, Coté, Elizabeth Arden), national and local women's and children's clothing manufacturers and designers, manufacturers of personal hygiene products (e.g., Johnson and Johnson, Tampax, Kimberly-Clark) as well as food processors whose products are purchased largely by women (General Foods, Kraft, Oscar Meyer meats, etc.) and supermarket chains (Safeway, A & P, etc.). Also examples of firms with vested interests in the good will of women are the large and wealthy department stores, such as Neiman-Marcus in Dallas, Dayton's in Minneapolis, Bullock's in Los Angeles, Filene's in Boston, Marshall Field in Chicago, etc., and nationwide chains such as Woolworth, Sears Roebuck, and Montgomery Ward. Most of these firms spend large amounts advertising to reach women. Some have owners who have gained legendary wealth through their sales success.

These firms should be approached by representatives of local and state coalitions of several women's organizations supporting ERA. The approach should be by letter first and then by personal visit of a small delegation. The presentation to manufacturers and distributors should be in careful but forceful language to make two points. On the "carrot" side, note that by contributing to the support of ERA they will be winning the good will of the *majority* of American women, who support it. However, note also the "stick" side of boycott. In other words, make clear that this contact is part of a *nationwide* move to assemble an *honor roll list* of manufacturers and distributors who have contributed vital funds to support passage of ERA—but also a list of firms to be *boycotted* by women if they fail to support their largest customer group at a time of unparalleled historic need.

Stick Your Neck Out—for ERA

The League of Women Voters is selling an ERA necklace—they even have a 14-karat gold version of it. This is a good item to wear to dinner and cocktail parties to inject into these vital information-swapping occasions a useful conversation piece. Contact your local League for information.

Other Money-Making Ideas

It has suddenly become fashionable to advertise everything from tennis shoes to tricycles on T-shirts and other items of apparel. Let's advertise for ourselves instead of for these various commercial interests. How about "ERA is as American as Apple Pie" T-shirts. Other possible items would be ERA tote bags. And in Springfield, Illinois, they've even thought of ERA gift certificates, "a unique and timely gift for the person who has everything but equal rights." These gift certificates, noting a donation has been made to help ratify ERA, are available through Paula Johnson (District 50 Coordinator), 2413 S. Whittier, Springfield, Illinois 62704.

A Gift of Time

Remember, our time—the skills we have, the things we each can do—has economic value. We are the "volunteering sex" of America. Volunteer your time, for anything from typing to phoning, to organizations working to pass ERA. Or to important individuals or organizations that will *endorse* ERA with a statement that can be publicized. Or for political candidates who have endorsed ERA.

Local Genius

Fund raising is not easy. If you're not gung ho for it already and equipped with good experience from the past with other causes, pull in your best local advisors for a brainstorming and motivating session. Women have been fund raising for years, for all the good causes. Women in the PTAs, B'nai B'rith, the Junior League, the United Way, etc., have successfully raised funds for all the many causes that keep this country operating. Draw upon this local fund of inspiration and information—and get them working with you. We've done it before for everybody else. Let's do it now for ourselves!

Where to Send the Money

Names and addresses for activist organizations on national, state and city levels can be found in the extensive lists ending chapter 10.

9

Educational Strategies and Tactics

Education must take place in two time frames: immediate and long range. We cannot expect to overcome deep-seated prejudices overnight. But we can, and must, make our fellow citizens and our representatives in government aware of the real situation of American women and the great need for ERA.

A poll by Market Opinion Research in 1975 for the National Commission on the Observance of International Women's 'Year came up with the following alarming picture of how large the information gap has been that we must overcome. Despite all the discussion, publicity, and controversy up until then, a bare majority of American women, 53 percent, were even aware of ERA. Only 24 percent could correctly identify whether their state had ratified it. No large group of women shared any one idea of what the effect of ERA would be. Even among women aware of ERA, 74 percent said they didn't know enough about it to have an informed opinion on the subject![1]

This chapter has three sections. Under the subheading "Person to Person," you will find ideas that involve primarily person-to-person contact as a means of persuasion or building promotional strength. The section entitled "Schools, Churches, and Other Organizations" summarizes ideas for promoting ERA in women's studies courses and on college campuses, possibilities for ERA "Freedom Summers," suggestions for approaching ministers, and a discussion of the stake of children in ERA. The last section, "Media and Newsmaking," offers practical advice on talking to the media and using letters to the editor and advertising. Also included are some ideas for making news (additional to big newsmakers such as the silent vigil or the boycotts outlined in the economic chapter) and for giving ERA Advancement Awards. Again, in all these sections, wherever possible, credit for ideas has been given to the women and

110

men who have written and phoned from all over the country to contribute their suggestions and thoughts. Finally, the chapter closes with some quick access facts to answer questions, rebut falsehoods, and spark up speeches.

Person to Person

Talk to Friends

While many of your friends may hold the same view of ERA as you do, most of them will not be as motivated as you are to *fight* for its passage. Others will have reservations about it or be actively or passively against it. Do not hesitate to use the respect they have for you as a friend to motivate them to work for ERA or to let them know why you disagree with reservations or positions against ERA. A practical reason for doing this is that psychological studies show most people are seldom very well informed or really fixed in their opinions and thus can be heavily influenced by persons they respect who have *firm* opinions based on good information.

Blood Is Thicker Than Water

"Supporters in ratified states should write relatives as well as friends in unratified states, giving good arguments for ratifying ERA and urging them to contact their legislators," says Connie Threinen, ERA Coalition contact for Wisconsin. To this I would add my own suggestion. Go ahead and rough-draft a letter to a hypothetical legislator advancing the points you feel should be made. Then send it to your relative or friend asking them to copy it on their own letterhead and sign and mail it from their state. For most people, this makes letter writing many, many times easier than trying to find the time to draft anything on their own.

In the Neighborhoods

Because of mobility and other reasons, few of us get to know our neighbors anymore. This leaves a great underlying hunger for some sense of community that pro-ERA women can satisfy and use to advantage in all the unratified states.

Announce an ERA coffee or tea at your home for a certain day and time by distributing Xeroxed, letter-size invitations to every house in your neighborhood. (These can be attractive and inexpensive.) Also post this invitation on the four telephone poles that seem to mark your neighborhood's boundary. Have ERA literature on hand, but mainly try to get acquainted with the handful of neighbors who show up and work to get them *also* to announce and hold similar coffees in their homes in order to "smoke out" and strengthen local ERA support. *Do not let that first gathering break up without designating another house and time for another coffee very soon, even if you're forced to hold it again at your own house.*

At the very next coffee, gather support for door-to-door canvassing of the neighborhood to graciously and non-threateningly identify all neighbors' positions on the issue. Now that you have built a core of local supporters, you can begin personally to invite fence-straddlers in. Keep going in this way and, next, personally invite the "antis" in along with a group of firm ERA supporters. Be sure to give those opposed a good chance to air their fears, however, rather than foolishly trying to shut them up. Then work quietly with your facts and mainly your friendly neighborly presence to try to calm their fears and at least neutralize them on ERA.

Sack Lunch Meetings

The sack lunch meeting discussion is a useful, low profile idea. All you have to do is to put up a little announcement on the bulletin board or otherwise pass the word at your place of employment inviting those interested in talking about ERA to join at noon in Conference Room X or Office X. By telling interested parties to bring their own sack lunch, you quickly take care of one of the biggest hassles for lunch meetings and make an easy thing of blending it into the working setting.

Speak Up, Speak Out

"ERA supporters must speak up—loudly and clearly," says Edi Kjos of Bismarck, North Dakota. "No amount of advertising can compare to the impact of a thousand letters to state legislators. And no media campaign can be

as effective as one friend coming out of the 'ERA Closet.' "
To which I would like to add that, if you wait for exactly
the right place and time to talk about ERA, you'll miss
nine out of ten opportunities to effect its passage.

"If you're in an unratified state and are involved in
community activities, speak out on ERA whenever you
can," Elizabeth Dribben of the national office of the League
of Women Voters, advises. "It is our responsibility to se-
cure the needed three additional states," urges Liz Snyder
of Los Angeles. *"This may be the only opportunity in our
lifetimes to write something into the Constitution."*

Schools, Churches, and Other Organizations

ERA On Campus

Those of us who remember what a difference college
campus activism meant for black rights and peace in the
1960s keep hoping for significant movement out of the
campuses to help with ERA. The fact is, few issues light
motivational fires on the campus these days, and there
just may not be time to get any sizable head of motivational
steam going there for ERA if we have a March 22, 1979
deadline.

But should we have an extension—or should ERA fail
this time—major attention *must* be directed toward the
young women on college campuses. They must be reached
and, as jobs after graduation are the big concern these days,
the single most effective tactic is to see that they are informed, by every available means, of what is at stake for
them economically if ERA is not passed. (See chapter 5
of this book—as well as chapter 6 of my book *Dissolution:
No-Fault Divorce, Marriage and the Future of Women,*
McGraw-Hill, 1977.) Young women must be mobilized
to work for a better future for themselves, which is what
ERA is all about.

Women's Studies

Contact with women's studies classes and women's centers
is one immediate tactic for getting already interested and
committed women to bring the issue to their roommates
and friends, to hold meetings and programs, and to use

their energy and efforts to spark, first, interest and, then, active support for the single most important issue affecting young women today.

"Students enrolled in women's studies classes throughout the country should speak and act on behalf of ERA as a class project," suggests Judge Sara Radin of Santa Monica.

When I was teaching a class on the social and legal status of women at Immaculate Heart College several years ago, I used a similar approach. Basically the class project, in which each individual participated, was to come up with a study kit for a similar course which would be suitable for high school classes. This is a model that could be used effectively in connection with ERA. High school civics, history, and women's studies teachers are interested in such materials, particularly if they come with an attractive and articulate college student who can be a guest lecturer in their classes.

Setting up a *students' speakers bureau* on ERA, helping to pass out and disseminate materials, and coming up with their own creative and innovative ideas and actions are other approaches that can get their start in women's studies classes and spread from there.

ERA Rallies

"We have a program of noon speakers," says Cindy Sprague of UCLA, "but there hasn't been anything at all on ERA." She suggests that students, through their own speakers bureau and by drawing from the college and outside community, can remedy that situation. She also suggests ERA rallies, where national celebrities from movies, television, or sports come to speak. Three names that come immediately to mind are Billie Jean King, Valerie Harper, and Alan Alda. But there are countless more (see my list in the next chapter) who are more than willing to tell why ERA is so important to them and to us all.

Students' Newspapers, Films, Radio, and Television

"Just about everybody on campus reads the school papers," points out Cindy Sprague. "They need articles on important and interesting issues. We can make it our business to provide these articles, as well as letters to the editor, and they are bound to get printed."

Campus radio stations are also interested in material and additionally give time to express viewpoints and editorials, so here again is a natural for making facts about ERA known. Programs do not have to be about ERA itself. There is a great interest today in such important issues as rape, abortion, and of course employment opportunities for women when they get out of school. Young women are entitled to this important and interesting information about their present and future.

Campus publications of all kinds, as well as campus radio and television stations, are a natural vehicle. These are the kinds of issues that bring ERA home, that make it evident that we aren't talking about some remote and theoretical question, but about the present and future lives of every one of us.

Student film festivals, focusing on the best films by and about women, are another natural means of sparking interest in ERA. Such film festivals could lead to a national contest, and they can also be combined with appearances by entertainment world celebrities, particularly women, who can talk about their own experiences in that world and tell why they support ERA.

Faculty and Other University Leaders

Faculty and other university leaders must be better integrated into the fight for ERA. ERA is the most important—and only—constitutional amendment concerning human rights since the middle of the nineteenth century. Surely the intellectual community must take a more active part in working for a better society, a society that will *not* come about without ERA. Lectures and discussions on ERA by established and respected faculty members, both outside and inside the universities, are a must. On an organizational level, faculty associations and clubs as well as professional organizations and groups can do a very important job. For example, the Society for the Psychological Study of Social Issues (SPSSI, the activist division of the American Psychological Association), played an important role in the APA decision to boycott nonratified states.

Women's caucuses in all faculty and professional organizations can play a much more important role than they think. This is what the APA experience demonstrates. We may still be a minority in university and other professional organizations, but we can be persuasive, and we can appeal to the conscience and goodwill of our colleagues—whether they are women or men.

Professional Journals

Every field, from law to sociology to economics to the arts, has its own professional journals. ERA and related issues concerning women are naturals for articles and editorials in these publications. The economic impact of ERA is one important and fascinating subject. ERA legal implications is, of course, a natural and there are many other possibilities. But these articles are not going to get written by themselves. *We* must write them or interest others to do so.

Again, the focus need not be on ERA per se—there are certainly numerous interesting, challenging, and intellectually stimulating aspects to the contemporary revolution in sexual roles. There is also much fascinating data coming to light every day about women's history, both facts and stories that have simply not been included in the traditional sources, plus the exciting contemporary events that are being recorded throughout the country today (as, for example, by the International Women's Year Oral History Project).[2]

High Schools and Elementary Schools

Education about women and ERA (wherever possible with interesting illustrative materials) must be made available to school teachers at all grade levels. Teachers associations, curriculum design committees, and PTA meetings are all avenues to this end. Other approaches are through Girls' Day, which is observed in most high schools, through girls' clubs, and also through community projects. One such project is the California-based Constitutional Rights Foundation, which brings education about legal rights and problems faced by young people into the classroom. Certainly our children, both girls and boys, are entitled to information about their present and future legal rights— and ERA.

ERA Posters

Poster art is a major American art form. Why not hold university-sponsored national contests for the best ERA poster? Be sure to hook this in with a publishing house, to publish an art book containing the winners of the national prizes. Not only will handsome posters come out of it, but it is another means of bringing ERA to people's attention: in art classes, in universities, on campuses holding the contests, and finally—visually and beautifully—through the resulting posters and art books.

ERA Freedom Summers

If ERA fails to win passage or the deadline is extended, here is an important idea, passed on by attorney Karen Kaplowitz of Los Angeles. "Judy Stiehm, who teaches at the University of Southern California, recently suggested a Freedom Summer for ERA comparable to the Freedom Summers for civil rights in the South. Students would receive some financial support to go to key states such as Oklahoma, Illinois, North Carolina, South Carolina, and Florida to work for ERA passage in those states."

The Role of the Church

ERA has the endorsement and support of major American religious organizations (see list in chapter 10), but support must be turned into action, and that is our job. One way is to encourage religious conferences to include on their agenda workshops on ERA and the changing roles of women and men. Another logical place to kindle interest and understanding about ERA is through religious retreats, where the agenda should again include these vitally important subjects. For materials on the family, chapter 5 can be very useful, as there are very natural concerns—and unfortunately also many unfounded fears—based on misinformation about what ERA will do to the American family. Many religious leaders are today concerned about civil liberties and fundamental human rights. Here chapter one can be particularly useful.

Talk to the Ministers

Many ministers will shy away from saying anything about ERA, fearing they may alienate conservatives in their congregations. However, many others will be very sympathetic because of the humanistic thrust of most religions when they are at their best. Both types of ministers should be encouraged to schedule discussions and church workshops and to devote sermons to the subject of sexual equality. Point out to them that a relatively safe way to do this is to examine sex equality and ERA as one of the "most pressing social issues of our day." The Bible of both Christians and Jews is, of course, laden with instances and attitudes of sexual inequality, being the historical product of an earlier time in patriarchal society when women's rights were seldom mentioned. But the thrust not only of the great religious thinkers but, according to psychologists, of the religious impulse or need itself, is toward *equality* among humans before God. Ministers should be urged to confront this conflict within organized religion and work it through in sermons and workshops.

Women's Conferences and Continuing Education

Both individually and through organizations, women can do a great deal to focus attention on ERA, to allay fears, and to inspire active interest. Women's conferences on *all* issues affecting women—from rape protection to government representation, from economic discrimination to our hidden history—are natural vehicles. So are the many continuing education classes, held both on and off our campuses, designed to bring women the knowledge and the skills that so many of us now need to enter the labor market and to manage our lives more productively and effectively.

Know Your Laws

"There is a need for women to be educated as to the laws under which we live. All organizations supporting ERA should have workshops to explain the issues and what ERA will and will not do in terms of laws," notes Pat Callon of

Little Rock, Arkansas. The material in chapters 2 and 3, "Facts and Fancies," and the chapters that follow on interpretation and enforcement of ERA are good starting points.

Media and News Making

What We Expect From Media

As a minimum standard of fairness, the National Commission on the Observance of International Women's Year made this recommendation to the media: "Women's activities and organizations should be treated with the same respect accorded men's activities and organizations. The women's movement should be reported as seriously as any other civil rights movement; it should not be made fun of, ridiculed, or belittled. Just as the terms 'black libbers', 'Symbionese libbers', or 'Palestine libbers' are not used, the term 'women's libbers' should not be used. Just as jokes at the expense of blacks are no longer made, jokes should not be made at women's expense. The news of women should not be sensationalized. Too often news media have reported conflict among women and ignored unity. Coverage of women's conferences is often limited solely to so-called 'splits' or fights. These same disputes at conferences attended by men would be considered serious policy debates."[8]

The media are the single most important force in shaping American public opinion. It is therefore essential that we work hard, not only to obtain more coverage for ERA, but to obtain fairer and better coverage as well.

Talk to Media People

Many of the reporters, researchers, and other staff on newspapers, radio, and television are women. They may not have policymaking positions, but they are often, from their own experience, very aware of the need for ERA. Additionally, there are many men in the media who are concerned and committed to issues affecting civil rights. Find these media people, make contact with them, and see whether you can put your heads together to improve and increase the coverage of women and ERA. For example, read local newspapers to identify reporters and columnists who seem sympathetic. Then form or join a media committee for your local women's organization and, on behalf of your organization, call in asking to see them. Go in equipped to give them as good a list as you can compile at the time of potentially newsworthy activities your group will be engaged in over the next few months. Ask them for any ideas they may have of interesting stories for which your organization might provide some aid with research and legwork. In other words, enlist their help—and offer yours in return.

Letters to the Editor

An interesting phenomenon of our time is the growth of more space for "letters to the editor" sections in newspapers. Take advantage of this highly influential forum by regularly reading these sections and becoming an active contributor as often as possible. Ideally, one interested local women's group should appoint a "letters to the editor" committee, with volunteers agreeing to read specific local sections regularly and then alert other volunteer letter writers to initiate discussion or respond to threats or opportunities that the readers identify. Also, examine papers for *un*sympathetic reporters, columnists, and editorial writers. Immediately follow up all appearances of their material downgrading ERA with a letter to the editor, or ideally a guest editorial, to present the truth about ERA.

Demand and Provide Accurate Information about ERA

In a speech at the National Press Club on September 12, 1975, Jill Ruckelshaus drew attention to the imbalance of media coverage that gives the same weight to the opinions of the Stop-ERA forces as to the majority report of the Senate Judiciary Committee on the Amendment. *"This isn't a question of one opinion about the ERA having equal standing with a contrary opinion,"* she said. "When the courts interpret the Equal Rights Amendment, they will *not* turn to a Stop-ERA pamphlet; rather they will look to the one authentic piece of legislative history we have; the Senate Judiciary Committee Report on the

Amendment which answers well many of the questions the Amendment opponents are raising."[4]

It is essential that we stress this point, over and over again. The media are *not* being interesting by featuring "both sides of the ERA question." They are being plain *irresponsible*. If a responsible journalist were presented with a claim that milk causes cancer in babies, he or she would never dream of giving it equal time with the truth about milk, as studied and reported by scientists and doctors. The same rule should apply to ERA.

Emphasize the Positive

"Somehow we need to encourage the media to emphasize the positive instead of enjoying female-versus-female fighting, or ERA losses," notes Nancy Neuman of Philadelphia. "Hardly anyone knows Indiana ratified in 1977, but everyone knows Florida and North Carolina didn't!"

Start clipping ERA stories pro or con from your local newspapers. Rate these stories "positive" or "negative." When you've got enough to make a comparison—say, twenty or so—write the operating head of your local paper on behalf of your organization, acquainting him or her with your survey and your desire to discuss the results with interested staff members. Ideally, to get anywhere with such a newspaper contact, the letter should be written by the president of the largest and best-established local women's organization. But, however you manage to get the attention of reporters and editorial writers, at least start by asking their advice on how you can gain more positive and less negative coverage for ERA—which tends to be more effective than accusing them of working against you.

Newsmaking Events

Feature articles on important issues can only get a certain amount of space in the media, so we have to find other ways of getting coverage. One way is the human interest story, the feature on a celebrity or a political personality or simply the story of a woman or man whose life has been seriously (or comically) affected by the need for ERA. One of our main ways of getting media coverage, however, remains the *making* of news. This need of the media for the new and the unusual has in the past tended to cause us troubles: as for example, the greater coverage given to a few alleged bra burnings than to serious and important issues and events. But it's something that we're stuck with, and so the question is how can we use it creatively. One way is—to borrow from the contemporary art scene—to create our own event, our own "happening."

The more creative and inventive these ideas are, the better, but for most of us, the more conventional methods are going to have to do. For example, star-studded benefits are always a way to get media coverage. "Enlist the aid of women in the media—especially television," urges Louise Manuel of Los Angeles. "Get Linda Ronstadt to do a benefit for the ERA at the Forum with as heavy a line-up as you can muster—for example, Barbra Streisand, Bonnie Raitt, Natalie Cole. Call it Women at the Forum and make it a benefit for ERA passage." All cities have local entertainment stars, so use this tip from the "entertainment capital" to produce your own.

A more unusual approach was used in Florida. Under the heading of "blood money," Florida women launched a blood donation program to dramatize the depth of their commitment to the passage of ERA while also raising money for the cause. The slogan was "Give Your Blood for Your Rights." Both women and men sympathizers gave their blood to blood banks and donated the payments to a coalition backing passage of ERA.

Another newsgetter is the Homemakers Rally and Walk for Equality. In 1976 ERA proponents rallied and walked five miles in subfreezing temperatures to the Virginia State Capitol. Their purpose was to present a petition supporting ERA to James Thomson, then chairman of the Virginia House of Delegates Privileges and Elections Committee. ERA opponent Thomson refused to see them, but the press coverage of the walk got across their basic message: that their petition from Thomson's home district contained one more signature than the total number of votes Thomson received in his last election. The International Women's Year conference in Houston in 1977 opened with another nationally publicized walk. This is a proven tactic that can pay off in your state.

If all else fails, ERA dinner meetings attended by local luminaries such as a sympathetic mayor can always get a little bit of media time and space. Members of women's organizations, such as the Business and Professional Women's Clubs, should encourage as many ERA dinner meetings as possible. Topics for speakers and/or panelists should be ERA related, e.g., "Violence Against Women," "Women in Today's Job Situation," etc. You can encourage other organizations to use ERA dinner programs by forming a committee in your organization to develop a local speakers' bureau and ERA-related topics making use of their names and expertise to build attendance.

Pro-ERA Advertising

As we go to the wire in key states, advertising can play an important role. Royce Neuschatz of Los Angeles recommends "ads in papers bearing the names of prominent ERA supporters, men and women. Radio spots by noted men and women with facts countering the myths can also be helpful during a calm but forceful media push by a good ad agency."

Other styles of advertising that we can all use—whether or not we have the money or access to newspaper, radio, poster, or television space—are automobile bumper stickers, signs on club bulletin boards, and, of course, ERA buttons and jewelry. To make the cause more visible, ERA T-shirts are effective. Lucy Pierson urges the purchase and wearing of ERA T-shirts. In her area, they are sold by the Washington ERA Coalition, P.O. Box 1002, Seattle, Washington 98103.

Better Use of Professional Publications

"I have dealt quite extensively with business and professional women in my efforts to gain support for ERA," writes ERA Illinois Co-chairperson Ann Ida Gannon of Springfield. "I find that many of them are ignorant about the basic constitutional principle and the history of the amendment, and they make their judgements primarily on the basis of headline news about 'radical activities.' It is important that professional journals and newsletters carry information that is precise and convincing."

Talk Shows

National and local talk shows are a staple in American living rooms these days. They are an excellent way to reach women and men about ERA. The way to do this is to get local and national celebrities who are guests on these shows (preferably regularly) to work positive mention of ERA into their appearances. Wherever possible, they should be encouraged to engage their hosts or hostesses into conversation about ERA, to explore issues, and most important to personalize these in terms of their own lives and their own aspirations, hopes and needs.

Look over the schedules of all local radio and TV stations to identify potentially sympathetic disc jockeys and talk show hosts and hostesses. Tell them you would like more coverage of ERA. Or be direct: perhaps even approach them with copies of this book—or your typed items from it—to see if they will work factual briefs and techniques for ERA passage into regular programs.

ERA Advancement Awards

Develop an ERA Advancement Award, Judy Chirlin of Washington, D.C., suggests. On a regular basis, your award committee should screen and select a "Woman or Man of the Week" or "Woman or Man of the Month" who has done the most to advance ERA during the period under review. This will be a good way to acknowledge the support of key legislators, of major funding sources, and of favorable editorial writers and to get publicity for ERA.

Some Ammunition

Quick Facts about the Position of Women

(from the proposed National Plan of Action drafted for the National Women's Conference, Nov. 18–21, 1977, in Houston, Texas. Statistics are generally for the years 1974, 1975, or 1976).[5]

* Seventy percent of the dramatic roles on television are for men.

* Women hold only 1 percent of the top paying senior library jobs in the country.
* Authorities estimate as many as 28 million "battered women."
* More than six million children under six have mothers working outside the home.
* Women professors on the average earn $3,000 less annually than men professors.
* Eighty percent of all law school fellowships go to men.
* Public school teachers are 63 percent women, but only 18 percent of primary school principals and 2 percent of secondary principals are women.
* Only 5 percent of the elective offices in the United States are held by women.
* Nine percent of state legislators are women.
* Only ten women have ever been appointed to federal courts and only 8 percent of the judges listed in the 1970 census were women.
* Of juvenile girls in custodial institutions, 75 percent are charged with disrespectful behavior or sexual misconduct—offenses for which adults could not be confined. Only 25 percent of boys are detained for these same offenses, and they're usually confined for shorter periods of time than are girls.
* Women offenders account for 10 percent of violent crime.
* Eighteen percent of all women sixty-five and over have incomes below the poverty level—this goes up to 42 percent for black women age sixty-five and over.
* Women sixty-five and over have the lowest median income of any age or sex group, around $1,900 a year, about half what men in the same group receive.
* Between 1970 and 1975 the number of reported rapes in the U.S. increased 48 percent.
* In 1975 alone there were 56,090 rapes—one reported to authorities every nine minutes.
* Of rapes reported to authorities, barely one-half resulted in an arrest, only 58 percent of those arrested are prosecuted, and almost half of the cases prosecuted result in acquittals or dismissals.
* Of the 24.3 million poor people in the U.S., 19.6 million are women and children.
* In 1976, twice as many women age sixteen and over than men lived below the poverty level.

All the Presidents' Wives

When "antis" claim "no real lady" supports ERA, point out that Rosalyn Carter, Betty Ford, and Lady Bird Johnson all support ERA. Read or give the opponents what these three Presidents' wives had to say during their stirring appearance together at the International Women's Year Conference in Houston, November 17, 1977.

"We must guard against obscuring valid issues with defensiveness and anger. The glue that holds us together is the firm knowledge that our basic goals are the same."[6] ——Rosalyn Carter.

"We may have different interests, but we shouldn't be dismayed by the clash of opinions and ideas. It has been said the 'evils' of a controversy will pass, but its benefits are permanent."[7]——Betty Ford.

"I once thought the women's movement belonged more to my daughters than to me. But I've come to know it belongs to women of all ages."[8]——Lady Bird Johnson.

Political Quotable Quotes

President Carter, in support of ERA, said that equal rights for women are an inseparable part of human rights for all. "As women achieve equality, men, too, are liberated from ancient prejudices and relieved of arbitrary barriers to personal fulfillment."[9]

President Gerald Ford stated, "The time for ratification of the Equal Rights Amendment has come, just as surely as did the time for the Nineteenth Amendment. . . . Americans must deal with those inequities that still linger as barriers to the full participation of women in our nation's life."[10]

Supreme Court Justice William J. Brennan commented: "There can be no doubt our nation has a long and unfortunate history of sex discrimination. Traditionally, such discrimination was rationalized as an attitude of romantic paternalism which, in practical effect, put women not on a pedestal but in a cage. . . ."[11]

Report No. 92-689, Senate Judiciary Committee: "The social and economic cost to our society, as well as the psychological impact of sex discrimination, are immeasur-

able. That a majority of our population should be subjected to the indignities and limitations of second class
citizenship is a fundamental affront to personal human
liberty."[12]

Remember, it's only a few powerful old-line politicians
that are blocking women's right to equality. ERA would
have passed in 1975 except for sixteen legislators in five
states; in 1977 the margins were even narrower: Florida
rejected the amendment by two votes, both turnarounds by
men who had previously committed their support to the
principle of equal rights.

Churches on ERA

*The 1976 General Conference of the United Methodist
Church:*

> The Gospel makes it clear that Jesus regarded women
> and men as being of equal worth. Nowhere is it re-
> corded that Jesus treated women in a different man-
> ner than he did men. . . . We therefore commend
> the U.S. Congress for its passage of the Equal Rights
> Amendment to the U.S. Constitution and call upon
> the various states to ratify this amendment in order to
> insure that "equality of rights under the law shall not
> be denied or abridged by the United States or by any
> state on account of sex." Be it resolved that all United
> Methodists work through the appropriate structures
> and channels toward ratification of the amendment
> by their respective states.[13]

*The 112th General Assembly of the Presbyterian Church
in the United States:*

> God made both women and men equal in his sight;
> hence, any discrimination on the basis of sex which
> assumes an inherent inferior-superior relationship is
> contrary to the will of God. . . . This 112th General
> Assembly . . . urges its members to work in society to
> promote the equal status of women, specifically . . .
> to call on their state legislatures, if those legislatures
> have not already done so, to ratify the Amendment . . .
> to provide specifically for equal rights for women.[14]

The 1973 General Assembly of the Christian Church (Disciples of Christ):

> While admitting that it has not always lived up to its own teachings, the church has long proclaimed that laws and practices which prevent women from exercising their freedom as children of God are morally indefensible. . . . Therefore, be it resolved that the General Assembly . . . endorse the Equal Rights Amendment and urge its ratification by those states where that has not yet occurred. . . .[15]

The 1970 General Assembly of the Unitarian Universalist Association, the 1970 Annual Conference of the Church of the Brethren, and the 1970 General Assembly of the United Presbyterian Church USA, the 1975 Governing Board of the National Council of Churches and the 1975 General Synod of the United Church of Christ have passed similar resolutions.

(From the leaflet "The Church, Religion, and the Equal Rights Amendment," available for $5 per hundred from ERA Support Project, 100 Maryland Avenue, N.E., Washington, D.C. 20002. Order No. W6000.)

Biblical Support for ERA

Old Testament passages are quoted as authority for the subservience of women. And the Bible does contain such passages. But there are others too, with a contrary message. For example, the equality of men and women is affirmed at the very beginning of the Old Testament: "So God created man in his own image, in the image of God he created him; *male and female he created them.* And God blessed them, and God said to them, 'Be fruitful and multiply and fill the earth and subdue it and have dominion over the fish of the sea and over the birds of the air and over every living thing that moves upon the earth.' " (Genesis 1:27–28)

In the New Testament too, authority for both positions can be found. Jesus certainly repeatedly acknowledges women as human beings in his relationships, so much so that one theologian has stated: "Jesus was a feminist, that is, a person who promoted the equality of women with men, who treats women primarily as human persons and willingly contravenes social customs in so acting."[16]

The rejection by Jesus of prevailing customs is seen throughout the Gospels: women were permitted to study the scriptures; to use their intellectual skills, to speak in public, and to bear witness.

Throughout both the Old and New Testaments women are remembered for their distinctive contributions: Deborah (prophet and judge), Miriam (prophet and musician), and Queen Esther (who saved the Jews); and in the New Testament, Anna (prophet), and Lydia (a businesswoman who founded an early house church).

(Adapted from the leaflet "The Church, Religion, and the Equal Rights Amendment," available for $5 per hundred from ERA Support Project, 100 Maryland Avenue, N.E., Washington, D.C. 20002. Order No. W6000.)

Information-Coordinating Agencies

On the national level, one of the functions of ERAmerica is to disseminate and coordinate information about ERA. It is located at 1525 M Street, Washington, D.C. 20005. Phone: 202/833-4354.

Equally important is the California-based Institute for Studies in Equality, located at 926 J Street, Suite 1014, Sacramento, California 95814, Phone: 916/444-9196. "ISE is a nationwide information exchange," writes Director Anita Miller, who also chairs the California Commission on the Status of Women. "Our goals are to serve as a data clearinghouse and facilitate people working together by putting individuals and organizations in contact with one another. To this end, we have an information resources desk, and an equality hotline, offering immediate information on topical subjects, a data bank, and a referral service. We also have a media outreach program, offering materials for the development of feature and news stories, as well as film documentaries and other materials, a conference and program consultation service, a speakers' bureau, and a number of our own publications on ERA, with particular emphasis on impact on state and local laws."[17]

Additional information-coordinating organizations are state ERA coalitions, the League of Women Voters, the

American Association of University Women, NOW, the National Women's Political Caucus, and other activist organizations listed at the end of the next chapter.

Some Entertainment Celebrities for ERA[18]

Alan Alda	Nancy Kulp
Adrienne Barbeau	Linda Lavin
Rona Barrett	Cloris Leachman
Candice Bergen	Norman Lear
Polly Bergen	Shirley MacLaine
Ruth Berle	Rue McClanahan
Karen Black	Richard Masur
Georgia Brown	Lee Meriwether
Gary Burghoff	Mary Ann Mobley
Carol Burnett	Mary Tyler Moore
Diahann Carroll	Kathleen Nolan
Judy Collins	Mary Kay Place
Leslie Curtis	Dory Previn
Altovise Davis	Tony Randall
Ossie Davis	Donna Reed
Ruby Dee	Madlyn Rhue
Linda Evans	Nancy Sinatra
Mike Farrell	Bruce Solomon
Barbara Feldon	Jean Stapleton
Jane Fonda	Loretta Swit
Betty Furness	Marlo Thomas
Lee Grant	Lily Tomlin
Lorne Greene	Cicely Tyson
Joan Hackett	Jessica Walter
Valerie Harper	James Whitmore
Fay Kanin	Nancy Wilson

10

Who Is the Enemy — and Who Are Our Friends: Useful Lists, Names, and Addresses

This chapter has two parts. It opens with specific informa-tion about the adversaries to ERA: who they are and what to do about their opposition. (More about the "antis" can be found in Part I, particularly chapters 2 and 3, on "Facts and Fancies.") The second part of the chapter is composed of lists and names and addresses for the organizations supporting and actively working for as well as against passage of ERA, with suggestions on how to use this information.

Know the Enemy

Who Opposes ERA?

The following organizations are on record as opposing ERA: the American Conservative Union, American Women are Richly Endowed (AWARE), the Communist Party U.S.A., the Daughters of the American Revolution (DAR), Eagle Forum, Humanitarian Opposes the Degrading Our Girls (HOT DOG), John Birch Society, Knights of Co-lumbus, Ku Klux Klan, League of Housewives (formerly HOW), Liberty Lobby, National Council of Catholic Women, Rabbinical Alliance of America, Stop ERA, the American Party, Veterans of Foreign Wars, Young Amer-icans for Freedom, and the Family Preservation League.[1]

According to Phyllis Schlafly's Stop ERA, the list also includes some state branches of the American Legion, the Farm Bureau, and the PTA. Also on that list are the Mormon Church, Catholic Daughters of America, the Missouri Synod of the Lutheran Church (Commission on Theology and Church Relations), and the Union of Orthodox Rabbis and the Union of Orthodox Jewish Congregations as well as the Illinois, Michigan, Florida, Arkansas, Virginia, and New York Federations of Women's Clubs, the Conservative Party of New York, and the League of Large Families.

There have been questions raised about the accuracy of the Stop ERA list, but the most important fact to remember—and to point out—is this: Unlike the organizations that support ERA, many of the organizations on record against ERA are *not* real organizations with true memberships. While the organizations supporting ERA have membership lists which can readily be obtained (with memberships of thousands of people), many of the "anti" organizations appear to be just another name. One good example is HOT DOG (Humanitarian Opposes the Degrading Our Girls), which turns out to be just another John Birch Society sub-organization, a front. According to the Institute for Studies in Equality, other such "ad hoc" groups are the Family Preservation League, the League of Housewives, and the Liberty Lobby.

It is also important to note that the major organizations that are opposed to ERA, such as the Veterans of Foreign Wars, the American Party, the Ku Klux Klan, the Knights of Columbus, and the John Birch Society, are primarily male. However, they sometimes have women as spokespeople, and it is important to understand the situation of these women—how it is that they have permitted themselves to be used to fight against their own best interests.

Who Are the Leaders: Two Profiles

Billy James Hargis

Two streams of opposition to ERA are right-wing extremism, which is against equality in any form, and fundamentalist religion, which views woman not only as a second-rate creation from the rib of a man but also as a source of evil. These two streams are perhaps best personified today in the figure of anti-ERA evangelist Billy James Hargis, whose scandal-ridden, once nearly bankrupt radio "ministry" now reportedly grosses more than $10 million a year. Hargis's opposition to ERA follows his earlier denunciation of the late Martin Luther King, Jr., as a Red instigator, his opposition to high school education as a communist plot, and his support for the B-1 Bomber. In 1975 *Time* magazine published an interesting exposé. "According to *Time*," summarized a recent *Los Angeles Times* article, "a couple married by Hargis discovered on their wedding night that each had had sexual relations with him. A number of other students, both male and female, also told *Time* reporters of similar experiences." Hargis denied the allegations as an attempt by the "leftist Eastern press" to defame him. Contributions to his causes did drop off sharply for two months after the scandal broke, he told the L.A. *Times*, but then rebounded "stronger than ever."[2]

Phyllis Schlafly

The opposition to ERA was mainly a matter of right-wing uneasiness until Phyllis Schlafly jumped in and—with the financial backing of the most retrogressive forces in the nation—proceeded to whip the opposition into top fighting shape.

Here is some of her background. A physically attractive woman who worked in an ammunition plant to support herself through college, she graduated Phi Beta Kappa and then gained a master's degree at Harvard. She was working as a research assistant in a bank when "Fred Schlafly came along and saved me."[3] They had six children, and husband Fred ran successfully for Congress. They began to participate together in more and more right-wing causes: Phyllis reportedly joined the John Birch Society in 1960, for example, and began to appear often on rightist radio and television programs like those of Billy James Hargis and Dean Manion. Together with Fred's sister, Eleanor, the three also went to work creating a small network of right-wing funding "fronts" centered in their hometown of Alton, Illinois.[4]

With this kind of support, Phyllis Schafly has been running for political office off and on since 1952. She is the author or coauthor of eight rightist books, including *A*

Choice Not An Echo, identified by the *Chicago Daily News* in a 1965 editorial as "one of the gamiest" of a group of "grubby paperback books written and published by right-wing Republicans" in support of Barry Goldwater's 1964 presidential quest.[5] It sold three million copies. Her regular *Phyllis Schlafly Report* (see chapter 2 for excerpts) has eighteen thousand subscribers. She regularly reaches millions of listeners through CBS Radio's "Spectrum" program, through a syndicated newspaper column, and through speeches and special radio and television appearances all over the country.[6]

People keep asking, "Where does Phyllis Schlafly get all the money to support such a huge and amazing enterprise?" Her publications intimate that the money comes either from subscriptions and small contributions to the Eagle Forum, which publishes the *Phyllis Schlafly Report*, or from impassioned supporters who bake and sell thousands of cakes and cookies for her cause. However, the evidence mounts that the rightist "big money" sees this bright, hard-hitting woman as the best thing that has happened to them since the heydays of Father Coughlin and Senator Joseph McCarthy. Not only do corporations like the Adolph Coors Company (see the economics section on boycotts) support her, but her hometown has for years now been a nest of funding "fronts" for receiving rightist money. The Cardinal Mindszenty Foundation, America Wake Up, and Defenders of American Liberties are groups that have not only been located in Alton, Illinois, along with the Eagle Forum, but also seem to have been interlocked with Schlaflys and well-known local Birch Society members as officers or supporters.[7]

"I think I am a good example of how women can do whatever they want with their lives," Mrs. Schlafly says. "They don't need legislation to have a fun, exciting, fulfilling life."[8]

What Are Their Tactics?

Some Opposition Quotes

"The National States Rights Party is opposing ratification of the so-called Equal Rights Amendment to the United

States Constitution because it is another Jewish scheme to destroy marriage, the family, the home, and motherhood. The leaders of the ERA Women's Lib movement are radical Jews, such as Gloria Steinem, Betty Friedan and Bella Abzug."[9]——J.B. Stoner, president of the National States Rights Party, in the *Thunderbolt*, April, 1973.

"ERA is an attack on holy scriptures, the family unit, the marriage relationship, parental duties and rights, the roles God has given men and women, and the right to be a woman! ERA will *not* give a woman dignity. . . . Her faith in GOD does that!"[10]——From a cartoon booklet published by Phyllis Schlafly's Eagle Forum.

(For more quotes, see chapter 2 and 3)

How Antis Defeated ERA in Florida

With the South providing the big block of states remaining opposed to ERA, knowing how the amendment was defeated in Florida in April 1977 can be useful. According to *Time* magazine, despite a poll showing that 62 percent of Florida voters favored ERA, some legislators were more impressed by the "road-show acts of Phyllis Schlafly," who told them that "women already enjoy superior rights." Members of her Stop ERA brigades wore long, formal dresses and "descended on legislators, bearing gifts of homemade bread 'from the breadmakers to the breadwinners.'" The most effective tactic of the opponents, according to *Time*, was "the misleading rhetoric that they have used to cloud the issues," e.g., claiming that ERA would force the legalization of homosexual marriage, end the support of wives by their husbands, and require use of the same public toilets by men and women. "With scant effect," concluded *Time*, "legal experts insist that the ERA requires none of these measures." Senator Lori Wilson, sponsor of the Florida ERA resolution, also blamed defeat on the good old boy image in southern life—the "good old boy who stubbornly fought against change, opposing to the last women's right to vote and black civil rights," and who, according to the *Time* magazine assessment, found the anti-ERA antics an excuse "to vote their predilections."[11]

How They Stopped ERA in North Carolina and Nevada

"By a vote of 26 to 24, the North Carolina State Senate, on March 1, rejected a liberal campaign coordinated through the White House to have North Carolina ratify ERA's adoption as an amendment to the U.S. Constitution," crowed a rightist newsletter afterward. Then it revealed how this was done. "Just a week earlier, on February 23, the Conservative Caucus had financed a mailing, signed by Phyllis Schlafly, National Chairman of Stop-ERA, which was sent to more than 86,000 North Carolina residents, urging each of them to contact their legislators to block passage of ERA. We are told that tens of thousands of postcards were sent to members of the North Carolina Senate as a result of the TCC mailing, which is credited with a decisive role in the outcome. We are also proud that Pacific Coast regional director Jaine Hansen, on detail to Phyllis Schlafly, played a very effective leadership role in stopping ERA in North Carolina, as she had just a few weeks earlier in her home state of Nevada."[12]

One lesson: If the opposition can send "tens of thousands of postcards" to legislators, we must too. And if they can collect signatures, we can and must do the same.

Falsehoods and the Media Double Standard

To prove their contention that ERA will legalize homosexual marriages, force coed public toilets, etc., etc., anti-ERA propagandists have circulated false stories through the media. For example, there is the widely circulated story that when Colorado adopted an ERA in 1972, homosexual marriages were legalized in that state. The truth is that *one* local clerk issued marriage licenses to men. *The Attorney General of Colorado then held that the licenses were invalid.* Further, the district attorney, who originally advised the clerk that he could do this, thought that the marriage law, *not the ERA,* authorized the licenses.[18] As for the charge that the state of Washington ERA has resulted in coed public toilets and coed prison cells and sleeping quarters in public institutions, Washington Governor Daniel J. Evans had this to say:

"The accusations concerning integration of facilities are so ridiculous, we in Washington have ceased to reply to them. Rights of privacy remain fully protected in this state and thus our restroom facilities, prison cells, and sleeping quarters of public institutions remain totally segregated."[14]

Yet the press continues to give this kind of anti-ERA propaganda a great deal of coverage—and weight. Eileen Shanahan, a *New York Times* reporter, has guessed that the reason is that it has been difficult for the press, because of typically short deadlines, to check out Phyllis Schlafly's "systematic misrepresentations."[15] But surely this kind of excuse cannot be countenanced and, indeed, seems absurd. There are short deadlines for every story. Substitute for Phyllis Schlafly the foreign minister of the Soviet Union, the Atomic Energy Commission, President Carter, or a spokesperson for the Dodgers, and see what kind of a media double standard this reveals!

Where Do They Get the Money?

To give an idea of the amounts of money that have been going into the anti-ERA propaganda campaign, here is a list of contributions from radical right sources:

1. The John Birch Society—$800,000 per year
2. Schlafly-Eagle Forum—$70,000 per year, based on the number of subscriptions to the *Schlafly Report*
3. The Conservative Caucus—$64,000 the first half of 1977 (The actual contribution was probably much higher.)
4. Local lobbyists—$75,000 ($25,000 per state for three major efforts during 1977)
5. Other radical right organizations—$50,000 per year (The estimate is based on the volume of literature and publicized activities of groups such as Patriotic Letter Writers of America, National Association of Pro-America, Young Americans for Freedom, the American Party and its affiliates, the Cardinal Mindzsenty Foundation, etc.)
6. Religious organizations—large but unknown sums

Total: $1,059,000 plus additional sums that cannot be determined.[16]

Source: *The Advocate*, November 16, 1977.

What to Do

Friends, Not Enemies

It is important to know the enemy, but it is also important to deal with one large portion of the opposition as potential friends. Make no mistake about it, the ambitious demagogues trying to stop ERA are true enemies and will try every trick in the book to gain their ends. But a large part of the opposition is composed of women who are fearful and anxious, and unused as yet to thinking for themselves. As Erica Jong writes, "Most of the women who are against ERA don't know what it really means and have been brainwashed by well-organized reactionary groups (Mormons, Birchers, etc.)." But they *can* be reached. Perhaps the most effective approach here is woman to woman. As Midge Evans of Tucson, Arizona, puts it, "Sit down and relate ERA to the everyday needs of women on a woman-to-woman basis instead of treating all antis as if they were enemies."

Laugh 'em Off

We made a very big mistake in not taking the opposition seriously until hard-driving rightists had stopped ratification in state after state. Nevertheless, "laughing off" the anti-ERA arguments is an effective tactic in many situations. As ERA coalition contact Constance Kite of Montpelier, Vermont, advises, "Take the position that no one can possibly take them seriously. It makes such a difference in the way the media will handle the situation. People will do anything to avoid being laughed at. Anger and political opposition they have learned to deal with, but low-keyed ridicule is something that anybody in public position cannot handle—it's wholly demoralizing."

Offense versus Defense

Mrs. Hermine D. Tobolowsky of Dallas, Texas—who from the tenor of her advice must be quite a battler—sends these tips on how to deal with the anti-ERA folk. "Have factual information at your fingertips to refute the many misrepresentations about ERA made by our opponents, but *don't* be defensive—counterattack! Express righteous indignation when opponents object to drafting women—why, how could anyone be unwilling to serve his or her country in a time of emergency!"

Shirley Heitland of Brookings, South Dakota, specifically advises us to go for the antis with questions like, "What have *you* ever done for women on welfare? Or for women alone? Or for displaced homemakers?" "You are so patriotic—should you not want to serve your country?"

Set the Record Straight

The best tactic against the opposition is the plain, honest truth. Refuse to let opponents make ERA a divisive issue between men and women, liberals and conservatives. *Show them that ERA is not a "women's issue," but a "people's issue"* benefiting men, women, and children. Do this by pointing out that it's supported by such conservatives as Strom Thurmond in the U.S. Senate and such liberals as Senator Birch Bayh; that the ultraliberal Representative Emanuel Celler prevented the passage of ERA for many years by keeping it bottled up in the Judiciary Committee of the House of Representatives; that the opposition has ranged from the Ku Klux Klan and the John Birch Society to the Communist Party.

To Debate or Not to Debate

"Refuse to be pulled into negative debates with opponents," some ERA workers advise. "Don't give respectability to their distortions by sharing a platform and being put on the defensive." This is often good advice, but I'd like to add a lawyer's qualification. There are times when it is better to confront the enemy and others when it is just impossible to avoid them. The secret of success in these situations is not to let yourself get bogged down answering your opponent's charges or in responding to his or her points. Brush most of them aside as being of little consequence and steadily advance your own pro-ERA arguments and points.

This is what lawyers are trained to do. We do *not* debate opposing counsel. We do *not* try to convince them of the justice of our cause. Our aim is to convince the judge—in this case, the unconvinced, the fence-straddlers, and those who are frightened or misinformed. We can accept debates without feeling we have to answer opposition claims and distortions on every count. We can concentrate on making our own important points—and in selling ERA with our commitment, our faith, and just good humor and charm. It's often just as important to be confident, courteous, pleasant, and even funny than to rebut every single argument brought against ERA—arguments which can sometimes just be dismissed by the simple and accurate statement that they are just not true.

Our Supporters and Friends

Who They Are

Our friends and supporters include individual women and men from all over this country, from Jimmy Carter, the President of the United States, to Anne Follis, president of Housewives for ERA; from Governor Ella Grasso of Connecticut to AFL-CIO delegate Earl Wilson who helped shape the AFL-CIO resolution that passage of the ERA would be a top AFL-CIO priority in the 1978 legislative session.[17] Our friends and supporters also include just about every major American political and civic organization from the Girl Scouts of America to the Democratic and Republican National Committees, from the American Bar Association to the YWCA.

A list of some of the best-known endorsing organizations follows. Use it to persuade doubters of the widespread, established group support for ERA and if any organizations to which you belong have not endorsed the amendment show them the list to get off the fence and take a stand.

Among, and in addition to, these endorsing organizations is a smaller number of organizations either organized specifically to advance sex equality, ERA, and women's rights or with especially active units devoted to this cause. These are the organizations to join—they need every active woman they can get. Volunteer to help them, even if you don't join, and use them as an information source. Names, addresses, and phone numbers can change, of course, but often some name and number can be better than none, if only to serve as a starting point.

A third way of relating to the fight for ERA passage through organizations is by giving money directly. Many women activated by this book and other information sources will want to send a contribution immediately to some place where it can do good. The best rule of thumb here is to make your first priority ERA state coalitions and other activist groups working on specific goals and time-tables. See the lists that follows, or call activist friends in your own area and ask who is getting the job done and where contributions will do the most good. Then decide on somebody to send your money to *and do it!*

National and Regional Organizations Supporting ERA[18]

Actors' Equity Association

Advisory Committee, Women's Rights and Responsibilities (HEW)

Amalgamated Clothing and Textile Workers Union

Amalgamated Meat Cutters and Butcher Workmen of North America

American Association of College Deans

American Association of Law Libraries

American Association of University Professors

American Association of University Women (AAUW)

American Association of Women Ministers

American Baptist Women

American Bar Association

American Civil Liberties Union

American Federation of Government Employees

American Federation of Labor-Congress of Industrial Organizations (AFL-CIO)

American Federation of Soroptimist Clubs

American Federation of State, County and Municipal Employees

American Federation of Teachers

American Federation of Television and Radio Artists

American Home Economics Association

American Jewish Committee

American Jewish Congress

American Medical Women's Association

American Newspaper Guild
American Nurses' Association
American Political Science Association
American Psychiatric Association
American Psychological Association
American Public Health Association
American Society for Public Administration
American Society for Microbiology
American Society of Women Accountants
American Society of Women Certified Public Accountants
American Veterans Committee
American Women in Radio and Television
American Woman's Society of Certified Public Accountants
Americans for Democratic Action
Association of American Women Dentists
Association of Flight Attendants
Association of Junior Leagues, Inc.
Association of the Bar of the City of New York
Association of Women in Science
Bakery and Confectionery Workers' International Union of
    America
B'nai B'rith Women
Brotherhood of Railway, Air Line & Steamship Clerks,
    Frt. Handlers, Express & Station Employees
California Press Women
Catholic Caucus, Ecumenical Task Force on Women and
    Religion
Catholic Women for the ERA
Catholics for ERA
Christian Church (Disciples of Christ)
Christian Feminists
Church of the Brethren
Citizens' Advisory Council on the Status of Women
Coalition of Labor Union Women (CLUW)
Common Cause
Communications Workers of America
Council for Christian Social Action, United Church of
    Christ
Council for Women's Rights
Council of AFL-CIO Unions for Professional Employees
    (CPE)
Delta Sigma Theta
Democratic National Party

ERA Ratification Council, Washington, D.C.
Evangelists for Social Action
Federally Employed Women (FEW)
Federation of Organizations for Professional Women
Friends Committee on National Legislation
Future Homemakers of America
General Federation of Women's Clubs
Girl Scouts of the U.S.A.
Gray Panthers
Hadassah
Insurance Workers International Union
Intercollegiate Association of Women Students
International Association of Human Rights Agencies
International Association of Machinists and Aerospace
    Workers
International Brotherhood of Painters & Allied Trades
International Brotherhood of Teamsters
International Federation of Professional and Technical
    Engineers
International Ladies' Garment Workers' Union
International Union of Electrical, Radio and Machine
    Workers
International Union, United Automobile, Aerospace &
    Agricultural Implement Workers of America (UAW)
Ladies Auxiliary of Veterans of Foreign Wars
Leadership Conference of Women Religious (Catholic)
Leadership Conference on Civil Rights
League of American Working Women
League of Women Voters
Los Angeles Advertising Women
Lutheran Church of America
National Association for the Advancement of Colored
    People (NAACP)
National Association of Colored Business and Professional
    Women's Clubs
National Association of Colored Women's Clubs
National Association of Commissions for Women
National Association of Negro Business and Professional
    Women's Clubs, Inc.
National Association of Railway Business Women
National Association of Social Workers, Inc.
National Association of Women Deans, Administrators and
    Counselors

National Association of Women Lawyers
National Black Feminist Organization
National Coalition of American Nuns
National Commission on the Observance of International
    Women's Year—1975
National Council of Churches
National Council of Church Women
National Council of Jewish Women
National Education Association
National Federation of Business and Professional Women's
    Clubs
National Federation of Press Women
National Federation of Republican Women's Clubs
National Federation of Temple Sisterhoods
National Gay Task Force
National Jewish Welfare Board
National Order of Women Legislators
National Organization for Women (NOW)
National School Boards Association
National Secretaries Association
National Welfare Rights Organization
National Women's Education Association
National Women's Party
National Women's Political Caucus
NETWORK, Catholic Nuns
Office and Professional Employees International Union
Oil, Chemical and Atomic Workers International Union
President's Task Force on Women's Rights and Responsi-
    bilities
Professional Women's Caucus
Republican National Party
Republican Women's Task Force
Retail Clerks International Association
Retail, Wholesale and Department Store Union
St. Joan's International Alliance
Screen Actors Guild
Service Employees International Union
The Newspaper Guild
Transport Workers Union of America
Union of American Hebrew Congregations
Unitarian Universalist Association
Unitarian Universalist Women's Federation
United Church of Christ

United Jewish Congress
United Methodist Church
United Methodist Church, Board of Church and Society
United Methodist Women's Division
United Mine Workers of America
United Presbyterian Church
United Rubber, Cork, Linoleum and Plastic Workers of
    America
United States Commission on Civil Rights
United States Conference of Mayors
United States Department of Labor
Women in Communications (founded as Theta Sigma Phi)
Women's Bureau, U.S. Department of Labor
Women's Campaign Fund
Women's Christian Temperance Union (WCTU)
Women's Equity Action League (WEAL)
Women's International League for Peace and Freedom
Women's Joint Legislative Committee for Equal Rights
Women's National Democratic Club
Women United
Writers Guild of America, West, Inc.
YWCA, Young Women's Christian Association
Zero Population Growth

Religious Organizations for ERA[19]

American Baptist Women
American Jewish Committee
American Jewish Congress
B'nai B'rith Women
Catholic Women for ERA
Christian Church
   (Disciples of Christ)
   Division of Homeland Ministries
Christian Methodist Episcopal Church, The Missionary
    Council
Church of the Brethren
Church Women United in the U.S.A.
Evangelical Women's Caucus
Friends Committee on National Legislation
Hadassah
Intercommunity Center for Justice and Peace
Joint Strategy Action Committee

Las Hermanas
Leadership Conference of Women Religious
Lutheran Church Women
National Assembly of Women Religious
National Coalition of American Nuns
National Council of Churches, Division of Church and
  Society
National Council of Jewish Women
National Federation of Temple Sisterhoods
NETWORK
Presbyterian Church in the U.S.
  General Assembly
  Mission Board
  Committee on Women's Concerns
Sisters of Loretto
  Denver, Colorado
The United Methodist Church
  Board of Church and Society
The United Methodist Church
  Women's Division
  Board of Global Ministries
Union of American Hebrew Congregations
Unitarian Universalist Association
Unitarian Universalist Women's Federation
United Church of Christ
  Advisory Commission on Women in Church and Society
United Church of Christ
  Board of Homeland Ministries
United Jewish Congress
United Presbyterian Church in the U.S.A.
  Council on Women and the Church
Women's League for Conservative Judaism
National Board of the Young Women's Christian Asso-
  ciation of the U.S.A.

Catholic Organizations for ERA[20]

(Listed separately to emphasize that the anti-ERA propaganda that *all* good Catholics are against ERA is false)

Catholic Women for the ERA
Catholic Caucus of the Ecumenical Task Force on Women
  and Religion

Las Hermanas
Leadership Conference of Women Religious (Exec. Board)
National Assembly of Women Religious
National Coalition of American Nuns
NETWORK
St. Joan's International Alliance (American Section)

ERA Coalition Contacts in Unratified States[21]

Alabama

Joanne Bloom
3301 Delia Lane, NW
Huntsville, AL 35810
(o) (205) 876-1206
(h) (205) 852-4425

Arizona

Lucille Huebner
5354 N. 3rd Avenue
Phoenix, AZ 85013
(o) (602) 267-5318
(h) (602) 265-1886

Arkansas

Gloria Cabe
ERA Arkansas
904 W. 2nd Street
Little Rock, AR 72201
(o) (501) 372-2151
(h) (501) 663-0202

Florida

Hon. Elaine Gordon
Good Government Society
561 N.E. 79th
Miami, FL 33138
(305) 895-1066
(904) 488-8315 Tallahassee

Georgia

Beth Shapiro, Chairperson
GA Council for the ERA
1992 McLendon
  Avenue, NE
Atlanta, GA 30307
(312) 969-2240

Illinois

ERA Illinois
Jean Maack
4735 Seeley Avenue
Downer's Grove, IL 60515
(312) 969-2240

Louisiana

Emily Hubbard, State
  Coordinator
ERA United of LA
6038 Jefferson Highway
Baton Rouge, LA 70806
(504) 925-9265

Missouri

Doris Quinn
MO ERA Coalition
108 S. Main Street
Independence, MO 64050
(o) (816) 461-8178
(h) (816) 254-1910

Nevada

Nevadans for ERA
1212 S. Casino Center
    Boulevard
Las Vegas, NV 89104
(o) (702) 385-1780
Cynthia Cunningham
(h) (702) 382-7736

Mylan Roloff
Northern Nevadans for
    ERA
3487 Skyline Boulevard
Reno, NV 89101
(h) (702) 826-7307
(o) (702) 826-6714

North Carolina

Maria Bliss
NC ERA
834 Shamrock
Ashboro, NC 27203
(o) (919) 625-2224
(h) (919) 625-5423

Oklahoma

OK-ERA, Oklahomans
    for the ERA
400 N.W. 23 Street
Oklahoma City, OK 73103
(405) 525-5400

Penny Williams
1366 E. 25th
Tulsa, OK 74114

South Carolina

Marsha Duffy
315 Harden
Columbia, SC 29205
(o) (803) 252-5538

Utah

Lynne Van Dam
Equal Rights Coalition
989 E. 9th Street
Salt Lake City, UT 84002
Mailings: P.O. Box 1533
Salt Lake City, UT 84110
(o) (801) 532-5080;
    532-6190

Virginia

Marianne Fowler
ERA-Pac
Raleigh Hotel, Room 212
9th & Bank Streets
Richmond, VA 23219
(804) 648-8384

Southern Regional

Betsy Brinson
Women's Rights Project
American Civil Liberties
    Union Foundation
Suite 512, 1001 E. Main
    Street
Richmond, VA 23219
(804) 649-8140

ERA Coalition Contacts in Ratified States[22]

Alaska

Amalie Zasada
Wolverine Lane
Fairbanks, AL 99701
(907) 479-4160

California

Virginia Carter
California Coalition ERA
111 Via La Circula
Redondo Beach, CA 90277
(213) 462-7111

Colorado

Joan Novy
ERA Colorado
744 Planet Place
Denver, CO 80221
(303) 427-0898

Connecticut

Clara Weir
ERA All the Way
127 Whitney
Hartford, CT
(203) 232-7461

Delaware

Kit Kallal
518 Kerfoot Farm Road
Wilmington, DE 19803
(302) 571-8948

Hawaii

Judy Stitley
1545 Nehoa Street
Apt. 502
Honolulu, HI 96822
(808) 941-1214
(808) 433-6958

Idaho

Mary Mech
Idaho ERA Task Force
1711 N. 12th Street
Boise, ID 83702
(208) 375-8335

Indiana

Nancy Pappas
ERA Indiana
619 Illinois Building
17 W. Market Street

Indianapolis, IN 46204
(o) (317) 634-4216
(h) (317) 634-1515

Iowa

Jean Lloyd-Jones
160 Oak Ridge
Iowa City, IA 52240
(h) (515) 279-8607
(o) (515) 282-6897

Kansas

Gloria O'Dell
Chair, KERA
P.O. Box 1791
Topeka, KS 66201
(o) (913) 295-2820
(h) (913) 379-5457

Kentucky

Martha Pickering
Pro ERA Alliance
3619 Hycliffe Avenue
Louisville, KY 40207
(h) (502) 893-3710
(o) (502) 585-2331

Maine

Pat Ryan
Governor's Commission on
   the Status of Women
State House
Augusta, ME 04330
(207) 289-1110

Maryland

Dale Balfour
5 State Circle
Annapolis, MD 21401
(h) (301) 363-1359
(o) (301) 269-0232

Michigan

Pat Houseman
Laura Callow, Co-chairs
Michigan ERA America
YWCA
217 Townsend
Lansing, MI 48933

Minnesota

Betty Bedor
MN Coalition to Support
  the ERA
3701 Colfax Avenue, S
Minneapolis, MN 55409
(612) 824-4610

Montana

Robin Hetel
Montana Ratification
  Council
P.O. Box 297
Helena, MT 59601
(406) 442-9837

Nebraska

Cheri Cody
League of Women Voters
5025 Grover
Omaha, NB 68106
(402) 391-0263
(402) 556-3919

New Hampshire

Aileen Katz
Box 462
Durham, NH 03824
(603) 868-2137
(603) 868-2141

New Jersey

Carmela Lunt
13 Brockden Drive
Mendham, NJ 07945
(201) 543-2229

New Mexico

Tasia Young
Commission on the Status
  of Women
Plaza del Sol Building
Albuquerque, NM

New York

Susie Glickman
Westchester County Task
  Force on Women
818 County Office Building
White Plains, NY 10601
(914) 682-2222

Or: Mark Gasarch
540 Madison Ave.
NYC 10022
(212) 826-6363

North Dakota

Donna Chalimonczyk
1625 South 14½ Street
Fargo, ND 58102
(701) 235-1793

Ohio

Helen W. Mulholland
560 Fox Lane
Worthington, OH 43085
(614) 885-5427
Or: Mary Miller
(616) 488-7260

Oregon

Wanda Mays
494 State Street
Suite 216
Salem, OR 97301
(503) 581-5722

Pennsylvania

Barbara Abbott
1436 Street Road
South Hampton, PA 18966
(215) 357-9204

Rhode Island

Jean Whipple
126 Waterman Street
Providence, RI 02906
(401) 421-1987

South Dakota

Shirley Heitland
310 19th Avenue, S
Brookings, SD 57006
(605) 692-4749

Tennessee

Ms. Silvine Hudson
1701 21st Avenue, S
Nashville, TN 37212
(o) (615) 297-7134
(h) (615) 383-2328

Texas

Mrs. Hermine Tobolowsky
Texans for ERA
7111 San Antonio
Austin, TX 78701
(512) 474-1798

Vermont

Ms. Constance Kite,
   Director
Commission on the Status
   of Women
Pavillion
Montpelier, VT 05602

Washington

Beth Quale
Wash. Equal Rights
   Amendment Coalition
6500 Ravenna Avenue, NE
Seattle, WA 98115
(206) 523-2121

West Virginia

Joyce Manyik
1146 Summit Drive
St. Albans, WV 25177
(304) 727-8191

Wisconsin

Constance Threinen
430 Lowell Hall
610 Langdon
Madison, Wisconsin 53706
(o) (608) 262-9760
(h) (608) 238-5489

Wyoming

Nancy Paternal
1001 Park Drive
Kemmerer, WY 83010
(307) 877-4729

National and Regional Organizations
Pro and Con: Names and Addresses[28]

The following is in part derived from one of the most extensive lists yet compiled of names and addresses for organizations relating to ERA in any way. It includes a few of the main organizations against it, such as the John Birch Society, as well as most of those for it, such as the League of Women Voters and NOW. It also includes many state chapters of activist national organizations as well as a variety of other entities whose names and addresses may be useful, ranging from state legislative judiciary committees to women's studies centers and official commissions on the status of women. The list is based on the work of the Equal Rights Amendment Project, Anita Miller, project director, Hazel Greenberg, editor and compiler. A more comprehensive list, with bibliography, is available in the extremely useful text *The Equal Rights Amendment*, published by the Greenwood Press, 51 Riverside Avenue, Westport, Conn. 06880.

AAUW. See American Association of University Women.

AFL-CIO (815 16th Street, NW, Washington, D.C. 20006).

Albuquerque Women's Center (University of New Mexico, 1824 Las Lomas, NE, NM 87106).

Alliance Link (Equal Rights Alliance, 2140 N. Magnolia Avenue, Chicago, IL 60614; 5256 Fairmont Avenue, Downers Grove, IL 60515).

Alliance of Media Women (12310 Chandler Boulevard, Suite 8, North Hollywood, CA 91607; Inter-Studio Feminist Alliance, Box 2268, Hollywood, CA 90028).

American Association of University Women (2401 Virginia Avenue, NW, Washington, D.C. 20037).

AAUW, California Division (Marilyn Poluzzi, Pres., 3229 S. Bonita Street, Spring Valley 92007).

AAUW, Illinois Division (Mary Carlson, Pres., 207 East School Lane, Prospect Heights 60070).

AAUW, North Carolina Division (Gloria Blanton, Pres., 1322 Dogwood Lane, Raleigh 27607).

AAUW, North Dakota Division (Lila Nelson, Pres., 1314 Cherry Street, Grand Forks 58201).

AAUW, Texas Division (Polly Orcutt, Pres., 10015 Lakedale Drive, Dallas 75218).

AAUW, Utah Division (Helen Camp, Pres., 4187 Shanna Street, Salt Lake City 84117).

American Bar Association (1155 E. 60th Street, Chicago, IL 60637).

American Business Women's Association (9100 Ward Parkway, Kansas City, MO 64114).

American Civil Liberties Union, Women's Rights Project (22 E. 40th Street, New York, NY 10016).

American Federation of Labor (815 16th Street, NW, Washington, D.C. 20006).

American Federation of State, County and Municipal Employees (1155 15th Street, NW, Washington, D.C. 20005).

American Home Economics Association (2010 Massachusetts Avenue, NW, Washington, D.C. 20036).

American Library Association, Social Responsibilities Round Table, Task Force on Women (50 E. Huron Street, Chicago, IL 60611).

Anchorage Women's Liberation (7801 Peck Avenue, AK 99504)

Arizona Legislative Council (324 State Capitol, Phoenix 85007).

Arkansas Governor's Commission on the Status of Women (Room 08, State Capitol, Little Rock 72201).

Arkansas Legislative Council, Committee on Judiciary (Room 315, State Capitol, Little Rock 72201).

Association of American Colleges, Project on the Status and Education of Women (1818 R Street, NW, Washington, D.C. 20009).

Association of the Bar of the City of New York (42 W. 44th Street, NY 10036).

ASUC L.A. Communications Board (Associated Students, University of California, 112 Kerckhoff Hall, 308 Westwood Plaza, Los Angeles 90024).

Baltimore Women's Liberation (101 E. 25th Street, Suite B-2, MD 21218).

Bay Area National Lawyers Guild (Box 673, Berkeley, CA 94701).

Berkshire Women's Liberation (Box 686, Lenox, MA 01240).

Bloomington Women's Liberation (Women's Center, Inc., 414 N. Park Street, IN 47401).

Board of Church and Society (100 Maryland Avenue, NE, Washington, D.C. 20002).

California Assembly Judiciary Committee (State Capitol, Sacramento 95814).

California Commission on the Status of Women (926 J Street, Suite 1003, Sacramento 95814).

California Commission on the Status of Women, Equal Rights Amendment Project (926 J Street, Suite 1014, Sacramento 95814).

California State Women's Caucus, California Democratic Council (5371 Wilshire Boulevard, Los Angeles 90036).

Caucus for Women in Statistics (American Statistical Association, 165 West End Avenue, New York, NY 10023).

Center for Information on America (Washington, CT 06793).

Center for Women's and Family Living Education, University of Wisconsin (Madison 53706).

Center for Women's Studies and Services (908 F Street, San Diego, CA 92101).

Church and Society Task Force. See Board of Church and Society.

Citizens' Advisory Council on the Status of Women (Department of Labor Building, Room 1336, Washington, D.C. 20210).

Coalition for the Passage of the Equal Rights Amendment in Arkansas (11 Ardmore Drive, Little Rock 72209).

Coalition of St. Louis Women (612 N. 2nd Street, St. Louis, MO 63102).

Colorado Coalition for Equal Rights (Box 18481, Denver 80218).

Colorado Commission on the Status of Women (Colorado Women's College, 1800 Pontiac Street, Denver 80220).

Colorado Legislative Council (46 State Capitol, Denver 80203).

Committee for the Protection of Women and Children (Box 502, Jefferson City, MO 65101).

Committee to Ratify the Massachusetts State Equal Rights Amendment (344 Boylston Street, Boston 02164).

Committee to Restore Women's Rights (717 Burkshire, Corpus Christi, TX 78412; 4203 Smoke Ridge, San Antonio 78217).

Common Cause (2100 M Street, NW, Washington, D.C. 20037).

Communication Workers of America (1925 K Street, NW, Washington, D.C. 20006).

Communist Party, U.S.A. See National Women's Commission of the C.P.U.S.A.

Congress of Women's Auxiliaries, CIO (815 16th Street, NW, Washington, D.C. 20006).

Connecticut Office of Legislative Research (120 State Capitol, Hartford 06115).

Continuing Education for Women, University of Hawaii (Krauss Hall, 2500 Dole Street, Honolulu 96882).

Council for the Continuing Education of Women, Miami-Dade Community College (300 N.E. 2nd Avenue, Miami, FL 33132).

Council of State Governments (Iron Works Pike, Lexington, KY 40505).

Davis Women's Center (University of California, Davis 95616).

Dayton Women's Liberation (Box 187, Dayton View Station, OH 45406).

Democratic National Committee, Women's Division (1625 Massachusetts Avenue, NW, Washington, D.C. 20036).

Denver Women's Liberation (1452 Pennsylvania, #17, CO 80203).

Equal Employment Opportunity Commission (2401 E Street, NW, Washington, D.C. 20506).

Equal Rights Alliance. See Alliance Link.

Equal Rights Amendment Project. See California Commission on the Status of Women, Equal Rights Amendment Project.

Equal Rights Coalition of Utah (473 1st Avenue, Apt. #3, Salt Lake City 84103).

ERAmerica (1525 M Street, NW, Suite 602, Washington, D.C. 20005).

ERA Central (53 W. Jackson, Chicago, IL 60604).

ERA Law Project (Attorney General's Office, State Office Tower, 30 E. Broad Street, Columbus, OH 43215). See Ohio Task Force for the Implementation of the Equal Rights Amendment.

ERA United (1219 Forsyth Street, Winston-Salem, NC 27101).

ERA United of Louisiana (Box 22363, Baton Rouge 70803).

Every Woman's Center (Munson Hall, University of Massachusetts, Amherst 01002).

Federally Employed Women (621 National Press Building, Washington, D.C. 20004).

Federation of Organizations for Professional Women (1818 R Street, NW, Washington, D.C. 20009).

Female Liberation (Box 344, Cambridge A, Cambridge, MA 02139).

Florida Office of Attorney General (Robert L. Shevin, Dept. of Legal Affairs, The Capitol, Tallahassee 32304).

Florida State '76–'77 Coalition (c/o Cele Niffenegger, Treasurer, 211 21st Avenue, W, Bradenton 33505).

Ford Associates, Inc. (701 S. Federal Avenue, Butler, Ind. 46721).

General Assembly of Ohio. See Ohio General Assembly.

General Assembly of the State of New York. See New York State General Assembly.

General Federation of Women's Clubs (1734 N Street, NW, Washington, D.C. 20036).

George Washington University Women's Liberation (Washington, D.C. 20006).

Georgia Commission on the Status of Women (Georgia Dept. of Human Resources, 47 Trinity Avenue, Atlanta 30334).

Hawaii Women's Liberation (Box 11042, Honolulu 96814).

Hoosiers for ERA (Room 321, Illinois Building, 17 W. Market Street, Indianapolis, IN 46204).

Housewives for ERA (1108 South Boulevard, Evanston, IL 60202).

Human Rights for Women (1128 National Press Building, Washington, D.C. 20004).

Idaho ERA Task Force (1211 N. 12th Street, Boise 83702).

Illinois Legislative Council (State House, Springfield 62706).

Illinois Stop ERA. See Stop ERA.

Indianapolis Women's Liberation (Box 88365, IN 46208).

Institute for American Democracy (1330 Massachusetts Avenue, NW, Washington, D.C. 20005).

Institute of Women's Professional Relations (Connecticut College, New London 06320).

Intercollegiate Association of Women Students (Box 2, 2401 Virginia Avenue, NW, Washington, D.C. 20037).

International Glove Workers Union of America (Amalgamated Clothing Workers of America, 15 Union Square, New York, NY 10003).

Interstate Association of Commissions on the Status of Women (Room 204, District Building, 14 and E Street, NW, Washington, D.C. 20016).

Inter-Studio Feminist Alliance. See Alliance of Media Women.

Iowa Commission on the Status of Women (State Capitol Building, Des Moines 50319).

John Birch Society (395 Concord Avenue, Belmont, MA 02170).

Kansas City Women's Liberation Union (5138 Tracy Street, MO 64110).

KNOW, Inc. (Box 86031, Pittsburgh, PA 15221).

Ladies Auxiliary of Veterans of Foreign Wars (406 W. 34 Street, Kansas City, MO 64111).

Lancaster Women's Liberation (230 W. Chestnut Street, 1st Floor, PA 17603).

L.A. Women's Liberation Center (746 S. Crenshaw Boulevard, Los Angeles, CA 90005).

League of Women Voters of the United States (1730 M Street, NW, Washington, D.C. 20036).

LWV of Arizona (1439 N. 1st Street, #202, Phoenix 85004).

LWV of California (126 Post Street, Room 512, San Francisco 94108).

LWV of Georgia (3272 Peachtree Road, NE, Room 353, Atlanta 30305).

LWV of Indiana (619 Illinois Building, 17 W. Market Street, Indianapolis 46204).

LWV of Jefferson Parish (Box 7583, Metairie, LA 70002).

LWV of Louisiana (343 Riverside Mall, Suite 304, Baton Rouge 70801).

LWV of Maryland (Vayley Road, Owings Mill 21117).

LWV of Massachusetts (120 Boylston Street, Boston 02116).

LWV of Michigan (202 Mill Street, Lansing 48933).

LWV of New Mexico (219 Shelby Street, Santa Fe 87501).

LWV of New York State (817 Broadway, New York City 10003).

LWV of North Carolina (2637 McDowell Street, Durham 27705).

LWV of Ohio (65 S. 4th Street, Columbus 43215).

LWV of San Diego (2454 4th Avenue, CA 92101).

LWV of Washington (1406 18th Avenue, Seattle 98122).

Liberation News Service (160 Claremont Avenue, New York, N.Y. 10027).

Library of Congress, Congressional Research Service (10 1st Street, SE, Washington, D.C. 20540).

Link. See Alliance Link.

Maryland Commission on the Status of Women (1100 N. Eutaw Street, Baltimore 21201).

Merritt College Women's Collective (5714 Grove Street, Oakland, CA 94609).

Michigan Women's Commission (24424 Fairmont Street, Dearborn 48124).

Minnesota Coalition to Support the ERA (Mary Weller, Chairperson, 16695 Galena Avenue, Rosemount 55068).

Minnesota Planning and Counseling Center for Women (301 Walter Library, University of Minnesota, Minneapolis 55455).

Missouri Commission on the Status of Women (210 E. Dunklin Street, Jefferson City 65101).

Missouri ERA Coalition (829 Edgar Road, St. Louis 63119).

Montana ERA Ratification Council (Box 297, Helena 59601).

Nassau County Department of General Services, Vocational Center for Women (1 Old Country Road, Carle Place, NY 11514).

Nassau County Women's Liberation Center (14 W. Columbia Street, Hempstead, NY 11550).

National Ad Hoc Committee for the Equal Rights Amendment (2310 Barbour Road, Falls Church, VA 22043).

National Association of Counties Research Foundation (1735 New York Avenue, NW, Washington, D.C. 20006).

National Association of Women Lawyers (American Bar Center, 1155 E. 60th Street, Chicago, IL 60637).

National Consumers League (1785 Massachusetts Avenue, NW, Washington, D.C. 20036).

National Council of Administrative Women in Education, National Education Association (1815 Fort Meyer Drive, N, Arlington, VA 22209).

National Council of Catholic Women (1312 Massachusetts Avenue, NW, Washington, D.C. 20005).

National Education Association (1201 16th Street, NW, Washington, D.C. 20036). See National Council of Administrative Women in Education.

National Federation of Business and Professional Women's Clubs (2012 Massachusetts Avenue, NW, Washington, D.C. 20036).

California BPW (609 Sutter Street, Room 202, San Francisco 94102).

Florida BPW (2118 W. Elm Street, Tampa 33604).

New York State BPW (Audrey F. Lanfare, Pres., 488 Simons Avenue, Hackensack, NJ 07601).

National Federation of Republican Women (310 1st Street, SE, Washington, D.C. 20003).

National Lawyers Guild. See Bay Area National Lawyers Guild.

National Organization for Women (NOW National Action Center, 425 13th Street, NW, Suite 1001, Washington, D.C. 20004).

Albuquerque NOW (Box 26262, NM 87125).

Ann Arbor NOW (1683 Broadway, #303, MI 48104).

Anne Arundel NOW (P.O. Box 788, Annapolis, MD 21404).

Atlanta NOW (Box 54045, Civic Center, GA 30308).

Baton Rouge NOW (580 Sharplen, #512, LA 70815).

Berkeley NOW (Box 7024, CA 94707).

Boston NOW (99 Bishop Richard Allen Drive, Cambridge, MA 02139).

Boulder NOW (P.O. Box 3452, CO 80303).

Brooklyn NOW (840 E. 40th, NY 11210).

California NOW (Mary M. Smith, State Coor., 1820 S. Bentley, #108, Los Angeles, CA 90025).

Central Connecticut NOW (41 Richard Road, East Hartford, CT 06108).

Central New Jersey NOW (32 Bank St., Princeton 08540).

Central New York NOW (119 Strong Ave., Syracuse 13210).

Champaign-Urbana NOW (1803 Golfview Dr., Urbana, IL 61801).

Chicago NOW (53 W. Jackson Blvd., Suite 1501, IL 60604).

Cincinnati NOW (3544 Edwards Rd., OH 45208).

Cleveland NOW (Box 91157, OH 44101).

Columbus NOW (P.O. Box 12053, OH 43212).

Dade County NOW (P.O. Box 330265, Miami, FL 33133).

Denver NOW (P.O. Box 3101, CO 80204).

Detroit NOW (1301 Orleans, #801 E, MI 48207).

DuPage NOW (258 E. Church St., Elmhurst, IL 60126).

Durham NOW (P.O. Box 3194, NC 27705).

East Bay NOW (Box 7024, Berkeley, CA 94707).

El Paso County NOW (P.O. Box 732, Colorado Springs, CO 80901).

Erie County NOW (P.O. Box 57, Hiler, NY 14223).

Essex County NOW (P.O. Box 201, Maplewood, NJ 10210).

Fox Valley/Elgin NOW (104 McKinley, St. Charles, IL 60120).

Fresno NOW (420 N. Van Ness, CA 93701).

Georgia NOW (Barbara J. Murrin, State Coor., P.O. Box 3686, Columbus, GA 31903).

Hammond NOW (105 Sherry St., LA 70401).

Harrisburg NOW (YWCA, 4th & Market, Rm. 319, PA 17101).

Hollywood NOW (1126 Hi-Point St., Los Angeles, CA 90035).

Houston NOW (P.O. Box 66351, TX 77503).

Illinois NOW (Naomi Ross, State Coor., 820 Judson, #3, Evanston, IL 60202).

Imperial Valley NOW (135 W. 7th St., Holtville, CA 92250).

Indianapolis NOW (3530 Donald Drive, IN 46224).

Jacksonville NOW (P.O. Box 1762, FL 32201).

Jefferson Parish NOW (P.O. Box 23094, Harahan, LA 70123).

Kitsap County NOW (P.O. Box 805, Bremerton, WA 98310).

Lehigh Valley NOW (P.O. Box 1994, Allentown, PA 18105).

Lexington NOW (P.O. Box 651, MA 02173).

Lincoln NOW (6127 Huntington, NE 68502).

Lompoc Valley NOW (P.O. Box 1237, CA 93436).

Long Beach NOW (P.O. Box 15306, CA 90815).

Los Angeles NOW (8271 Melrose Ave., Suite 109, CA 90046).

Madison NOW (P.O. Box 2512, WI 53701).

Maine NOW (JoAnn Dauphine, State Coor., 23 March St., Bangor, ME 04401).

Marin County NOW (Box 2924, San Rafael, CA 94901).

Merced NOW (P.O. Box 94, CA 95340).

Midland NOW (P.O. Box 1243, MI 48640).

Milwaukee NOW (1560 S. 75th St., West Allis, WI 53214).

Minneapolis NOW (3246 Girard Ave., S., MN 55408).

Missoula NOW (1744 S. 12th West, MT 59801).

Missouri NOW (Dorothy Tegeler, State Coor., 2743 N. Hanley Rd., St. Louis, MO 63114).

Monmouth County NOW (P.O. Box 823, Red Bank, NJ 07701).

Monterey Peninsula NOW (Box 1661, CA 93940).

Montgomery NOW (1336 Marco Road, AL 36116).

Montgomery County NOW (11707 Milborn Dr., Potomac, MD 20854).

Muncie Delaware NOW (3200 Brook Dr., IN 47304).

Nassau-Long Island NOW (P.O. Box 179, Bank Plaza Sta., Merrick, NY 11566).

New Haven NOW (P.O. Box 6119, Hamden, CT 06518).

New Orleans NOW (5509 Coliseum St., LA 70115).

New York City NOW (47 E. 19th Street, NY 10003).

New York State NOW (Zelle Andrews, State Coor., 30 Greenridge Ave., #5-H, White Plains, NY 10605).

Northern Nevada NOW (1100 W. Plum 6 Ln., Reno 89509).

Northern New Jersey NOW (57 Leonard Dr., Tappan, NJ 07675).

Northern Virginia NOW (3326 Hartwell Ct., Falls Church, VA 22042).

North Orange County NOW (Box 10453, Santa Ana, CA 92711).

North Suburban Chicago NOW (10 A Dundee Quarter, #108, Palatine, IL 60067).

Oklahoma City NOW (817 Parker Rd., OK 73127).

Palo Alto NOW (P.O. Box 135, CA 94302).

Passaic County NOW (46 Sixth Ave., NJ 07055).

Pennsylvania NOW (Dixie White, State Coor., P.O. Box 1996, Allentown, PA 18105).

Pensacola NOW (P.O. Box 19016, FL 32503).

Peoria NOW (913 W. St. James, #B-1, IL 61606).

Phoenix NOW (P.O. Box 16023, AZ 85011).

Pomona Valley NOW (P.O. Box 909, Claremont, CA 91711).

Portland NOW (Box 843, OR 97207).

Quad Cities NOW (1126 54th St., IL 61265).

Rhode Island NOW (Patricia M. Dwyer, State Coor., 176 Magill St., Pawtucket, RI 02860).

Richmond NOW (P.O. Box 25831, VA 23260).

Riverside-CB NOW (c/o YWCA, 16 East Olive St., Redland, CA 92373).

Roanoke Valley NOW (943 Welton Ave., S.W., Roanoke, VA 24015).

Rockford NOW (215 Hunter Ave., IL 61108).

Sacramento NOW (P.O. Box 1404, CA 95819).

Salinas Valley NOW (635 Kirkwood, CA 93901).

San Diego County NOW (P.O. Box 80292, CA 92138).

San Fernando Valley NOW (11361 Kelowna St., Lakeview Terrace, CA 91342).

San Francisco NOW (300 Broadway, Suite 23, CA 94133).

San Gabriel Valley NOW (P.O. Box 1315, South Pasadena, CA 91030).

San Joaquin NOW (P.O. Box 4073, Stockton, CA 95204).

San Jose NOW (P.O. Box 2-G, CA 95109).

Santa Barbara NOW (562 La Marina, CA 93109).

Snohomish County NOW (P.O. Box 525, Lynnwood, WA 98036).

South Bend NOW (230 Wakewa, IN 46556).

Southeastern Connecticut NOW (P.O. Box 817, New London, CT 06320).

Springfield NOW (108 E. Union, IL 62702).

Springfield NOW (P.O. Box 1312, MA 01101).

St. Louis NOW (2130 Marconi, MO 63110).

St. Paul NOW (P.O. Box 80065, MN 55108).

Sunnyvale-South Bay NOW (P.O. Box 2304, CA 94087).

Tacoma NOW (P.O. Box 1030, WA 98402).

Tallahassee NOW (P.O. Box 2732, FL 32304).

Tampa NOW (3608 Ridge Ave., FL 33603).

Temple Hills NOW (Box 31296, MD 20031).

Thurston County NOW (P.O. Box 2713, Olympia, WA 98501).

Tippecanoe NOW (5830 St. Rd. 26 E, Lafayette, IN 47905).

Tucson NOW (Box 4770, AZ 85715).

Tulsa NOW (5347 E. 26 Pl., OK 74114).

Union County NOW (P.O. Box 824, Westfield, NJ 07090).

Virginia NOW (Jean Marshall Clarke, State Coor., 2313 Rosedown Drive, Reston, VA 22091).

Washington, D.C. NOW (c/o Quest, 2000 P St. N.W. #308, 20036).

Witchita NOW (328 N. Main, KS 67152).

National Woman's Party (144 Constitution Avenue, NE, Washington, D.C. 20002).

National Women's Commission of the C.P.U.S.A. (Communist Party, U.S.A., 23 W. 26th Street, New York, NY 10010).

National Women's Political Caucus (1921 Pennsylvania Avenue, Washington, D.C. 20006).

Alameda County (Northern California) WPC (Sybil Galazin, Coor., 1470 Creekside Drive, Walnut Creek 94598).

Arizona WPC (Joyce Hunter, Chair., 5519 N. Marion Way, Phoenix 85018).

Minnesota WPC (Re: *Gold Flower*, Box 8341, Lake Street Station, Minneapolis 55408; Marlene Johnson, Chair., 574 Lincoln Avenue, St. Paul 55102).

New Mexico WPC (Box 25925, Albuquerque 87125).

Oregon WPC (#12, West Lynn 97068).

Philadelphia Women's Political Caucus (640 Rodman, PA 19147).

San Fernando Valley NWPC (7105 Hayvenhurst Avenue, Van Nuys, CA 91406).

Southern California NWPC (1133 Hacienda Place, Los Angeles 90060).

Wisconsin WPC (428 Lowell Hall, 610 Langdon Street, Madison 53706).

Nebraska Governor's Commission on the Status of Women (1700 Crestline Drive, Lincoln 68506).

Network (224 D Street, SE, Washington, D.C. 20003).

Nevadans for ERA (Box 1682, Carson City 89701).

New Jersey Assembly Judiciary Committee (State House, Trenton 08625).

New Jersey Department of Community Affairs, Division on Women (363 W. State Street, Box 2768, Trenton 08625).

New Mexico Equal Rights Legislation Committee (Box 3271, Station D, Albuquerque 87110).

New York City Commission on Human Rights (80 Lafayette St., NY 10013).

New York Coalition for Equal Rights (11 W. 42nd Street, New York City 10036).

New York State General Assembly (State Capitol, Albany 12224).

New York State Legislature (State Capitol, Albany 12224).

New York State Women's Division (Executive Chamber, 1350 Avenue of the Americas, New York City 10019).

North Dakota Coordinating Council for the ERA (1625 S. 14 1/2 Street, Fargo 58102).

North Dakota Women's Coalition (c/o Bonnie Austin, NL Editor, Box 464, Bismarck 58501).

NOW. See National Organization for Women.

Ohio Bureau of Employment Services, Women Services Division (145 S. Front Street, Columbus 43216).

Ohio Coalition for Equal Rights Amendment (1463 Berkshire, Columbus 43221).

Ohio Commission on the Status of Women (798 Craig Parkway, Newark 43055).

Ohio General Assembly (State House, Columbus 43215).

Ohio Legislative Service Commission (State House, Columbus 43215).

Ohio State University Library (Columbus 43210).

Ohio Task Force for the Implementation of the Equal Rights Amendment. See ERA Law Project.

Oregon Council for Women's Equality (Box 8186, Portland 97207).

Pennsylvania Commission on the Status of Women (512 Finance Building, Harrisburg 17120).

Peoples Christian Coalition (5104 North Christiana, Chicago, IL 60625).

Philadelphia Task Force on Women on Religion (Box 24003, PA 19139).

Philadelphia Women's Liberation Center (4634 Chester Avenue, PA 19143).

President's Commission on the Status of Women (Defunct). Now Interdepartmental Committee on the Status of Women (1336 Main Labor Building, Washington, D.C. 20210).

Pro ERA Alliance (Room 120, 200 S. 7th Street, Louisville, KY 40202).

Publisher's Auxiliary (491 National Press Building, Washington, D.C. 20004).

Republican National Committee (310 1st Street, SE, Washington, D.C. 20003).

Richmond Women's Center (610 S. Laurel Street, VA 23220).

Roanoke Valley Women's Coalition (1212 Keffield Street, Roanoke, VA 24019).

Saint Joan's International Alliance (435 W. 119th Street, New York, NY 10027).

Seattle Radical Women (3815 5th Street, NE, Washington 98105).

Seattle Women's Liberation (YWCA, 3rd and Seneca, WA 98101).

Slippery Rock Women's Liberation (Re: *The Hand That Rocks the Rock*, c/o Ronny Howard, Department of English, Slippery Rock State College, Slippery Rock, PA 16057).

Society of American Archivists, Women's Caucus (National Archives and Records, Pennsylvania Avenue at 8th Street, NW, Washington, D.C. 20408).

South Carolina Coalition for the Equal Rights Amendment (311 Springlake Road, Columbia 29206).

South Carolina Office of the Attorney General (300 Wade Hampton State Office Building, Columbia 29201).

Stop ERA (Box 618, Alton, IL 62002).

Storrs Women's Center (Box 18, CT 06268).

Tennessee Commission on the Status of Women (921 Andrew Jackson Building, Nashville 37219).

Texans for Equal Rights Amendment (603 W. 13th Street, No. 203, Austin 78701).

Texas Stop ERA. See Stop ERA; Women Who Want to Be Women.

Texas Subcommittee on H.C.R. 57 of House Committee on Constitutional Revision (State Capitol, Austin 78711).

Twin Cities Female Liberation (2953 Bloomington Avenue, S, Minneapolis, MN 55407).

Union W.A.G.E. (2137 Oregon Street, Berkeley, CA 94705).

Unitarian Universalist Women's Federation (25 Beacon Street, Boston, MA 02108).

United Auto Workers—CIO, Women's Department (8000 E. Jefferson, Detroit, MI 48214).

United Church of Christ, Task Force on Women in Church and Society (297 Park Avenue, S, New York, NY 10010).

United Methodist ERA Support Project (100 Maryland Avenue, NE, Washington, D.C. 20002). See Board of Church and Society; Church and Society Task Force.

United Methodist Women's Caucus (2121 N. Sheridan Road, Evanston, IL 60201).

United Presbyterian Church of U.S.A., Council on Women and the Church (475 Riverside Drive, New York, NY 10027).

United Sisters (Box 5984, Tampa, FL 33675).

United Sisters (Re: *Puce Mongoose*, Box 41, Garwood, NJ 07027).

United States Commission on Civil Rights, Women's Rights Program Unit (1121 Vermont Avenue, NW, Washington, D.C. 20425).

United States Department of Labor (Washington, D.C. 20210). See Women's Bureau.

United States Department of Justice (10th and Pennsylvania Avenue, NW, Room 1614, Washington, D. C. 20530).

United States National Women's Agenda (Women's Action Alliance Information Center, 370 Lexington Avenue, New York, NY 10017).

University of New Mexico Law Students (Albuquerque 87106).

University of Virginia, Continuing Education for Women (4210 Roberts Road, Fairfax 22030).

Urban Research Corporation (5464 S. Shore Drive, Chicago, IL 60615).

Utah Governor's Committee on the Status of Women (210 State Capitol, Salt Lake City 84114).

Utah Office of Legislative Research (326 State Capitol, Salt Lake City 84114).

Vermont Legislative Council (State House, Montpelier 05602).

Vocational Center for Women. See Nassau County Department of General Services.

Washington Forum (915 19th Street, NW, Washington, D.C. 20006).

Washington Legislative Council, Judiciary Committee (Room 147 North, State Capitol, Madison 53702).

Waterbury Women's Center (25 Grand Street, CT 06702).

Wayne County CIO Council (2310 Cass Street, Detroit, MI 48201).

Wisconsin Equal Rights Coalition (713 E. Johnson Street, Madison 53703).

Wisconsin Governor's Commission on the Status of Women (Room 427, Lowell Hall, 610 Langdon Street, Madison 53706).

Wisconsin Legislative Council, Special Committee on Equal Rights (428 Lowell Hall, 610 Langdon Street, Madison 53706).

Wisconsin Legislative Reference Bureau (State Capitol, Madison 53702).

Wisconsin Psychiatric Institute (330 E. Lakeside, Madison 53715).

Woman Activists in New York State (T. Hommel, 10 St. Marks Place, New York City 10003).

Women at A.T.&T. (1601 41st Avenue, Seattle, WA 98102).

Women for Change Center (3220 Lemmon Avenue, Suite 290, Dallas, TX 75230).

Women's Action Alliance Information Center. See United States National Women's Agenda.

Women's Advisory Group at Bonneville Power Administration (1002 N.E. Holladay, Portland, OR 97230).

Women's Bar Association of the District of Columbia (5272 River Road, Suite 690, Washington, D.C. 20016).

Women's Bureau (U.S. Dept. of Labor, Employment Standards Administration, 14th Street and Constitution Avenue, NW, Room 5330, Washington, D.C. 20210).

Women's Caucus for Political Science (Box 12859 University Station, Gainesville, FL 32601).

Women's City Club (2110 Park Avenue, Detroit, MI 48201).

Women's Equity Action League (821 National Press Building, Washington, D.C. 20045).

New Jersey WEAL (78 Alberta Avenue, Trenton 08619).

Texas WEAL (P.O. Drawer 12185, Dallas 75225).

Women's Division, State of New York. See New York State Women's Division.

Women's Liberation groups of Salt Lake City (Women's Liberation Action Group, 363 E. 600 South, Utah 84111).

Women United (Box 300, Washington, D.C. 20044; 2001 Jefferson Davis Highway, Crystal Plaza 1, Ste. 805, Arlington, VA 22202).

Women Who Want to Be Women (Box 2324, Fort Worth, TX 76101).

Young Americans for Freedom (Woodland Road, Sterling, VA 22170).

YWCA News of Atlanta (Midtown Atlanta YWCA, 45 11th Street, NE, Georgia 30309).

YWCA Women's Center (395 Main Street, Orange, NJ 07052).

Zero Population Growth (1346 Connecticut Avenue, NW, Washington, D.C. 20036).

11
What Happens When ERA
Is Ratified:
Ground Rules for Interpretation

The Equal Rights Amendment will not go into effect immediately: it provides for a two-year period of study to conform existing laws and pass new ones, as required. *During this two-year period, before the amendment takes full effect, legislatures and administrative agencies will be charged with the task of conforming our legal system to the amendment's requirements. Thereafter, it will be the job of our courts to determine if conformity has been achieved if and when laws are challenged.*

In short, ERA will require a comprehensive reexamination and, where necessary, amendment of our federal and state laws, local ordinances, and administrative rules and procedures. This is why Section 3 of the proposed Twenty-seventh Amendment to our Constitution provides for a two-year interim period: to allow sufficient time to study these laws, ordinances, and rulings and to come up with fair and nondiscriminatory changes wherever necessary.

It is only once ERA goes into effect—that is, two years after ratification—that it will provide citizens with a legal vehicle to make sure our laws do not discriminate on the basis of sex. It will then be up to our courts to hear any challenges to existing laws and to determine whether they meet the new constitutional requirements.

In stating this legislative intent, *U.S. Senate Report #92-689* specifically provides that "the legislatures of the several states will have the primary responsibility for revising those laws which conflict with the Equal Rights Amendment. Indeed, the purpose of delaying the effective date of the Equal Rights Amendment for two years after ratification is to allow legislatures—particularly those which meet only in alternative years—and agencies, an opportunity to review and revise their laws and regulations."[1] Thus, the way has been paved for an orderly and systematic transition after ERA is ratified. There is also every reason to expect that we will finally have a comprehensive system of federal and state laws governed by the principles established by the Equal Rights Amendment. Without the amendment, efforts to eliminate sex discriminatory legislation would continue for decades, if not centuries.

But none of this will happen by itself. It will require our active and vigilant participation. ERA ratification is only the beginning, the first round. Our next task, and a major one it is, will be to make sure that the Twenty-seventh Amendment to our Constitution is properly interpreted and enforced.

ERA's Intent: The Legislative History

How our lawmakers and our courts will interpret the Equal Rights Amendment will, as we have seen in part 1, be determined primarily by the amendment's legislative history. (See particularly chapter 1, Fancies 1,2,3,4,5, and 10). To recapitulate briefly, the legislative history of any piece of legislation, be it an ordinance or a constitutional amendment, contains the legislative intent of those who introduced and passed it. It therefore consists of the arguments presented by the sponsors and proponents of the Equal Rights Amendment and their witnesses, *not* the arguments advanced by the opposition, as these were rejected by Congress when it voted for passage.

As indicated in chapter 1, there are two major sources for ERA legislative history. The first and more concise is the majority report of the Senate Committee on the Judiciary contained in *U.S. Senate Report #92–689*, 92nd Congress, second session (sometimes referred to as "Equal Rights for Men and Women" or just the "Senate Majority Report"). The second primary source is the *Congressional Record for 1971–1972*, recording the House and Senate floor *debates* as well as the *hearings* before both the House and Senate Judiciary Committees.

These debates and hearings include the opinions of legal

experts whose testimony was requested by ERA sponsors (see for example chapter 1, Fancies 5 and 6). One very important such resource is a legal treatise that was placed in the *Congressional Record* by ERA sponsor Senator Birch Bayh and distributed to all representatives by Sponsor Representative Martha Griffins. This is the Yale law review article of April 1971, "The Equal Rights Amendment: A Constitutional Basis For Equal Rights For Women," 80 *Yale Law Journal* 871 (1971) by Brown, Emerson, Faulk, and Friedman. But, again, one important caveat (as pointed out in part 1) is that this article has been much distorted and misquoted by anti-ERA propagandists such as Senator Sam Ervin and Phyllis Schlafly, causing much confusion which could, unless we are vigilant, again creep into the interpretation of the amendment after it is ratified (see in particular chapter 1, Fancy 10).

What Happens When ERA Is Ratified

Much of the legislative history of the Equal Rights Amendment has been set forth in chapter 1. There is, however, one point that is so important that it warrants repeating again. This is that the specific legislative intent of ERA is that laws which confer rights and benefits to one sex only shall *not* be struck down, but amended by our legislatures or interpreted by our courts to extend these rights and benefits to both sexes. Only those laws (or portions of laws) which deny women or men a right or benefit on the basis of their sex are to be invalidated. The legislative mandate is clear. In rewriting legislation, sex-neutral and functional considerations, rather than sexual stereotypes, must be followed. Similarly, in interpreting legislation, whenever possible, laws must be construed as sex-neutral by our courts.

For example, suppose a state has the following provisions regarding spousal support:

Section 1. Courts in divorce proceedings may, in their discretion, make awards of spousal support.

Section 2. Courts shall have no power to award spousal support to husbands.

If this law were reexamined by the legislature, to conform it to ERA, only Section 2 would need to be amended.

In accordance with the requirements of ERA, it would
have to read as follows:

Section 2. Courts shall have the power to award
spousal support to either spouse (or to both husbands and
wives).

Should the legislature fail to amend such a law accordingly, it would be subject to challenge in court. Again,
the legislative history of ERA would require that a judge
hearing a constitutional challenge to that law, would have
to rule that "spousal support" under Section 1 should be
construed to include both husbands and wives and that
only Section 2 of the law must be struck down.

It is essential that we be aware of this legislative intent
to prevent abuses of legislative and judicial discretion, as
it has unfortunately not been unheard of for some judges
(particularly in the lower courts) to try to use egalitarian
laws and principles to punish women for seeking equality
by attempting to deprive them of their rights. Such attempts
have happened before ERA and will undoubtedly happen
again, but they will *not* be successful if we are vigilant and
insist that ERA be interpreted properly—that is, in accordance with the legislative intent.

The Meaning of the State ERAs

The constitutions of sixteen American states contain
guarantees against sex-based discrimination. State ERAs
have recently been included in the constitutions of fourteen
states: Alaska (1972), Colorado (1972), Connecticut
(1974), Hawaii (1972), Illinois (1971), Louisiana (1974),
Maryland (1972), Massachusetts (1976), Montana (1973),
New Mexico (1973), Pennsylvania (1971), Texas (1972),
Virginia (1971), and Washington (1972). In addition, the
original constitutions of Utah and Wyoming included
clauses guaranteeing civil and political rights without regard to sex.[2]

Although there have been variations in the interpretation of these provisions from state to state (pointing to
the need for a single uniform federal standard, which ERA
will provide), the legislative and court actions taken under
these provisions have, in the words of the Presidentially
appointed National Commission on the Observance of International Women's Year (IWY), been "particularly re-

assuring."[3] They should therefore be monitored and studied carefully, as in appropriate situations they can be an important secondary source of guidance for the proper implementation of the Equal Rights Amendment.

In 1975, the IWY Commission, appointed by President Ford, contracted with the Women's Law Project of Philadelphia to collect and study the reported judicial interpretations from states with ERAs in their constitutions. One of the most important findings of their study was that *"fairer decisions to divorced homemakers, to children, and to husbands are resulting from state ERAs."*[4]

For example, a Pennsylvania case, which was decided after that state enacted its ERA, held that a wife is entitled to half the household goods at divorce even though her husband paid for them, whereas under prior Pennsylvania law she would have been entitled only to what she could prove she had paid for.[5] (More about this in chapter 12.) The study also found that rape laws have not been invalidated by state ERAs. Furthermore, no laws prohibiting homosexual marriage have been invalidated, and no laws providing for separate toilets have been overturned.[6]

Nevertheless, horror stories about the terrible things that these recent state ERAs have wrought are one of the great anti-Equal Rights Amendment propaganda staples (see chapter 10). This is ironic, for the evidence is very definitely that, on the contrary, women in these states have made significant gains.

The Truth About State ERAs

Governor Daniel J. Evans of the state of Washington wrote the following in February 1976: "I am aware of no classification of 'privileges' which a woman has lost because of adoption of the ERA. . . . The passage of the ERA has brought Washington state a new commitment to the right of equal treatment for all our citizens."[7]

From Pennsylvania, Marie R. Keeney, director of the Commission For Women, wrote in January 1976:

> Pennsylvania women have not lost rights or privileges because of the Equal Rights Provision, nor will they when the federal ERA is ratified. To the contrary,

women are in a stronger position, particularly in the domestic relations area, as a result of the ERA. . . . Implementation has not proven costly or unwieldy, although the necessary statutory changes cannot be expected to occur with no special assignment of staff and effort. . . . There has been neither a mandate nor any action to integrate public restrooms or sleeping quarters in public institutions or prison cells. Absolutely no invasion of privacy in these areas has been encountered in the nearly five years the amendment has been in effect.[8]

From Alaska, Lou Anne Maxwell, Equal Employment Opportunity officer, wrote as follows in February 1976:

Women have not lost any rights in Alaska. To the contrary, although we have no actual studies to prove it, credit, housing, and employment have improved. Women are becoming more aware of their rights, and the records of The State Human Rights Commission clearly indicate this—forty percent of the complaints filed are based on sex discrimination. Many women are being employed in jobs not usually open to women. For instance, there are now approximately 1,900 women employed in the Trans-Alaska Pipeline.[9]

In a letter to the *Wall Street Journal* in October 1976, the Maryland commission to study implementation of the Equal Rights Amendment said, "Rather than producing a loss of rights or privileges for our citizens, the amendment has been a stimulus for constructive change and has produced a greater equality of the sexes."[10]

When a member of the board of directors of the League of Women Voters of New York wrote to the governors of states with ERAs and asked whether women had lost any rights, she received replies from ten states. All of them—Alaska, Colorado, Connecticut, Hawaii, Maryland, New Mexico, Pennsylvania, Virginia, Washington, and Wyoming—said "no" on all counts, and with the letter from the governor of New Mexico was enclosed a publication of the League of Women Voters of New Mexico summarizing the more important statutory changes resulting from the state ERA, including the right for wives of comanagement in community property.[11]

Lessons from State ERAs

What this means is that the experience with state ERAs can and should be used to make sure that the Twenty-seventh Amendment gives us the kinds of laws and court decisions it was intended to give. But again, there are some cautions here. For example, some of the earlier decisions in Utah and Wyoming, whose original constitutions contained equal rights provisions, cannot legitimately be used as models. The reason is that the ERA-type provisions in these state constitutions were primarily intended to preserve for women only the right to vote. Further, since they were adopted before the turn of the last century, they have not been interpreted consistently with our contemporary standards of justice and equality. Even in the fourteen states that added ERAs during this past decade, it will still be up to us to examine what has worked well and what has not.[12]

How vigorously lawmakers and judges act in implementing and enforcing the requirements of the Equal Rights Amendment will inevitably vary, at least at the beginning. It is up to us to be vigilant and to use some of the fine precedents that have already been set in states with ERAs in their constitutions to make sure that the legislatures and judges in all of our states interpret the Equal Rights Amendment properly and fairly (more about this in chapter 13). For example, the court decisions of Pennsylvania and Washington have diligently enforced the requirements that their state laws not discriminate on the basis of sex.[13] The high courts of Alaska, Colorado, Connecticut, Maryland, and Texas have also indicated that strict scrutiny—that is, the same test that is required in discrimination based on race—must be employed in deciding cases under their state ERAs. The same conclusion was reached by the Illinois Supreme Court in the case of *People v. Ellis*,[14] a case concerning a statute under which female offenders were treated as juveniles up to age eighteen but males only up to age seventeen. The court found that the legislative history of the Illinois ERA indicated that the amendment's proponents wanted women to have "the same type of equality" as had "long been held to apply to blacks." Accordingly, the court held that classifications based on sex must be considered "suspect" and that the more lax "rational test," requiring only that the discrimination not be "invidious, or arbitrary," is not strict enough.[15]

This too is the intent of the proponents of the Equal Rights Amendment to our constitution—that sex discrimination deserves the same strict scrutiny as discrimination based on race—and this is the test that should be applied by legislators and judges in interpreting ERA.

12

What Should ERA Do: Ten Goals for Implementation

The Equal Rights Amendment requires full constitutional recognition of the right of women and men to be treated as individuals before the law. ERA is necessary because this recognition has been sadly lacking until now. It can, and must, result in the comprehensive revision of federal and state laws, as a first step toward equalizing the inferior social and economic position of American women. It can also and must provide women and men with a simple, direct, and permanent means of access to our courts in order to right individual and social injustices based on sex.

Goal 1
Equalize and Strengthen the Position of Homemakers

Despite the claims of anti-ERA propagandists that the Equal Rights Amendment will rob married women of great privileges and rights, the legal position of the American homemaker in most of our states is far from good. In fact, in many states, it is downright dismal.

Only a handful of states (California, Arizona, Idaho, Louisiana, Nevada, New Mexico, Texas, and Washington) have a community property system—which at least in theory treats marriage as a partnership. In most American states we have what is called a "common law" system of law which, essentially, means that, unless the breadwinner (usually the husband) places assets bought with his earnings in both his and his wife's name, under the law they are exclusively his.

As for the much publicized right of support during marriage (which anti-ERA propagandists falsely say is terribly threatened by the Equal Rights Amendment), this right, if it exists at all, is no more than an abstraction. This was vividly demonstrated by one of the few litigated cases on the subject, *McGuire v. McGuire*.[1] When Mrs. McGuire got so sick that she had to go to court and ask for an order for her husband to perform his legal obligation to "furnish a proper home for his wife and to maintain her there in a degree of comfort authorized by the circumstances," the Nebraska Supreme Court flatly turned her down. Mrs. McGuire was the wife of a well-to-do farmer. She sued her husband in 1953 after a marriage of thirty-four years. In her complaint she stated that she had "worked in the fields, [done] outside chores, cooked and attended to her household duties, raised as high as 300 chickens, sold poultry and eggs, and used the money to buy clothing and groceries." She complained that she lived in a house without a bathroom, had to get water from a well, drove a 1929 Ford without a working heater, and that although her husband had the means to do so, he refused to fix the house or the car and that in the last four years, he had hardly given her any money.[2]

When the Nebraska Supreme Court threw out the case, they said that "*to maintain an action such as the one at bar, the parties must be separated or living apart from each other.*" Beyond that, the court had this to say: "The living standards of a family are a matter of concern to the household and not for the courts to determine," and this is so, "even though the husband's attitude toward his wife, according to his wealth and circumstances, leaves little to be said on his behalf"[3] (emphasis added).

The fact that a husband's legal duty to support a wife will be judicially defined only in divorce court is (despite the anti-ERA propaganda) a very well-known and established rule of law. Consequently, it is absurd to state that the ERA can be interpreted to deprive married women of the support of their husbands or, as Phyllis Schlafly has claimed, to throw homemakers out of their homes and force them to go out and get jobs.

On the contrary, what the Equal Rights Amendment can and must do is to strengthen the position of the married homemaker so that she is less dependent on her mate's largesse, both during and after marriage. The problem of dependency and its negative economic and social consequences is particularly acute for the widowed and divorced woman who, far from being privileged under existing laws, is more often than not legally discriminated against—a fact that is reflected in her generally low and often desperate economic position. But it is a problem that, at least potentially, affects every woman in America.

The legislative history of the Twenty-seventh Amendment clearly demonstrates that its intent is to improve the position of the American homemaker. To recapitulate briefly, the Senate Majority Report explicitly expresses the congressional intent that the ERA be interpreted specifically to recognize the value of the services of the homemaker. It also explicitly negates the anti-ERA propaganda claim that the amendment must be interpreted to require both spouses to contribute identical amounts of money to the marriage: "It is clear that the amendment would not require both husband and wife to contribute identical amounts of money to a marriage," states the Senate Majority Report.[4] "The support obligations of each spouse would be defined in functional terms based, for example, on each spouse's earning power, current resources and nonmonetary contributions to the family welfare. . . . *Where one spouse is the primary wage earner and the other runs the home, the wage earner would have a duty to support the spouse who stays at home in compensation for the performance of her or his duties*"[5] (emphasis added).

Clearly then, once ERA is ratified, one of our primary aims must be to ensure that, in the reexamination and revision of existing state laws, the homemaker is given better protection.

Can this be done? Again, the answer is, very definitely, "yes." Not only can it be done once ERA is passed, but it already has been done in some of the states that have ERAs in their state constitutions. For example, the state of Montana, which has an Equal Rights Amendment, amended its support laws in 1975 to specifically recognize the value of the services rendered by the homemaker: "Duties of husband and wife as to support: In so far as each is able, the husband and wife shall support each other out of their property and labor. As used in this section, the word 'support' includes the nonmonetary support provided by a spouse as homemaker."[6] Similar language is found in the Uniform Marriage and Divorce Act, a model family law act that has been proposed for adoption by the legislatures of all states.

In summary then, the ERA can be used to enforce the principle (now ignored in most states) that the home-maker's role in marriage has economic value that entitles her or him to full partnership under the law.

Goal 2
Equalize and Strengthen the Social and Economic Situation of Divorced Women and One-Parent Families

In Florida, which has no state ERA and which has voted against ratifying the Equal Rights Amendment, home-makers are facing the following situation. Florida is a common law state. What this means is that, upon divorce, the property of one spouse is *not* awarded to the other spouse unless he or she has contributed separate property to the acquisition of the estate. Consequently, Florida homemakers are primarily dependent on spousal support or alimony for postdivorce financial protection. When in 1971 Florida switched to no-fault divorce, the state legis-lature also introduced the concept of "rehabilitative," as opposed to "permanent," alimony. As interpreted by the courts, this provision resulted in the switch to short-term awards (rather than lifetime alimony) to "give a dependent spouse time to get back on her or his feet" or "become self-supporting following the divorce."[7]

This practice has continued despite a number of re-versals in higher courts. As a Florida appellate court com-plained in 1975, "There is apparently a feeling in some circles that the passage of the no-fault divorce law in 1971 had the effect of abolishing permanent alimony except where the wife (or the husband, as the case may be) is unable to get a job." (*Lash v. Lash*)[8]

So, in Florida, the homemaker is in a very precarious position indeed, and, ironically, it is probably because the Florida homemaker has good reason to feel frightened and insecure that the anti-ERA propagandists have been so successful there with their scare tactics about ERA. The truth, however, is that Florida women have nothing to lose and much to gain from the passage of ERA.

This becomes crystal clear when one examines—and contrasts—the experience of women in Pennsylvania, a state that adopted an ERA in 1971. Pennsylvania courts have taken a giant step toward protecting and equalizing the position of the homemaker *on the basis of their state ERA.* In the case of *DiFlorido v. DiFlorido,*[9] a Pennsylvania housewife was held entitled to half the household goods and other property at divorce *even though her husband paid for them.* In refusing to follow Pennsylvania case law decided *prior* to the state ERA (which held that she would have been entitled only to what she could prove she had paid for), the court said this: "We cannot accept an approach that would have ownership of household items on proof of funding alone, since to do so would . . . fail to acknowledge the *equally important and often substantial nonmonetary contributions made by either spouse.*" (*DiFlorido v. DiFlorido*).[10] Basically, then, the Pennsylvania Supreme Court declared the common law property doctrine inconsistent with the state ERA and, in so doing, very significantly expanded the property rights of divorced homemakers.

Texas, which adopted a state ERA in 1972, has also provided important legal precedents for the proper interpretation of the Equal Rights Amendment in the area of family law. When, in *Cooper v. Cooper,*[11] a Texas homemaker was awarded more than half the community property and $1,500 monthly in child support—plus expenses for private schools not to exceed $6,000 per year and all medical and dental expenses incurred by the children—her husband, a wealthy physician, appealed on the grounds that the award was in conflict with the state ERA.

But the court upheld both the unequal division of property and the award of child support.

With respect to the award of property, the Court of Civil Appeals held that "the difference in earning capacity and business opportunities would justify an unequal division of the community property" to Mrs. Cooper, who had been a homemaker for sixteen years.[12]

As for the child support award, the court had this to say: "If 'equality under the law shall not be denied or abridged because of sex,' it must be presumed that the legislature intended that the duty of the spouses to support their minor children is equal. *This does not mean, however, that the*

*court must divide the burden of support of the minor
children equally between the parties. The court's order
in this respect should reflect a due consideration of the
respective abilities of the spouses to contribute*"[18] (emphasis added).

Thus, in both common law and community property
states, the Equal Rights Amendment can give homemakers
better legislative and judicial protection upon divorce, just
as state ERAs already have done. It will be our task to
see to it that this result is achieved in all American states.

But our task goes further than that. As the IWY report
points out, even when trial courts award spousal and child
support, the duty to pay them remains largely unenforced.
For example, studies show that in 1975 only 44 percent
of divorced mothers were awarded child support, and only
45 percent of these collected regularly.[14] It will be up to
us to see that better laws are properly interpreted and
better enforced and that the problem of collection—one of
the most severe faced by divorced homemakers—is finally
addressed by our law enforcement officials. (More later
about implementation and enforcement.)

If these and other problems of the one-parent family
are not addressed, millions of American children (many
of formerly middle-class homes) will be doomed to grow
up in poverty and alienation—at incalculable personal cost
to them and social and economic cost to us all. According
to the U.S. census, in 1970 approximately one out of
every ten American families was headed by only one
parent, and in over 85 percent of these families, this parent
was the mother. Between 1955 and 1973, the number of
families in the United States headed by a woman increased
by 56 percent—from 4.2 million families to 6.6 million.
During the decade from 1960 to 1970 alone, the number of
such families increased by about 1 million, and during the
first three years of the present decade, the number has
again increased by another million.[15]

These one-parent families are the poorest in our nation.
One immediate reason is the immense earning differential
between women and men in the labor market. Another
reason is the lack of adequate child care facilities, which
makes it virtually impossible for many mothers to do anything other than go on welfare. And yet welfare is both
personally degrading and economically inadequate: it sim-

ply keeps the family on a poverty level. What is remarkable is that, with all of the many social, cultural, and economic strikes against them, a healthy minority of these families are headed by women who are able to provide themselves and their children with a good standard of living—often women who have made exceptional personal and career achievements.

While ERA does not directly address itself to the problems of these one-parent families, the Twenty-seventh Amendment can be used to equalize and strengthen their legal, social, and economic status. In proclaiming that women are legally as valued as men, ERA recognizes the value of families headed by women. It also provides a legal and moral commitment to the mothers of millions of children—of the one-sixth of all Americans under eighteen —who are still taught to see themselves and their families as "second-class." This commitment must be translated into action: better enforcement of spousal and child support awards, intelligent welfare reform (taking into account the social value of homemaking and child rearing), and effective equalization of employment opportunities (including adequate child care and educational facilities), so that these millions of families can be fully integrated into the mainstream of American life.

Goal 3
Equalize and Strengthen the Position
of Widows and Older Women

In 1973 there were 9,851,000 widows in the United States, a 41 percent increase since 1950.[16] What is their situation under current law?

The story of Mary Heath, reported by the IWY Commission, is typical.[17] Mary and her husband Floyd were ranchers near Cody, Nebraska, and they worked side by side for thirty-three years. They worked hard because Cody is in the Nebraska sandhills, where it rarely rains and twenty acres of grazing land is needed to supply just one cow. Mary worked the cattle, helped with the haying, and raised hogs as a sideline.

When Floyd died in 1974, Mary inherited their ranch. She didn't expect any real problems since they had both worked the farm together and the property was in both their names. But she was wrong. What she learned was that she would have to pay $25,000 inheritance tax whereas, if she had died first, Floyd would not have to pay one penny! Furthermore, as the Internal Revenue Service explained to her, under federal tax rules the farm belonged entirely to her husband unless she could prove she had contributed money to its purchase or improvement. Her years of work on the ranch did not count, and the joint title was meaningless.[18]

As the IWY report points out, Mrs. Heath's problem is not only one of farm women.

> Whenever an estate is more than $120,000, a widow must prove she has contributed money to the purchase or the improvement of the estate or face estate taxes. The homemaker's contribution to the family's worth does not count, no matter how many meals she has prepared, no matter how many hours she has cleaned house, cared for the children, or spent making and mending her family's clothings (and if you think a $120,000 estate is a large one, just consider the cost of houses today).[19]

For American widows, the Equal Rights Amendment can be the wedge to bring about much needed reform of estate and inheritance tax laws. By recognizing the economic value of a homemaker's contribution and by affirming the principle that discrimination based on sex is unconstitutional, the Equal Rights Amendment will provide the legal basis for ending the unequal treatment of wives and husbands under our estate and inheritance tax laws.

But the legal discrimination against widows under our laws is not confined to taxes. The inheritance rights of spouses vary enormously from state to state. In some community property states, one-half of the community property automatically goes to either spouse. In California, for example—after a battle that lasted for almost a century—widows were little by little protected from their husbands' giving away or mortgaging property that belonged to them, so that finally, today, widows in California are truly and equally protected.[20] In many other states, however—particularly those that still adhere to the common law system—widows have very little protection. In some of these states widows receive an automatic one-third share. But in others—for example Georgia, North Dakota, and South Dakota—there is no such share so that, if he chooses, a husband can legally disinherit his wife.

Clearly, ERA will require fairer intestacy laws (which protect family members where there is no will), for, as we have seen, under the common law rules it is only the wage earner's investment in property that is recognized, and the contribution of the homemaker is ignored. Similarly, ERA will also require that inheritance laws that deprive wives of any legal share in the marital property be reexamined because, as it stands now in most common law states, women can only will property that stands in their name.

One of the least publicized facts of American life is that women who are sixty-five and older have the lowest annual median income of any age or sex group. In 1975, according to Dr. Arthur Fleming, U.S. Commissioner on Aging, their median income was approximately $1,900 per year, and in 1974, 18 percent of all women sixty-five and over had incomes below the official poverty level.[21]

This, then, is our ultimate destination, our reward for being women, and for hoping that we will be protected and taken care of, instead of asserting and demanding our rights. The poverty, fear, and isolation in which millions of old women live today is not an accident. It is the result of lifelong legal, economic, and social discrimination. ERA can be used to change this shameful fact of American life, and it is up to us to make sure that it does.

Goal 4
Equalize and Strengthen the Position of Women Who Work Outside the Home

To recap, briefly, the *real* situation of women in the American labor force, as detailed in chapters 2 and 3: Over 37 million women work outside their homes, and women are today the fastest single growing segment of the labor force. *But instead of improving, our situation has worsened and the gap between male and female incomes is widening.* This has occurred despite the many laws that have been passed in recent years against employment discrimination based on sex.

Why is this? One major reason is that most of these laws simply lack teeth.

As it stands now, even the agencies of our federal government (the largest single employer of women) are not adequately enforcing the President's Executive Order requiring maintenance of equal employment programs—an order issued as far back as 1965! The Affirmative Action Program, calling for good faith efforts to achieve equal employment goals and timetables by federal contractors and grantees, is today practically unenforced, and the Equal Employment Opportunities Commission is severely hampered by lack of adequate staffing and funds.

ERA can provide the impetus for allocating more resources toward the vigorous enforcement of fair employment laws and regulations. This would entail better and larger staffs, reasonable budgets for information dissemination, and the education of agency and law enforcement officials to provide motivation for them to do the job. Only if this is done will Title VII of the Civil Rights Act of 1964—as well as Executive Orders 11246 and 11375 and other fine existing federal and state laws designed to end sex-based employment discrimination—change the alarming fact that in 1974, according to the Department of Labor statistics, men earned 75 percent more than women.[22]

Another reason for women's inferior position in the labor market is that only a small percentage of women workers are unionized. One factor has been that women are heavily overrepresented in occupations in which there have been no unions: clerical and secretarial jobs, education, health, housework, and social services. But another factor has been discrimination by the unions themselves in which, particularly in the crafts and trades, women have traditionally been excluded from both apprenticeship and training programs. Here, again, ERA can help bring about much needed changes. We already have laws prohibiting labor union sex discrimination, and the clear mandate of ERA should provide the impetus for their enforcement.

The situation of the woman entrepeneur—the woman who in the independent American tradition sets out to make it on her own—is today little better than that of her employed sisters. In some states, she is still legally hampered from setting up her own business if she happens to be married. In all states, she is at the bottom of the economic scale.

The vast majority of women-owned businesses are small, and, according to a 1972 Commerce Department survey, the average annual income of women-owner-operated businesses was only $10,000.[23] Once again, we are faced with an area in which there are already some good laws on the books, but they are not enforced when it comes to women.

For example, the Small Business Administration was set up specifically to help the small entrepreneur through low-interest loans, information, and other forms of aid. Moreover, under Section 8a of the Small Business Act of 1953, the SBA is specifically directed to assist socially or economically disadvantaged owners of businesses. But the SBA has refused to include women in this category because they are technically not a minority.[24]

In 1975 the U.S. Civil Rights Commission reported that "small Business Administration officials assert that assisting the development of female-owned businesses is not the current national policy."[25] Not surprisingly, it also found that women-owned firms were encountering "problems of staggering proportions in obtaining information on federal, state, and local government contracting opportunities in time to submit timely bids, and in obtaining the working capital necessary for effective marketing and bidding."[26]

In reporting to the President on the situation of women entrepreneurs and women in the labor force, the IWY Commission expressed grave concern about "the apparent failure of the Office of Federal Contract Compliance to enforce compliance with the nondiscriminatory provision of its enabling legislation as they pertain to sex."[27]

As an interesting and ironic sidelight, the IWY Commission also pointed out that there is evidence of sex-based employment discrimination in the very heart of the U.S. government: the Congress. At present, we have no law or executive order directly prohibiting sex-based discrimination against federal employees of the legislative branch. The results, as shown by a 1974 study by the Capitol Hill Women's Political Caucus, are large discrepancies in the pay received by women and men. (The median salary for women press professionals, for example, was $10,878 compared with $26,600 for men.)[28] Since ERA specifically requires that equality of rights shall not be denied or

abridged by the United States or by any state on account
of sex, this should certainly apply to the Congress of the
United States.

In business and industry, as in education and government, the problem of the woman who works outside her
home—like that of the woman who works inside her
home—is one of attitudes and values. Ours is still a society
that, despite all the rhetoric, does not give real economic
or social value to anything women do. This is not to say
that, again, the potential legal and symbolic impact of the
Equal Rights Amendment is not enormous. But in the last
analysis, it will be up to us to see that this potential is
translated into reality.

For a comprehensive analysis of the situation of women
in the labor force, as well as of women entrepreneurs, see
*To Form a More Perfect Union: the Report of the National
Commission on the Observance of International Women's
Year, 1976*, particularly the section on "Women In The
Work Place," page 57, and "The Recommendations of the
Women in Employment Committee," page 303.

Goal 5
Equalize and Strengthen the Position
of Women in Education

Education shapes our social values. It determines how we
see ourselves and others. It is also the major route for
personal advancement: it provides us with the training that
we need to make a place for ourselves in our society and
our world.

In both these respects, ours is an educational system that
casts women in supporting roles. Women continue to move
into educational programs that either do not prepare them
for paid employment or prepare them only for work in the
lower paying "female" jobs. Women are grossly under-
represented in training programs in the higher paying
trades. Women are still being discouraged from entering
the prestigious (and almost totally male dominated) professions. As far as counseling and role models are concerned—not just in textbooks but in every phase of education, be it inside or outside of schools, on television or in
the movies—women are still predominantly portrayed in
the "traditional" roles: that is, as supportive characters, as

men's secretaries and wives, as nurses where men are doctors, as helpers where men are doers.

The symbolism of ERA—the explicit and unequivocal declaration in the highest law of our land that sex is not a reasonable basis for discrimination—can go a long way toward beginning to cure what this is all about: the social disease of sexism. More directly, ERA will help strengthen laws and executive orders aimed against educational discrimination, such as Title IX of the Education Amendments of 1972, which prohibits sex discrimination against students and employees by educational institutions receiving federal aid. ERA should immediately bring about stricter enforcement of Title IX as it clearly and unequivocally states that sex discrimination is unconstitutional. That such a statement is necessary is demonstrated by the fact that Title IX has hardly been enforced. The Department of Health, Education, and Welfare, whose chief enforcement weapon against sex discrimination under Title IX is the right to cut off federal money to noncomplying institutions, has never done so to date—despite the countless complaints that have been filed![29]

HEW significantly influences education in the United States today through its regulations and through the $6 billion of federal aid it provides education each year. Yet, three years after a task force appointed by the Commissioner of Education set forth specific and extensive steps that HEW was to take to improve educational opportunities for girls and women, HEW still had failed to act.[30]

HEW's failure to enforce our laws, executive orders, and regulations against sex discrimination has, in the words of the IWY report, "led many community groups and concerned individuals to question HEW's sincerity in enforcing the law against sex discrimination."[31]

It has also left the position of women in the educational field virtually unchanged. On the employment side, according to the National Center for Educational Statistics, from 1974 to 1975 the proportion of women faculty members in private and public institutions of higher learning (relative to men) actually *declined* at the higher ranks of professor and associate professor, and the mean salaries of men continued to exceed those of women at every academic rank.[32] In primary and secondary schools, the situation was no better. While in 1975 women were 63 percent of all public school teachers, only 2 percent of secondary school principals and 18 percent of primary school principals were women.[33]

Women must be given an equal chance to affect and shape educational policy. Counseling, texts, and curricula must be reexamined and, where necessary, adjusted to the contemporary needs and aspirations of women. The educational programs of all schools, universities, vocational colleges, and apprenticeship programs must give us an equal chance and prepare us for the world of tomorrow, a world in which science and technology (from which we have been traditionally excluded) are critically important.

Goal 6
Equalize and Strengthen the Position of Women in the Media

Beyond education in our schools, there is the ubiquitous education through our media which—social scientists are now proving—definitively affects our attitudes and behaviors. We live in a time when the television set in the average American household is on almost seven hours each day (or 2,400 hours per year), a time when the impact of television on American institutions and the American public can perhaps best be expressed in the astonishing statistic that television has increased the time Americans spend on mass media by 40 percent.[34]

How are women portrayed? In the vast majority of programs men are the heroes, and we are the supporting cast: the secretary, the nurse, the mistress. In the commercials, we are seen either as unreal glamour pusses or as housewives whose major aim in life is to have their wash turn out whiter than their neighbors'. In the great TV and film outpourings of "action" entertainment, it is the men who do the active things: the chasing, the fighting, and the killing. Except for an occasional and totally unreal Wonder Woman or Bionic Woman, we are again the second string: the wives, the girl friends—and the victims. Even at best, when we are not trivialized, sensationalized, commercialized, satirized, or exploited, we are—in the words of the 1977 U.S. Commission on Civil Rights Report— "rarely represented accurately in radio, television, newspapers, magazines, films, entertainment programming, and advertisements."[85]

This is true at a time when American children receive more education from television than from their elementary schools and high schools, when, during an average year, a junior high school student attends school 980 hours—and spends 1,340 hours watching television![86]

How can ERA alter this dismal situation? First, the passage of ERA in itself has enormous symbolic value. The constitutional affirmation of the principle that women are full-fledged human beings, entitled to the same aspirations and opportunities as men, is in itself a giant step toward changing the image of women. Second, ERA provides us with a weighty legal weapon: we must use it ourselves and make sure that it is used by federal and state regulatory agencies—particularly the Federal Communications Commission—in properly discharging their duties.

The FCC is the federal agency that grants licenses to radio and television broadcasters. Under the law, these licenses may be granted only to those networks and stations that do not violate their responsibility to use the airways in the public interest. The airwaves belong to the American people, and the commercial and educational stations that are licensed to broadcast on these airways have only a privilege to do so, not an absolute right. Licenses should be denied when a station fails to serve the public adequately, and clearly, the definition of public must include women—51.3 percent of the population. The Equal Rights Amendment requires that women be treated in a nondiscriminatory manner by all government agencies. The FCC's continued failure to see that licenses are granted only to stations that take the interests of women into account in their definition of "public interest," violates this requirement.

The same type of approach must be taken with public television, and here we should be able to get even more immediate results. Certainly, stations that are publicly funded or established through acts of Congress must be required to make affirmative efforts to expand the portrayal of women to include a variety of roles and to represent accurately the numbers and life-styles of women in society. They should be in the forefront in the campaign to de-emphasize the exploitation of female bodies and the use of violence against women in the mass media, as should other federally and state aided cultural institutions, such as libraries, museums, and universities.

It is essential that the false and sexually stereotyped image of women found in our mass media be changed right away. It is not only demoralizing and demeaning to women and misleading and harmful to girls; it is dangerous, in the light of the contemporary increase in crimes of violence against women. Women must cease to be portrayed predominantly as victims, often even willing victims, in our mass media. Such images teach us that women are safe, easy, targets for brutal behavior; that rape, wife beating, and psycho-type murders are interesting, entertaining, and even sexually stimulating. It is essential that women no longer be perceived in this manner, both as a matter of safety and as a question of plain human dignity. This is particularly essential for older women: according to Dr. George Gerbner, who has been monitoring and cataloging television programs for the past decade, they are practically never seen on television at all except as helpless and passive victims of crime.[37]

To insure that these changes come about, the Equal Rights Amendment must also be used to require immediately stricter enforcement of laws which prohibit employment discrimination against women working in the mass media. At present women constitute only 25 to 35 percent of the work force *and only 5 percent of the policymakers!*[88] With the mandate of the ERA behind us, appropriate federal and state agencies—including the Federal Communications Commission, the United States Commission on Civil Rights, the Department of Health, Education, and Welfare, the Department of Justice, and state civil rights commissions—can vigorously enforce the laws we already have on our books which prohibit employment discrimination, in television, in movies, in newspapers, in libraries, in museums—in short, in all forms of mass education that shapes our attitudes, values, and beliefs.

But even *with* ERA, this will not happen by itself. It will still be up to women, individually and through organizations, to see that we are finally taught to see ourselves—and to be seen by others—as full-fledged, equal human beings.

Goal 7
Equalize and Strengthen the Position of Women in Government and the Military

There is no woman in the United States Senate. There has never been a woman on the United States Supreme Court. There are now only 18 women among the 435 members of the United States House of Representatives.[39]

If our role in shaping national policy is minuscule, our role in determining foreign policy is almost nonexistent.

In the military leadership we are also conspicuous only by our absence. Even today, despite all the pressure, publicity, and law suits, differential enlistment standards and quotas still severely hinder career opportunities for women in our nation's armed services.[40]

It is up to us to equalize and strengthen our position in all of these institutions that so vitally shape and affect our lives and the lives of our children—the institutions which are the seats of power in our society.

How can ERA be used to achieve this goal? While ERA will not require that women be given equal delegate representation at political conventions or proportionate representation in all elected and appointed offices, it will require that we be given equal treatment under all governmental laws and practices and that appointments to state boards and commissions, as well as to our courts, not discriminate on the basis of sex.

In government, as a first step, appointed offices should be made a prime target. Lawsuits are one approach. Whenever a sex-based pattern of discrimination against qualified candidates for judicial and administrative positions can be established, ERA would come into play, and a court action could be filed. Another approach is political. Here the ERA requirement of equality of rights under the law must still be used, but in conjunction with political pressure. The carrot is political, the stick is legal—and we should use both.

One recommendation of the IWY Commission is that we set as our immediate goal the appointment of more women to the numerous boards and commissions which advise and set policy at all levels of government. At this point, according to a report prepared by the Center for the American Woman and Politics, Eagleton Institute of Politics, Rutgers University, the average proportion of women on such boards and commissions is only 15 percent.[41] To increase this number to the 51.3 percent that would be representative of our proportion in the population, the IWY recommends that organizations establish rosters of women candidates, that we monitor upcoming appointments carefully, and that we make it known to all concerned (the governor, the immediate appointing officer, the media, and the public at large) that we have qualified candidates to propose for appointments in order to insure that our rights and interests are adequately considered in making both national and international policy.[42]

As for the military, ERA requires that women who choose to enlist have equal opportunity to do so and have access to valuable military benefits such as in-service training, GI loans and mortgages, and veteran preferences for civilian jobs. ERA will also require that women be drafted if men are drafted. But even if the draft is reintroduced, ERA will not mean that infantry units must be half women or that women must constitute one half of all combat units. The military services will have the same right to assign women as they have to assign men on the basis of their ability to perform a particular task. Consequently, only those women who are capable in this respect will be assigned to such duties.

We have been excluded from participation in policy-making decisions for a very long time. We have a long way to go, and ERA can take us only part of the way. But if we work together, as 51.3 percent of the population in a democratic society, we can assume the rights and responsibilities that are rightfully ours.

Goal 8
Equalize and Strengthen the Position of Women Discriminated Against by Our Criminal Laws

Suppose a man is walking down the street and a gun is pointed at him and his wallet is taken. He is not required to produce a witness to the crime. Neither is he required to show evidence that he defended himself or that he did not consent to the removal of his wallet. However, if a woman is sexually assaulted, she may have to produce what is known as "corroborating evidence" and establish that the sexual assault occurred without her consent.

Moreover, in most states the sexual history of a rape victim is considered proper evidence at a rape trial, on the rationale that evidence that a woman is "unchaste" will support the defense of "consent."

The problem of the rape victim—the fact that the trial of her assailant becomes her trial instead, the lack of sympathy of law enforcement agencies, and the irrational attitudes and laws that still make prosecution of rape so difficult—have in recent years received publicity and consequent attention. In some states, there has been the beginning of legal reform. New Mexico, which adopted a state ERA in 1973, has struck down a prior law which allowed a judge to give special instructions to the jury in a rape trial, suggesting that the victim's testimony was less credible because of the nature of the crime.[48] In California, which has been revising its laws in anticipation of the ratification of the Equal Rights Amendment, a woman's past sexual history is now admissible only when it can be shown to be relevant: for example, the prior sexual relationship between the victim and the defendant.

But in order to equalize the laws of all American states to make them fair and to ensure that they really fulfill their function—that is, the protection of women from sexual assault and battery—the ERA now provides us with a more uniform and direct weapon. It is a weapon that we sorely need, for the image of woman as victim is so deeply entrenched in all of our minds that a major problem facing women is the failure of law enforcement agencies to enforce laws designed for our protection. This is so not only in the case of rape but also in the case of other assaults and batteries.

For example, if a man complains that a friend has beaten him, no law enforcement official would say that he will not interfere because it is a private matter. Yet, if a woman is beaten by her husband or even her boyfriend, police regularly refuse to "interfere" in "private matters." This— and the fact that many states still do not give wives adequate protection or even the right to sue their husbands— is another example of the kinds of inequities in our criminal laws that ERA can be used to correct.

Another area in which our criminal laws treat women

improperly is in sentencing. As the IWY report to the President pointed out, "Statutes in several states call for longer sentencing for female offenders than for males for the same offense. Cases upholding disparate legislative sentencing schemes based on sex have reasoned that, compared with male criminals, females are more amenable and responsive to rehabilitation and reform—which might, however, require a longer period of confinement."[44]

Perhaps most shocking, because it often results in an irremediably blighted life, is the fact that 75 percent of juvenile girls in juvenile custodial institutions are there because they were charged with "status offenses"—either disrespectful behavior or sexual misconduct. Not only are these offenses for which adults could not be confined, but the fact is also that only 25 percent of boys in custodial institutions are there for status offenses, and they are usually confined for shorter periods of time than girls.[45]

In addition, as the IWY commission points out, women's prisons are less likely than men's to have a full-time medical staff or adequate hospital facilities. General support services in prisons—health, counseling, library, religious, and recreational—are less available to women than men. And as far as rehabilitation goes, the findings of the IWY Commission were that "on a national basis, women in prison receive little or no vocational training or job placement assistance which would enable them to support themselves and their children upon release."[46]

Can the Equal Rights Amendment be used to eliminate these and other sex-based inequities in our criminal laws? The answer is yes. It can, and it must so that both women victims and women offenders are finally given equal protection of our laws.

Goal 9
Equalize and Strengthen the Position of Women Discriminated Against by Our Civil Laws

Despite the enormous amount of time, money, and energy that women have put into improving our legal system during the last two hundred years, there are still many sex-based inequities in both our federal and state laws.

On the federal level, a prime example is our social security system. As it stands today, if a woman who works as a homemaker becomes disabled, she is not entitled to benefits although her services to her family must be replaced. Likewise, the family of a homemaker who dies receives no benefits.

The reason is that women who work as homemakers are not covered by social security. Moreover, they are ineligible for unemployment insurance, health plan benefits, and retirement pensions because they have been engaged in unpaid labor at home.

Wives who are employed outside the home, except while their children are young, may have so small a social security benefit of their own that their benefit based on their husband's service is greater. This can occur because *absence from the labor force of more than five years is heavily penalized* in the formula for computing social security benefits. (Low earnings of women, of course, are also an important factor here.)

Wives divorced after fewer than twenty years of marriage may—even if they return to the labor force—be entitled to only a very small benefit because of the penalty for years out of it. They get no credit for the years they were homemakers and no benefits based on their former husband's employment.

As the IWY Commission Report points out, "The basic plan of the Social Security Act reflected the prevailing belief that the wife was an appendage of the husband— not a fully equal partner. If she had been considered equal, the system would have given her at a minimum a separate account with half the accruing right to benefits credited to her."[47]

This view, that women are *not* equal, is costing the American woman dearly. "Poverty, isolation, and fear are the plight of many of today's older women, victims of lifelong economic discrimination that has left them without security," reported the IWY Commission.[48] Women who are sixty-five and above have the lowest annual median income of any age or sex group, approximately $1,900 per year, or about half that of men in the same age group.[49]

The legislative history of the ERA clearly establishes the principle that the work performed by the homemaker is entitled to recognition under our family laws. Whether this recognition will be required in other areas of law, such as social security and disability insurance, is a question that remains to be answered. Again, an affirmative answer will come only if we make our needs heard.

There are other areas in which statutes, cases, and government regulations either discriminate against women or fail to take our needs and interests into account. In some areas, like credit discrimination on the basis of sex, a number of federal state laws already exist, but there is lack of uniformity and again problems of enforcement. In addition, as in the area of insurance discrimination, we are here often faced with gray areas in which actual disparities between the economic position of the sexes, rather than unlawful discrimination, also come into play.

In the area of family law, there are still many states with laws that blatantly discriminate against women, where ERA can—and must—be used to protect us. For example, as recently as 1974, Georgia enacted a law that basically defines the wife as her husband's chattel. It reads: "The husband is the head of the family, and the wife is subject to him; her legal existence is merged in the husband, except so far as the law recognizes her separately, either for her own protection, or for her benefit, or for the preservation of the public order."[50]

While most American states are waiting to see what happens with ERA before rewriting discriminatory laws, others, where there has been strong and vocal women's lobbying, have already begun the piecemeal reform of sexist laws. But this law-by-law and case-by-case process requires an enormous amount of time, energy, and financial resources. It is far from uniform, and it may take many years, even centuries. In the end, there would be no guarantee that these good laws would be enforced—or that they would not be repealed again and bad ones would be passed to replace them.

The only way to guarantee no legal backsliding is ERA.

Goal 10
To Finally Affirm the Principle That All Men
and Women Are Created Equal

In 1848 in Seneca Falls a handful of women held the first American women's rights convention. At that time they passed the following resolution: "Resolved, that all men and women are created equal; that they are endowed by their creator with certain inalienable rights; that among these are life, liberty, and the pursuit of happiness."[51]

The Equal Rights Amendment embodies this principle and enshrines it in the Constitution of the United States. In so doing, it provides us with an essential tool that we have lacked until now. How we will use it will depend on us, but the fact remains that, for the first time in American history, we will have a well-known, accessible, and permanent remedy that can be used by each one of us to insure that our laws become free of sexual prejudices and remain so for all time.

Beyond this, what ERA provides is a symbol that the time is here for women to assert their equal rights as human beings. It is a symbol that the time is past when women's goals and aspirations can be dismissed or ridiculed. It is proof that the women's movement must now be taken as seriously as any other civil rights movement, that we mean business, that we are over half of the population, and that we will no longer permit our needs to be ignored and our rights to be suppressed.

13

Some Suggestions for Effective Implementation and Enforcement

In interpreting legislation, lawmakers and judges may not substitute their views for the legislative intent. They can, however, wield their influence in many other ways. For example, in drafting, legislators can put real teeth in laws or simply put a token piece of legislation on the books. Similarly, in interpreting a law, judges can require strict conformance or merely ask for halfhearted compliance. There is, therefore, the danger that in recalcitrant, unsympathetic or simply uncommitted hands, ERA will not be properly implemented and enforced.

The single most important issue after ERA is passed is *who* is to interpret and implement its requirements.

As we have seen, the amendment provides for a two-year "moratorium" to give the state and federal governments time to revise existing laws and enact new ones when necessary. Already, state legislatures and federal agencies, bar conventions and committees, judges, lawyers, and sociologists are gathering throughout this nation to decide how this is to be done. *But as these groups are predominantly composed of men, unless we assert our right to participate in this process, the interpretation and implementation of ERA will be dependent upon male analysis, despite the fact that women constitute 51.3 percent of our population.*

We Must Make Better Use of Our Power and Skills

ERA offers a unique challenge to American women. We can sit back and let the men who have for so long defined our world and circumscribed our part in it, do so once more. Or we can take the responsibility and the risks and insist on taking part ourselves.

While it is essential that we exert our influence at the polls by nominating and voting for only nonsexist candidates, it is not realistic to expect that massive inroads will be immediately achieved through existing political machinery. Nor can we expect suddenly to amass enough wealth to gain the economic power necessary to achieve control in the male-dominated corporate boardrooms where so many social and political decisions are made. We must, therefore, continue to exert pressure along avenues that are immediately accessible and from which we have not been constrained by patriarchal acculturation. For example:

(1) We can use our already highly developed skills at *fund raising* to finance massive lobbying and media campaigns through national women's organizations.

(2) We can make our *organized presence* felt at every legislative hearing, bar convention and local bar association meeting, at every family law symposium, and at other forums where ERA, proposals for divorce reform, and laws and measures affecting women are currently being discussed, evaluated, and interpreted.

(3) Women's organizations can hold *public hearings* patterned along the lines of those already held by congressional and state legislative committees. Such hearings might be entitled to media coverage under the fairness and equal time requirements of the FCC and would bring implementation and enforcement issues for ERA to the attention of the nation.

We Must Insist on Full Participation in Evaluating and Drafting Legislation

While it is shocking that we have been enfranchised in this country for only fifty-five years, it is even more shocking that, during this time, the American political apparatus has successfully functioned to exclude us from any real participation. To begin to correct this situation, we must demand that state and federal governments hire qualified women to study and draft the legislative modifications that ERA will require.

Much, if not most, of the legislation introduced by federal and state legislators is drafted not by the elected representatives themselves but by paid members of their staffs, lobbyists, bar associations, law professors, or by special bodies such as the Commission on Uniform State Laws which commissioned and financed the development of the Uniform Marriage and Divorce Act.

I have personally seen how heavily legislators rely on outside help for ideas and even for drafting, particularly from the organized bar (that is, the various local and national bar associations). As a member of the Los Angeles Women Lawyers' Association, I have known firsthand how, through much hard work, lobbying and politicking, we have been able to obtain legislative sponsors for needed legislation and generally to influence a number of bills affecting women. But I have also known firsthand how frustrating, time-consuming, and basically limited the influence of women is when it is exerted only on a volunteer and unofficial basis. I have further seen that even officially appointed advisory agencies, like the President's Commission on the Status of Women and its state and local counterparts, also have very limited influence. Like other officially appointed study and advisory commissions about other serious social problems, they turn out detailed reports and excellent recommendations, which then receive a day's media publicity and are put away on a shelf.

If ERA is to be properly interpreted and forcefully implemented, we cannot rely on these basically inefficient traditional approaches. We must make sure that we, the majority of Americans who are women, participate *directly* in the reexamination and reformulation of our legal system mandated by ERA.

There are precedents in our legal system for requiring that those citizens most directly affected by an act of the government *meaningfully* participate in its planning and implementation. To get federal financing for such projects as urban renewal, land-use planning, and urban transportation, you have to show proof that community representatives have been included in the step-by-step planning activities, and large budgets are allocated by state and local agencies to this end. The same rationale certainly applies to women with respect to ERA, for we are the citizens who will be most fundamentally affected by its passage.

We must not accept any excuses from our state and federal governments for *not* hiring qualified women to study and draft legislation. Certainly, the old excuse that there are no qualified women is totally unacceptable. On the contrary, the fact is that women as a group today are *more* qualified to work on legislation affecting women than are men. The reason is not only that we understand our own needs and problems better than anyone else can. It is also that we have more experience and better skills in this field than men.

In the past decade large numbers of women, both inside and outside the legal profession, have thoroughly studied and investigated how our legal, social, and economic system affects us as women. It is women lawyers who have filed sex discrimination cases. It is women advocates who have lobbied for better legislation. It is women law students who have demanded and obtained courses in women's law. It is women who have gathered the social and legal data and who have spoken up for better laws and fairer court decisions. And it is women who must now be hired to conform our legal system to ERA, as it is essential that in this process we have a voice that is at least equal to men's.

We Must Be Active Social Inventors

One of the most promising phenomena of recent years is the fact that American women are overcoming one of the strongest of all patriarchal taboos: the prohibition against helping ourselves. During the past decade, women have developed a number of important social inventions specifically designed to that end. The most publicized of these, the so-called "consciousness-raising groups," have helped women to work together to examine their personal and social situations and to break through inner and outer patriarchal bonds. By means of another social invention, the practice of "court watching," other women's groups are systematically monitoring the legal system by going to court and recording the activities of judges and attorneys, particularly in relation to sexist practices and prejudices, and then publishing their results.

But if we women are to break through our ubiquitous patriarchal structure, a much more concerted and well-organized approach is required. *As one step in this direction, women should establish a network of institutes for the development of nonsexist social inventions. The top priority of these institutes would be the creation of im-*

proved methods for implementing desired social changes, with a crash program to create devices which would insure the inclusion of women in the interpretation and implementation of the ERA as fully functioning, recognized, and paid participants.

One way of financing such institutes would be to set aside for this purpose a certain portion (say, 25 percent) of all punitive damages awarded in sex discrimination cases. There are precedents for this type of approach, not only in class actions, in which damages are collected on behalf of an entire class of aggrieved persons, but also in the growing practice of using a social reparations approach in sentencing convicted individuals. Instead of being put in prison, convicted individuals—or groups— are organized to perform useful services for those they have harmed. For example, a group of milk company executives found guilty of price fixing was ordered to donate $175,000 to charitable organizations and to work forty-five days for community agencies that provide help for needy children. U.S. District Court Judge Charles ("Carl") Muecke said he was looking for a constructive alternative that would more closely compensate those injured by the milk companies' practice. "Any fine I would levy," he stated, "would go to the Government, and that would be like spitting in a blast furnace."[1]

We Must Demand Educated and Unbiased Public Officials

It is essential that a massive educational program accompany the study and implementation of ERA. Without a better awareness of the real situation and problems of women—on the part of both the public and our judges and law enforcement officials—better laws may simply not be enforced.

The problem is partly one of ignorance, as very often even our higher officials are simply uninformed or misinformed about issues and problems affecting women. But unfortunately, there is more to it than that. We already have many excellent studies and statistics and official reports. The fact is that, due to long-standing prejudices and biases, they are all too often just ignored by those in positions of responsibility and power.

While it is true that massive shifts in social attitudes cannot be immediately legislated or otherwise brought about, we are still entitled to public officials who properly discharge their duties, officials who are well informed and free from significant prejudice and bias.

In case after case, the Supreme Court has ruled that governmental action must be free from prejudice and bias. Executive orders aimed at eliminating bias in government contracts and in education have been an important step toward meeting this constitutional requirement. As a first step, *these executive orders should be expanded to include a massive drive to reeducate public officials so that they understand the real socioeconomic problems of American women.* The immediate area in which such a program is most urgently needed is in connection with the implementation of ERA—where by definition issues relating to women are involved.

As it stands now, it is unfortunately not uncommon for judges and law enforcement officials to make blatantly sexist statements, jokes, and put-downs of women. If judges made similarly disparaging remarks about blacks in a case dealing with laws affecting black people, they would be disqualified from the case immediately. The same principle should be applied in interpreting and implementing ERA.

Since attitudes can be as much a function of irrational bias as of rational knowledge, *judges and law enforcement officials should be required to take attitude tests along the lines of those given by the Peace Corps to weed out racists.* They would be used to sift out the most virulently sexist and racist individuals. For those who would argue that this is too strong a measure, the answer is that the principle that judges and jurors must be fair and impartial is a basic element of our system of jurisprudence. The essence of the voir dire[2] process of jury selection is the examination of jurors to weed out those with prejudicial attitudes. If the attitudes of jurors must be scrutinized and tested, surely the same principle should apply to judges who interpret the meaning of an amendment that will decisively affect our future. Eventually such a program could lead to civil service type examinations for all public officials charged with enforcing ERA. These would also test their knowledge and understanding of contemporary social and economic realities affecting women.

If these public servants had to prepare for such examinations, they would learn, for example, that over one-tenth of our families are headed by women, that the vast majority of America's poor are women and children, that older women, even more than older men, are practically unemployable, and that adequate child care is almost impossible to find. In the area of family law, if judges knew these facts, they might no longer treat the divorced woman as an abnormality, as simply a temporary aberration en route to another marriage, nor could they continue to rationalize minimal support awards as simply "interim measures." Law enforcement officials would have no excuse for failing to enforce spousal support orders or for refusing to take vigorous steps to collect child support awards, not only on behalf of women on welfare, but for other mothers as well. In these and other areas of law, the effect of such a program would be to lessen prejudice and to insure that ERA is interpreted in a rational and humane way.

It is important to emphasize that we are dealing here not with the problem of men versus women, but of sexist attitudes, which in patriarchal societies are internalized by both sexes. All too often, in fact, women who obtain positions of power, such as judgeships, bend backward in identifying with patriarchal values and prejudices to show that they are not in any way favoring their own sex. Male judges may be influenced by personal circumstances, such as problems in their own marriages, that make for unconscious biases against women. While a few judges and law enforcement officials are violently sexist, most are simply well-meaning people unconsciously locked into archaic and paternalistic approaches to male-female relationships.

We Must Form Political Coalitions

How ERA is implemented is, in the last analysis, essentially a political issue. It is unfortunately *not* enough that ERA is right and just. For centuries, women have *not* been treated equally under our laws. ERA represents a fundamental shift in public policy. It is unrealistic to expect that such a major change in public policy will happen overnight.

Established political and social institutions are by their

nature resistant to *any* kind of change. Additionally, we have to overcome deeply ingrained sexist prejudices and stereotypes. Looking at it realistically, just because ERA is ratified we cannot expect that the powerful forces that have opposed it will just roll over and die. They will continue to expend their time and money (which they obviously have in greater quantities than we have) fighting effective implementation. And it is much easier to fight against something than to come up with workable, effective, and positive programs.

Nevertheless, this is our task: the mobilization of sufficient political power to bring about systematic and enforceable programs for legal and social change.

To accomplish this we must form coalitions. As a first priority, *coalitions of women's groups* must be developed *now*. To some extent, this is already happening. ERAmerica is a national umbrella coalition supported by pro-ERA organizations all across the country, such as the National Federation of Business and Professional Women's Clubs, the League of Women Voters, the National Women's Political Caucus, the National Women's Party, the National Organization for Women, the American Association of University Women, Common Cause, and representatives from both church and labor coalitions. Similarly, there are also pro-ERA coalitions in the remaining unratified states.

The task that lies ahead is to coordinate our activities in all areas affecting ERA implementation, as a united effort is a hundred percent more effective than the same organizations working with limited resources on their own. That this is already being recognized is evidenced by the fact that in California, at this writing, a group of major women's organizations, ranging all the way from California Women Lawyers to the National Council of Jewish Women, are forming a coalition. The purpose is to work more closely on issues and goals affecting women and to hire a legislative advocate to help insure that these goals are translated into better laws. Whether we like it or not, lobbying is an essential political tool. It is an American reality, and it is used very effectively by our enemies, who have more money than we have. This new coalition recognizes this fact. It recognizes that each organization separately could not afford to hire its own legislative advocate but that, together, it can be done.

Another important area in which organizations can economize on time and money is the creation of *implementation task force coalitions*. All national and state organizations should form their own task forces to aid ERA implementation. But these task forces will function a hundred percent more effectively if information and advice is shared.

We must additionally form *task oriented* coalitions with civil rights organizations like the NAACP and ACLU, labor unions like the AFL-CIO and AAUW, and professional organizations such as the American Psychological Association and the American Association of Social Workers and all other groups interested in strengthening and expanding American human rights. Coalitions on the university level, both among students and faculty, are particularly important. There is a potential pool of student activism that can be tapped by a good cause, and far too little has been done in this direction to date. Faculty members, too, are extremely important. They are an important source of experts who will be necessary in the ERA implementation process (more about this later), and they also exert widespread influence on social attitudes and values.

It is essential that *educational coalitions* work on nationwide programs (including all the mass media) to bring accurate information about ERA to the nation. This is essential in two respects. First, it is an effective means of obtaining more supporters (both from individuals and from organizations). Secondly, it is a demonstration of political unity and strength, which will not be lost on our legislators, judges, and law enforcement officials and will put them on notice that we stand behind ERA and demand that they do too.

Otherwise, there is the danger that, instead of an effective implementation program, we face years of evasions, distractions, and draining petty battles over every little detail every step of the way. It is unfortunately also a political fact that nonaction is easier than action and that public officials are very effective at dragging their feet. They can simply hand over implementation to officials who know that the "real" goal is not implementation. They can keep congratulating us on how much progress we are making (as they have been doing now for a very long time) and tell us to keep up the good work while they themselves do little or nothing at all. And they know very well how to play the "expert witness game" in which so-called experts, ostensibly expressing truth and justice on either side, are paraded so that in the end a stalemate can be presented as the only just and reasonable "compromise."[3]

We will have to face all of these evasive tactics, and many more, but if we work together—and if we are aware that nothing is going to happen unless we make it happen—in the end we will prevail.

We Must Obtain Self-enforcing and Remedial Legislation

One very important way of making sure that something does happen is by actually writing this requirement into post-ERA laws. As we have seen, today many good laws just lie languishing on dusty shelves because they do not have provisions requiring that they be enforced. However, this need not be the case *if laws are properly drafted*. Self-enforcing devices must therefore be written into all antidiscrimination laws and orders. These must provide for adequate funding, for staff, and both internal and external education. Other self-enforcing devices include grievance procedures and requirements for periodic evaluations of programs and agencies. This is a way of making public officials accountable for the results of legislation, by putting it into the laws themselves. The necessity for these devices cannot be overemphasized, and it is still one more reason for making sure that we as women actually participate in the process of reexamining, amending, and drafting post-ERA laws.

When ERA is adopted, the first step in its implementation will be to examine all existing federal, state, and local laws to determine whether they contain classifications based on sex and if so, whether these classifications are constitutionally permissible. When a law is found to be in conflict with the Equal Rights Amendment, the second step will be to decide whether this law should be expanded to include both sexes, be nullified entirely, or, when necessary, be replaced by different legislation. I believe that a third step must also be studied: the enactment of laws specifically designed to make up for the disadvantaged position in which women now find themselves.

This approach is not without precedent. For example, the Supreme Court of the United States has accepted the proposition that there are situations in which the law must make allowances for differences between the rich and the poor. In the landmark case of *Griffin v. Illinois*, the Court held that state courts must provide free trial transcripts for indigents' appeals in criminal cases even though solvent defendants are required to pay for theirs.[4] And, in *Gideon v. Wainwright*, the Court extended that ruling to require that indigent defendants must be provided with court-appointed counsel in criminal proceedings.[5] The executive branch of our government has also adopted this approach, precisely in the area and the manner which I am suggesting. Executive Order 11246, passed in 1967, prohibits private firms with federal contracts from discriminating on the basis of race, creed, national origin, or sex. In 1972 the order was amended to require private firms to develop and implement "affirmative action programs" to ensure equal employment for women and minorities. The order requires an employer to give minority groups and women preferential treatment in hiring and promotion. Since the passage of Title IX of the Higher Education Act of 1972, similar requirements also apply to college campuses receiving any form of government financing or aid. In business and education, active recruiting and hiring programs are now presented by prescribed law to correct some of the damage caused by traditional discrimination against women.

ERA should be interpreted in line with this reasoning. Whenever sexism in our society has created sex-based inequalities and inequities, the amendment should be interpreted to require remedial legislation. This will ensure that ERA cannot be used to penalize women while pretending to treat them equally, as has unfortunately happened under some of our pre-ERA divorce laws. Thus, in the field of family law, these programs would require measures designed to equalize the economic position of a home-maker unemployed by divorce with that of her former mate. Such programs could also include procedures to facilitate collection of spousal and child support payments through specially adapted versions of already existent garnishment and attachment laws; they could also require new tax laws under which employed custodial parents could take child care as a legitimate business expense deduction.

In the light of contemporary social and economic realities and trends, the remedial programs should also specify that legislatures give priority to measures designed to minimize the social and economic imbalances and dislocations that women's transition into postindustrial society is bringing about. For example, adequate child care facilities should be provided for both single and married parents contributing child care services and, as advocated in Sweden, each parent should have the option of working only six hours a day.

We Must Use All Available Resources

For many years, throughout our nation, creative and dedicated women and men have been working to eliminate sex-based discrimination from our laws. They have studied our laws and our social and economic system. They have gathered essential data and done important research. They have written countless excellent official and unofficial reports setting forth their findings. And they have made detailed and comprehensive recommendations.

One of our major problems is that we have not had adequate financial resources to publish and disseminate this valuable information. Another problem is that we do not as yet have efficient lines of communication between the many individuals and groups working for social justice for women.

We must have better information-sharing procedures, better links between concerned individuals and groups, so that we can be more economical and less repetitive in our efforts. This is not to say that some amount of duplication is not natural or even desirable in as much as the process of acquiring information is in itself an important experience. But it is essential that we make better use of the resources we already have. Some of these are listed in the reference notes of this book. They include reports by the Citizens' Advisory Council on the Status of Women, such as *Interpretation of the Equal Rights Amendment in Accordance with Legislative History*, *The Equal Rights Amendment and Alimony and Child Support Laws*, and *The Equal Rights Amendment—Senator Ervin's Minority*

Report and the Yale Law Journal.[6] These are invaluable sources for easy-to-follow, concrete data on proper ERA interpretation. Another valuable source included in the references are law review articles on the subject of ERA and sexual discrimination under our laws. These include Barbara Brown, Thomas Emerson, Gail Falk, and Ann Freedman's, "The Equal Rights Amendment: A Constitutional Basis for Equal Rights for Women," which was read into the *Congressional Record* by ERA sponsor Birch Bayh, and Lujuana W. Treadwell and Nancy W. Page's "Equal Rights Revision: The Experience of the State Constitutions," 65 *California Law Review* 1086, on the interpretations that state ERAs have been given to date.[7] They also include books with important background information and statistics, such as Jane Trahey's *On Women and Power,*[8] Caroline Bird's *Born Female*[9] on the situation of women in the labor market, and my own book *Dissolution: No-Fault Divorce, Marriage, and the Future of Women,*[10] which focuses on the current situation of the homemaker under our rapidly changing family laws.

A very important work is *Impact ERA.*[11] It is a series of articles by national authorities edited by the Equal Rights Amendment Project of the California Commission on the Status of Women under the direction of Anita Miller and Dr. Hazel Greenberg. It examines the limitations as well as the possibilities of ERA plus its political, economic, social, and psychological impact. For example, Dale Rogers Marshall and Janell Anderson's "Implementation and the Equal Rights Amendment" provides excellent and specific suggestions for strategy and tactics, and Jean Mundy's "Female Fears of Equality" is a perceptive and illuminating analysis of some of the false fears that the opponents of ERA have been able to whip up. The Equal Rights Amendment Project has also compiled a compendium of sexist laws that need changing.[12]

Another document with which every person working for proper ERA implementation should become familiar is the report of the National Commission on the Observance of International Women's Year, *To Form a More Perfect Union—Justice for American Women.*[13] It is an invaluable source of statistical data and social, economic, and political background. Of particular interest is part 4, the "Recommendations of the Commission," notably the recommendations of the Enforcement of the Laws Committee (which offers a detailed list of good laws that need better enforcement) and the report of the Media Committee (directed toward the basic goal of improving and strengthening women's image in our society).

Some other useful publications are *The Equal Rights Amendment: A Bibliographic Study* (compiled by the Equal Rights Amendment Project, Anita Miller, project director, Hazel Greenberg, editor and compiler; Westport, Conn.: Greenwood Press, 1976); *1975 Handbook on Women Workers* (U.S. Department of Labor, Employment Standards Administration, Women's Bureau, Bulletin 297, Washington, D.C. 20210); publications of the Women's Bureau (U.S. Department of Labor, Employment Standards Administration, Women's Bureau, Washington, D.C. 20210); *Women in 1975* (Citizens' Advisory Council on the Status of Women, Washington, D.C. 20210); *From Reverence to Rape: The Treatment of Women in Movies* (Molly Haskell, Baltimore: Penguin Books, 1974); *Report of the Task Force on Women in Public Broadcasting* (Corporation for Public Broadcasting, 1111 Sixteenth Street, N.W., Washington, D.C. 20036); *Women's Washington Representative* (a newsletter reporting federal actions that affect women; issued from 410 First Street, S.E., Washington, D.C. 20003); and *The NOW Times* (a monthly newspaper published by the Los Angeles County chapters of the National Organization for Women; issued from 1126 HiPoint Street, Los Angeles, Calif. 90035).

But the most important and, as yet, largely untapped basic resource that we have is the goodwill and decency of millions of Americans—what President Carter's Special Assistant Mark Siegel has called "the decency constituency." "We must find a way to demonstrate very concretely that there is a motivated national constituency for the amendment," writes Siegel. "The intensity of the 'decency constituency' must be demonstrated. ERA should be worked into all speeches, no matter what the primary subject is. People must understand that the clock is ticking, and time is running against them. Business, labor, chambers of commerce, religious groups, media, etc., all should be mobilized to get the message out. Public momentum must be rejuvenated, not with a whimper but with a bang."

14

How to Continue the Fight for Sexual Democracy

March 22, 1979—and what it symbolizes—should become part of our national holiday calendar so that we and our children after us can remember the significance of this day.

If ERA passes, March 22 should be a day of national celebration. We should express our joy in our homes and our streets. There should be parades in all major cities and we should assemble in front of the White House and the capitols of every state to demonstrate our gratitude and our determination to complete the task we have set for ourselves: to bring about a truly democratic society.

If ERA fails, March 22 must be a day of national mourning. No woman should work on that day. No girl should go to school. Everything must come to a standstill. We must not buy anything. We must not produce anything, be it meals in our homes, or office work, or products at our jobs. In short, should ERA fail by March 22, 1979, we must demonstrate to the nation the depth of our sorrow and anger and the strength of our determination to wrest for ourselves the equality and dignity under the law that the Twenty-seventh Amendment to our Constitution will provide.

There will, of course, be women who will not participate: women who have been turned against their own best interests, who have been frightened and deceived into opposing equality for themselves and their sisters. But there have always been quislings and turncoats who collaborated with the enemy and were misled and frightened into fighting against their own cause. We must take this in our stride too because, unlike our enemies, we are fighting for choices, for options and opportunities. Our goal is not compliance and conformity and lack of deviation, and it is as unrealistic to expect complete unity among women as it is of any other social or political group.

If by March 22, 1979, the Equal Rights Amendment has finally become part of our Constitution, the date will symbolize a historic victory. But even then, we must recognize that ratification is only the beginning, the first round. If the significance of that day is to be that ERA was *not* ratified by the requisite states, we must also not forget that we have only lost the first round. If we have an extension, we must quickly get the few needed ratifying states. And if we have to start all over in Congress, we must be ready for that, too.

Whether there has been an extension or whether we have to start again from scratch, it is up to us to make any ERA defeat a turning point. There have been other times in history when all seemed lost. After major defeats by the British, Washington's army was starving and freezing at Valley Forge, but through determination and courage the troops turned the tide. We too can go on to victory. We too can, if we must, use the shock and anguish of defeat as a rallying cry to mobilize all women and men to stand up to those who will try to use an ERA defeat as a license to discriminate, to try to take away from us the gains we have already made.

The Goal of Sexual Democracy

Whatever happens, we must continue to fight for sexual democracy with every means at our disposal. On the legal front, ERA ratification must be followed by swift and proper implementation. In the political arena, representation commensurate with our numbers must be achieved. Economically, we can no longer tolerate our second-class status. Our dependency and powerlessness must come to an end.

One of our most important priorities has to be a fundamental change in our system of values. The patriarchal myths that portray us as inferior to men, be they in the Bible or on television, must be replaced by humanistic ones *not* based on the premise that one sex or race or nation is innately superior and meant to rule. And because these myths are inculcated from birth through the patriarchal family, we must work for the democratization of the family, for our sake and for the sake of all the generations still to come.

A truly democratic world will never come to pass as long as patriarchal values and institutions persist, for these pervade all authoritarian social relationships and are their basis from early childhood on. Sexual democracy is the only foundation upon which a humanistic world can be built, a fact that is, ironically, perceived more clearly by our enemies than by our friends.

A Full and Equal Voice

As we shift from industrial to postindustrial society, the roles of women and men will inevitably continue to change. The high divorce rate, the one-parent family, the accelerating entry of women into the labor force, the growth of the welfare family—all these are symptoms of this shift. But unless we achieve sexual democracy—a society offering equality of opportunity and meaningful life choices to both women and men—our roles may change, but our status will not.

In chapter 12, ten goals were set forth as immediate action targets in connection with ERA. Implicit in these, and equally essential, is the goal of achieving a full and equal voice in determining the present and future course of our society and our world.

In politics and government, many more qualified women must be encouraged to seek elective and appointed offices. We must support these candidates with our full organizational strength. We must not rest until our domestic and foreign policy is determined no longer *for* us, but *by* us as well.

In the private sector, we must encourage many more qualified women to seek and attain positions of leadership. We must remedy the shocking fact that, for all intents and purposes, women have *no* voice in the private economic sector of our society. As the *New York Times* pointed out in 1977, "No woman is chairman or president of any of the nation's top companies. Women at present hold fewer than 2 percent of the directorships of top American corporations and fewer than 1 percent of top management posts."[1] As Jane Trahey reports in *On Women and Power,* out of 20,800 board seats in the top American corporations, women hold 205. Out of the 846 board members of the top 50 industrial corporations in the United States, only 17 are women; out of the 1,621 executive officers of these companies, only 13 are women.[2]

We have long served the world of American business and industry as secretaries, as consumers, as laborers, as hostesses—in short, as supporting personnel. We are today 40 percent of the labor force, and this proportion is growing every day. Clearly, the time has come for us to take a more active role in the business and corporate decisions that so vitally affect our lives. For the decisions of America's business leaders affect all areas of our lives: what we read and what we eat, what we see and what we wear, what we spend and what we earn, and even what we enjoy. Their policies affect not only the quality of our products and services but the quality of our physical and social environment as well: our trees, our land, our air, our airwaves—and what they carry into our homes and our minds through television, movies, and radio.

Together, business and government constitute the major decision-makers in our lives, the established seats of power from which we have for so long been barred. But to say that we must gain equal access to these power centers is by no means to say that if women just get a bigger slice of the existing political and economic pie, all will be well.

Sexual democracy means more than the realignment of present power relationships. True sexual democracy can only be attained in a society where human values take priority over material ones, where profit is not calculated in dollars and cents but in terms of social well-being, and where global good, not just personal or even national good, is the primary aim.

Our task is to create such a society, both from the grass roots level and from positions of leadership. Only from positions of leadership can we ensure that we and our daughters have effective life choices—economically, socially, and personally—including the fundamental right of reproductive freedom of choice. Only from positions of leadership can we change conditions in the labor market, which women are entering today in such unprecedented numbers while earning merely a fraction of the wages of men. Only from positions of leadership can we make sure that older women in this country have the respect and economic security they deserve. Only from positions of leadership can we fundamentally alter our social priorities —putting peace ahead of war, cooperation ahead of competition, and nurturing ahead of killing.

We owe this to all women, and to all men, with whom we can only live in harmony in a sexually democratic world.

Our Choice

Today this country is being asked to make a choice. Should our Constitution be expanded to afford full and equal protection under our laws to 51.3 percent of our population? Should we go forward? Or should we go back?

We are being asked to make this pivotal choice less than a decade before *1984*, when both the prophets of science fiction and the forecasters of futurology warn us that our planet is in grave danger of taking an authoritarian path, a path foreshadowed in the 1930s by the rise of Hitler, Mussolini, and Stalin. All around us in the world today—in Africa, in Asia, in Europe, in South America, in the Middle East—we are surrounded by totalitarian societies, both old and new. At the core of these regimes—be they fascist, communist, monarchist, or capitalist—are patriarchal values and male-dominated structures in which power is wielded to repress both women and men.

When our country was established, it was also in the midst of a primarily authoritarian world. Our Constitution was fashioned to create something different and better for us and for all humanity. Throughout our history, our strength has been in that Constitution and in our commitment to its expansion to meet evolving popular aspirations and needs.

Now we are being given the precious opportunity to strengthen that Constitution, to add to it the essential component of sexual democracy we *must* have if we are to withstand the authoritarian menace from within and without.

We cannot falter at this critical time. We cannot be daunted by temporary setbacks and defeats. We cannot give in to old stereotypes that "feminine" means passive, dependent, and weak. We can no longer be "good little women" who will not assert our rights. We must demand that full social, economic, and political participation for ourselves and our daughters no longer be denied us on the basis of our sex. *We must assert these demands until they are met:* as women, as mothers, as the majority of the population in one of the few democracies left in this world.

If we fail to live up to that commitment, the prophecies of technocracy, dehumanization, and totalitarianism may very well come to pass. But to say that this *can* happen is not to say that it *must.* It will happen if the evolution of democracy is halted at this critical crossroads. It need *not* happen if we persevere until we achieve our goal: sexual democracy, and through it, a better world.

Reference Notes

Introduction

1. In *Reed v. Reed*, 404 U.S. 71 (1971), for the first time in its history the U.S. Supreme Court included women under the definition of "persons" protected by the equal protection clause of the Fourteenth Amendment. The Supreme Court struck down an Idaho statute providing that in determining the relative rights of competing applicants for letters of administration of decedent estates "males must be preferred to females."
2. David A. Binder and Riane Eisler, "Amicus Curiae Brief," Supreme Court of the United States, *Perez v. Campbell*, Docket No. 5175, October Term 1970.
3. *New York Times*, June 9, 1968, p. 56. In his eulogy at Robert Kennedy's funeral, Edward Kennedy quoted Robert as follows: "Some men see things as they are and say why. I dream things that never were, and say, why not."

Part I

Chapter 1

1. See note 1, Introduction.
2. In *Frontiero v. Richardson*, 411 U.S. 677 (1973), the U.S. Supreme Court struck down an air force rule which denied dependent benefits to husbands of female officers, while granting them to wives of male officers. However, three of the justices, while agreeing that the Air Force regulation was unconstitutional, made it clear that they considered the question of whether to apply the stricter compelling-state-interest test rather than the mild "rational-basis" test a political and not a constitutional issue. They critized their fellow judges who had based their decision on the stricter test, arguing that they should have waited to see if ERA was ratified first.

3. *The Earnings Gap Between Women and Men*, Women's Bureau, U.S. Department of Labor, Washington, D.C., 1976 (hereinafter cited as *The Earnings Gap Between Women and Men*), p. 1.

4. *Work in America*, Report of a Special Task Force to the Secretary of Health, Education, and Welfare, Cambridge, Mass.: MIT Press, 1973 (hereinafter cited as *Work in America*).

5. By 1976, after climbing steadily every year, the annual U.S. divorce rate had reached the 1-million mark (*Monthly Vital Statistics Report*, National Center for Health Statistics, Rockville, Md., October 27, 1976). Subsequent reports indicate that the U.S. divorce rate is no longer jumping upward every year, but seems to be leveling off at the 1-million rate.

6. The threat of an authoritarian future is posed as a grim alternative to humanism by many futurologists, including Robert Theobald (*Futures Conditional*, New York: Bobbs-Merrill, 1972) and Willis Harman (*An Incomplete Guide to the Future*, San Francisco, Calif.: San Francisco Book Co., 1976). George Orwell's *1984* (New York: New American Library, 1971) and Aldous Huxley's *Brave New World* (New York: Harper & Row, 1969) are its best-known literary expressions.

Chapter 2

1. *Congressional Record*, Vol. 117, No. 6, Washington, D.C., January 28, 1971, p. S-469 and p. S-469-2.

2. Mary A. Delsman, *Everything You Need to Know About ERA*, Riverside, Calif.: Meranza Press, 1975, pp. 33–34 (hereinafter cited as Delsman, *Everything You Need to Know About ERA*).

3. *H.R.J. Res.208, 92nd Cong., 2nd Sess.* (October 12, 1971); *S.J.Res.8, 92nd Cong., 2nd Sess.* (March 22, 1972).

4. See *Congressional Record* for the 92nd Congress, debates on ERA and U.S. Congress, Senate, *Senate Report 92-689*, "Equal Rights for Men and Women," 92nd Congress, 2nd Session, majority report submitted by Mr. Bayh (hereinafter referred to as *Majority Report of the Senate Judiciary Committee*).

5. *The Phyllis Schlafly Report*, July 1975, p. 4.

6. "Equal Rights Measure Killed in Florida," *Los Angeles Times*, April 14, 1977.

7. "Georgia Turns Down Equality for Women," *Los Angeles Times*, January 29, 1974.

8. *The Phyllis Schlafly Report*, January 1977.

9. *The Equal Rights Amendment—Senator Ervin's Minority Report and the Yale Law Journal*, Citizens' Advisory Council on the Status of Women, Washington, D.C., July, 1972, p. 5

(hereinafter cited as *ERA: Ervin's Minority Report and the Yale Law Journal*).

10. *The Phyllis Schlafly Report*, September 1974, p. 1.
11. Senator Birch Bayh, in debate of March 21, 1972, *Congressional Record* Vol. No. 118, Washington, D.C., p. S-4389.
12. *Majority Report of the Senate Judiciary Committee*, p. 13.
13. Senator Birch Bayh, in debate of March 21, 1972, *Congressional Record* Vol. No. 118, Washington, D.C., pp. S-4390 to S-4391.
14. U.S. Congress, Senate, *Senate Report 92-689*, 92nd Congress, 2nd Session, Minority Views of Mr. Ervin, p. 388 (hereinafter cited as *Senator Ervin's Minority Report*).
15. *ERA: Ervin's Minority Report and the Yale Law Journal*, p. 1.
16. *The Phyllis Schlafly Report*, July 1975, p. 4.
17. *The Proposed Equal Rights Amendment to the United States Constitution*, Citizens' Advisory Council on the Status of Women, Washington, D.C., 1970, p. 11.
18. *Majority Report of the Senate Judiciary Committee*, p. 11.
19. *Interpretation of the Equal Rights Amendment in Accordance with Legislative History*, Citizens' Advisory Council on the Status of Women, Washington, D.C., 1974, p. 2 (hereinafter cited as *Interpretation of the Equal Rights Amendment in Accordance with Legislative History*).
20. *Majority Report of the Senate Judiciary Committee*, p. 15.
21. *Ibid.*, p. 15.
22. *Congressional Record*, Vol. 117, No. 6, Washington, D.C., January 28, 1971, p. S-472.
23. *Ibid.*, pp. S-471 to S-472.
24. *Ibid.*
25. *Ibid.*
26. *Ibid.*
27. *Ibid.*, p. S-469-2.
28. *Ibid.*, p. S-470.
29. Vic Lockman, *The Equal Rights Amendment, a Trojan Horse*, Alton, Illinois: Eagle Forum, 1976, p. 6 (hereinafter cited as *ERA: A Trojan Horse*).
30. *Congressional Record*, Vol. 117, No. 6, Washington, D.C., January 28, 1971, p. S-471.
31. *Ibid.*
32. *Ibid.*
33. *Majority Report of the Senate Judiciary Committee*, p. 12.
34. Joan M. Krauskopf, "The Equal Rights Amendment: Its Political and Practical Contexts," 50 *California State Bar Journal* 79 (March/April 1975), pp. 139–140 (hereinafter cited as Krauskopf, "The Equal Rights Amendment").
35. Citizens' Advisory Council on the Status of Women, *The

Equal Rights Amendment and Alimony and Child Support Laws, Washington, D.C., January, 1972.
36. *Ibid.*, pp. 10–11.
37. *ERA: A Trojan Horse*, p. 3.
38. *Majority Report of the Senate Judiciary Committee*, p. 17.
39. *Ibid.*
40. *Ibid.*
41. *ERA: A Trojan Horse.*
42. *Califano v. Goldfarb*, 45 U.S.L.W. 4237 (1977).
43. *Ibid.*

Chapter 3

1. *Reed v. Reed*, 404 U.S. 71 (1971).
2. *Congressional Record*, Vol. 117, No. 6, Washington, D.C., January 28, 1971, p. S-469-2.
3. Mary C. Dunlap, "The Equal Rights Amendment and the Courts," in California Commission on the Status of Women, *Impact ERA*, Millbrae, Calif.: Les Femmes Publishing, 1976, p. 31 (References to *Impact ERA* will hereinafter be cited as *Impact ERA*).
4. 92 S.Ct. 1179 (1972).
5. For a discussion of these two different constitutional tests, see, e.g., Kenneth L. Karst, " 'A Discrimination So Trivial': A Note on Law and the Symbolism of Women's Dependency," 49 *Los Angeles Bar Bulletin* 499 (October 1974) and Krauskopf, "The Equal Rights Amendment."
6. 411 U.S. 677 (1973).
7. 94 S.Ct. 1734 (1974).
8. *DeFunis v. Washington*, 94 S.Ct.1704 (1974).
9. 94 S.Ct.1734, at p. 1740.
10. *Geduldig v. Aiello*, 417 U.S. 484 (1974).
11. *Ibid.*, quoting from *Frontiero v. Richardson.*
12. *Ibid.*
13. Barbara Brown, Thomas Emerson, Gail Falk, and Ann Freedman, "The Equal Rights Amendment: A Constitutional Basis for Equal Rights for Women," 80 *Yale Law Journal* 871 (1971). (Hereinafter cited as *Yale Law Journal.*)
14. *Senator Ervin's Minority Report.*
15. *ERA: Ervin's Minority Report and the Yale Law Journal*, Introduction.
16. *Ibid.*, p. 5.
17. *Ibid.*, p. 11.
18. *The Phyllis Schlafly Report*, April 1977.
19. *The Phyllis Schlafly Report*, July 1975, p. 4.
20. *Ibid.*

21. *Impact ERA*, p. 44.
22. *Interpretation of the Equal Rights Amendment in Accordance with Legislative History*, p. 8.
23. Delsman, *Everything You Need to Know About ERA*, pp. 116–117.
24. *Interpretation of the Equal Rights Amendment in Accordance with Legislative History*, p. 7.
25. Congressional debate, October 12, 1971, *Congressional Record* Vol. 117, Washington, D.C., p. H-9391.
26. *Congressional Record* Vol. 118, Washington, D.C., p. S-4411.
27. *Interpretation of the Equal Rights Amendment in Accordance with Legislative History*, p. 8.
28. *Ibid.*, p. 7.
29. Delsman, *Everything You Need to Know About ERA*, pp. 62, 63.
30. *Ibid.*, pp. 60–61.
31. *Ibid.*, p. 51.
32. *Impact ERA*, p. 44, footnote 38.
33. Carmen Ristorucci, "Why We Oppose the ERA," in *Political Affairs: Journal of Marxist Thought and Analysis*, March 1976, p. 8. *Political Affairs* is the "theoretical journal of the Communist Party, USA," and its editor is Gus Hall, General Secretary of the Communist Party, U.S.A.
34. *Ibid.*, p. 10.
35. Alva Buxenbaum, "The Equal Rights Amendment: New Trends, New Developments," *Political Affairs: Journal of Marxist Thought and Analysis*, January 1978, p. 17.

Chapter 4

1. See e.g., Henry A. Murray, editor, *Myth and Mythmaking*, Boston, Mass.: Beacon Press, 1959.
2. See, e.g., *Dred Scott v. Stanford*, 19 H.O.W. 393 (1857).
3. Donald Molin and Cullen Maiden, *Black America*, Stockholm, Sweden: Sveriges Radio, 1965, p. 57.
4. *The Holy Bible*, King James Authorized Version, Exodus, chapter 20.
5. *Ibid.*, Exodus, chapters 20 and 21.
6. *Ibid.*, Genesis, chapter 29.
7. H.D.F. Kitto, *The Greeks*, Baltimore, Md.: Penguin Books, 1958, p. 219.
8. Renford Bambrough, editor, *The Philosophy of Aristotle*, New York: Mentor, 1963, pp. 387–388. (Hereinafter cited as Bambrough, *The Philosophy of Aristotle*.)
9. *The Holy Bible*, Ephesians 5:22–23.

10. Blackstone, *Commentaries*, Nineteeth London edition, Vol. 1, Philadelphia, Pa.: Lippincott Co., 1908, p. 366.

11. *Ibid.*, p. 365.

12. Eleanor Flexner, *Century of Struggle*, Cambridge, Mass.: Harvard University Press, 1959, p. 65 (hereinafter cited as Flexner, *Century of Struggle*).

13. *Muller v. Oregon*, 208 U.S. 412 (1908), at pp. 421–422.

14. Caroline Bird with Sara Welles Briller, *Born Female*, New York: Pocket Books, 1968, pp. 33–35 (hereinafter cited as Bird, *Born Female*).

15. Leo Kanowitz, *Women and the Law*. Albuquerque, N.M.: University of New Mexico Press, 1969, p. 104.

16. Information provided by the Institute for Studies on Equality, Sacramento, California, and Stop ERA, Southern California Division, Riverside, California.

17. See notes 33, 34 and 35, chapter 3.

18. The communism and ERA association and the charge that ERA will destroy the American way of life are routinely made by Stop ERA spokespeople; e.g., Mary Schmitz v. Gloria Allred debate, Pasadena City College, Pasadena, Calif., May 14, 1977.

19. Bambrough, *The Philosophy of Aristotle*, pp. 387–388.

20. Flexner, *Century of Struggle*, p. 46.

21. *Ibid.*, p. 75.

Chapter 5

1. The first Married Women's Act was enacted in Mississippi in 1839. Other states soon followed and by the 1850's these acts, sometimes also known as Married Women's Property Acts, removed much of the legal subjugation of women to their husbands, by granting them the right to contract, to sue and be sued in their own names, to manage and control the property they had brought into the marriage, and to hire themselves out for paid employment without their husband's permission. For a discussion of the feminist struggle for these reforms, see Flexner, *Century of Struggle*, chapter 4.

2. Flexner, *Century of Struggle*, p. 131.

3. Bird, *Born Female*, p. 28.

4. For a comprehensive discussion of the struggle of American women to gain access to education, see Mabel Newcomer, *A Century of Higher Education for American Women*. New York: Harper, 1959.

5. *Ibid.*, chapter 2, particularly pp. 25–32. The arguments against the education of women ranged from the popularly believed and "scientifically established" principle that women

are mentally inferior to men to concern that women were too frail to stand the physical strain of study, which it was said would cause them brain fever, and, if they survived and still managed to have children, would surely result in unhealthy offspring.

6. Bird, *Born Female*, p. 26.
7. *Equal Pay Act of 1963*, 29 U.S.C., Section 206 (1964).
8. *Civil Rights Act of 1964* (Pub. Law 88–352, Section 701–716, 78 Stat. 241, 42 U.S.C. Section 2000e (1964).
9. *1969 Handbook on Working Women*, U.S. Department of Labor, Women's Bureau Bulletin No. 294, p. 15 (hereinafter cited as *1969 Handbook on Working Women*).
10. *Ibid.*
11. *Underutilization of Women Workers*, U.S. Department of Labor, Women's Bureau, 1971 (Revised), p. 9 (hereinafter cited as *Underutilization of Women Workers*).
12. *Ibid.*, p. 11.
13. *1969 Handbook on Working Women*, chapter 1.
14. *Underutilization of Women Workers*, p. iv.
15. Bird, *Born Female*, chapter 4.
16. *The Earnings Gap Between Women and Men*, p. 1.
17. *Ibid.*, pp. 2–3.
18. *Women Workers Today*, U.S. Department of Labor, Women's Bureau, Washington, D.C., 1976, p. 8.
19. See note 5, chapter 1, and *Monthly Vital Statistics Report*, National Center for Health Statistics, Rockville, Md., March 4, 1976 and April 20, 1976.
20. *Wyman v. James* 27 L.Ed. 408, 91 S.Ct. 381 (1971).
21. Fred Bruning, "How to Put Your Man on a Pedestal," *Los Angeles Times*, July 13, 1972.
22. Simone de Beauvoir, *The Second Sex*, New York: Modern Library, 1968 (hereinafter cited as de Beauvoir, *The Second Sex*).
23. John Kenneth Galbraith, *Economics and the Public Purpose*, Boston, Mass.: Houghton Mifflin, 1973.
24. *Ibid.*, pp. 30–31.
25. Blanche Crozier, "Constitutionality of Discrimination Based on Sex." 15 *Boston L.Rev.* 723, 727–8 (1935).
26. Alfred Adler, *What Life Should Mean to You*, New York: Capricorn Books, 1931, p. 267 (hereinafter cited as Adler, *What Life Should Mean to You*).

Chapter 6

1. Jessie Bernard, *The Future of Marriage*, New York: Bantam Books, 1972, (hereinafter cited as Bernard, *The Future of Marriage*); Carl Rogers, *Becoming Partners*, New York: Dela-

corte Press, 1972 (hereinafter cited as Rogers, *Becoming Partners*).

2. See, e.g., Marabel Morgan, *The Total Woman*, Fleming, N.J.: H. Revell Co., 1973.

3. *Ibid.*, pp. 96–97.

4. *Ibid.*, p. 82.

5. De Beauvoir, *The Second Sex*, pp. xxiii–xxiv.

6. *Ibid.*

7. Gunnar Myrdal, *An American Dilemma*, New York: Harper, 1944, Appendix 5.

8. Kate Millett, *Sexual Politics*, New York: Doubleday, 1970, p. 57.

9. Alfred Adler, *Understanding Human Nature*, Greenwich, Conn.: Fawcett Publications, 1954, p. 111 (hereinafter cited as Adler, *Understanding Human Nature*).

10. *Ibid.*, pp. 111–112, 122.

11. Bernard, *The Future of Marriage.*

12. Ashley Montagu, *The Natural Superiority of Women*, New York: Collier Books, 1970.

13. Bernard, *The Future of Marriage*, p. 53.

14. *Ibid.*, p. 301.

15. Adler, *Understanding Human Nature*, pp. 120–121.

16. *Ibid.*, p. 120.

17. *Ibid.*, p. 121.

18. Richard J. Gelles, *The Violent Home: A Study of Physical Aggression Between Husbands and Wives*, Beverly Hills, Calif.: Sage Publications, 1972; review by Charles Hennon in *Journal of Marriage and the Family*, May 1977, p. 433.

19. Susan Brownmiller, *Against Our Will: Men, Women, and Rape*, New York: Simon and Schuster, 1975, pp. 201, 212–229 (hereinafter cited as Brownmiller, *Against Our Will*).

20. *Ibid.*, p. 9.

21. *Ibid.*, p. 10.

22. *Ibid.*, pp. 300–312.

23. *Ibid.*, pp. 23–118.

24. Robert T. Francoeur and Anna K. Francoeur, eds., *The Future of Sex Relations*, Englewood Cliffs, N.J.: Prentice-Hall, 1974, p. ix.

25. Robert S. Weiss, "Marriage and the Family in the Near Future," in *The Family and Its Future*, Katherine Elliott, ed., London: J. and A. Churchill, 1970, p. 57 (hereinafter cited as Weiss, "Marriage and the Family").

26. Ronald Fletcher, "The Making of the Modern Family," in *The Family and Its Future*, Katherine Elliott, ed., London: J. and A. Churchill, 1970, p. 184. (hereinafter cited as Fletcher, "The Making of the Modern Family").

27. Weiss, "Marriage and the Family," p. 57.

28. Rogers, *Becoming Partners.*

29. Ben B. Lindsey and Wainwright Evans, *Companionate Marriage*, New York: Arno, 1972. A reissue of a book originally published in 1927, indicating how far back this term was coined.

30. William H. Masters, Virginia E. Johnson, *et al.*, *The Pleasure Bond: A New Look at Sexuality and Commitment*, Boston, Mass.: Little, Brown, 1975.

31. Robert Thamm, *Beyond Marriage and the Nuclear Family*, San Francisco, Calif.: Canfield Press, 1975, p. 166.

32. Fletcher, "The Making of the Modern Family," p. 184.

33. *Ibid.*

34. *Ibid.*, p. 183.

35. See note 6, chapter 1.

Part II

Introduction

1. Legal opinions of J. William Heckman, Counsel of the Subcommittee on Constitutional Amendments of the U.S. Senate and John M. Harmon, Assistant Attorney General, Office of Legal Counsel, Department of Justice, 1977.

2. E.g., The American Law Division of the Congressional Research Service, the Legal Counsel of the U.S. Senate Judiciary Committee, and the Attorneys General of the states of Idaho, Michigan and California.

3. *Coleman v. Miller*, 307 U.S. 433 (1939).

4. House Resolution Number 9703, introduced October 20, 1977.

5. Legal opinion of John M. Harmon, Assistant Attorney General, Office of Legal Counsel, Department of Justice, 1977.

6. Letter from Congresswoman Holtzman to Dr. Marjorie Bell Chambers, President, AAUW, October 18, 1977. Another interesting historical footnote is that, according to *Do It NOW* (the official journal of the National Organization for Women), the extension idea was first thought up by two law students, Katherine Timlin and Alice Bennett, both Hollywood NOW chapter members. The two women researched the concept and presented it to the NOW leadership, which took it from there, spearheading a vigorous campaign for a Congressional extension of time.

Chapter 7

Many of the ideas in this chapter result from my survey of ERA activists July 1977 through February 1978. The contributions are credited in the text and are not noted. The notes that follow are solely for comments or to cite other sources.

1. An example of survey response that will not be further footnoted. See explanation above.
2. Correspondence to Elizabeth Snyder, October 1977.
3. "Tribute to Alice Paul" by Winona McGuire, August 7, 1977.
4. *Ibid.*
5. ERAmerica.
6. This status report is based on the excellent up-dates provided by ERAmerica.

Chapter 8

As with chapter 7 notes, only sources other than my 1977–78 survey are cited here. (See preamble to chapter 7 notes for full explanation.)
1. *Time*, November 14, 1977, p. ₂8.
2. *Chicago Tribune*, October 23, 1977, p. 10.
3. *Time*, November 14, 1977, p. 28.
4. ERAmerica.
5. *Chicago Tribune*, October 23, 1977, pp. 1, 10.
6. Letter from James W. Hurst, Vice President, Atlanta Convention and Visitors' Bureau, to Charles A. Kiesler, Executive Officer, APA, August 18, 1977.
7. Letter from Edward J. McNeill, Executive Vice President, New Orleans Tourist and Convention Commission, to Charles Kiesler, APA, August 17, 1977.
8. Statement by Dr. J. D. Goodchilds, Council Representative for Division 9 (SPSSI), to APA Council, August 28, 1977.
9. *Los Angeles Times*, November 21, 1977, Part I, pp. 3, 28, 29.
10. Quoted in *ERA Illinois Newsletter*, Vol. 2, No. 1, October 1977, p. 4.
11. *Ibid.*, p. 3.

Chapter 9

As with previous chapters 7 and 8, only sources other than my survey are cited. (See preamble to chapter 7 notes for full explanation.)
1. *To Form a More Perfect Union: Justice for American Women.* Report of the National Commission on the Observance of International Women's Year, U.S. Government Printing Office, Washington, D.C., 1976 (hereinafter cited as *To Form a More Perfect Union*), p. 108.
2. The International Women's Year Oral History Project, organized by Constance Ashton Myers of the University of South Carolina at Aiken, Aiken, South Carolina, is recording the historically important IWY Conference of 1977.

3. *To Form a More Perfect Union*, p. 252.
4. *Ibid.*, p. 30.
5. *Proposed National Plan of Action*, National Women's Conference, Houston, Texas, November 18–21, Department of State, Washington, D.C., 1977 (hereinafter cited as *Proposed National Plan of Action*).
6. *Los Angeles Times*, November 20, Part II, p. 3.
7. *Ibid.*
8. *Ibid.*
9. Winona McGuire, "The Family and the Proposed Equal Rights Amendment," draft for pamphlet, December 7, 1977.
10. "ERA a Bread and Butter Issue." AAUW pamphlet.
11. "200 Years is Long Enough . . ." ERAmerica pamphlet.
12. *Majority Report of the Senate Judiciary Committee.*
13. "The Church, Religion, and the Equal Rights Amendment," p. 3.
14. *Ibid.*
15. *Ibid.*
16. *Ibid.*, quoting Leonard Swidler, "Jesus Was a Feminist."
17. Correspondence with author, January 1978.
18. I am indebted to B.J. Cling, Coordinator of the Women's Committee of Screen Actors' Guild and Chairperson, Celebrity Committee of the California ERA Coalition, for aid in developing this list.

Chapter 10

As with previous chapters 7, 8, and 9, only sources other than my survey are cited. (See preamble to chapter 7 notes.)
1. Information provided by the Institute for Studies in Equality, Sacramento, California, and Stop ERA, Southern California Division, Riverside, California.
2. Facts about Hargis are from "Billy James Hargis Riding High Again," by Brian J. Kelly in the *Los Angeles Times*, November 26, 1977, p. 13.
3. *Los Angeles Times*, November 11, 1977, Part IV, p. 11.
4. "Who's Phyllis Schlafly?" and "Schlafly's Role in Four Foundations Gives Researchers Tangled $$ Trial" in *Homefront* (publication of the Institute for American Democracy), February, 1973, pp. 9, 10.
5. "What Makes Phyllis Run," by Saundra Saperstein, *Chicago Daily News*, November 5–6, 1977.
6. *Ibid.*
7. *Homefront*, February, 1973, pp. 9, 10.
8. *Chicago Daily News*, November 5–6, 1977.
9. *ERA Monitor*, January 21, 1976. An excellent publication of the Equal Rights Amendment Project, Sacramento, California,

which has unfortunately discontinued publication as of this writing.

10. *ERA: A Trojan Horse.*

11. *Time,* April 25, 1977, p. 89.

12. From an anti-ERA pamphlet sent out by Senator Orrin Hatch accompanying a letter dated March 16, 1977. The letter solicited contributions from his "fellow supporters" of the Conservative Caucus to help underwrite the Stop-ERA campaign in Florida.

13. *To Form a More Perfect Union,* p. 30.

14. Letter from Governor Daniel J. Evans, February 5, 1976, quoted in *To Form a More Perfect Union,* p. 28.

15. *Ibid.,* p. 30.

16. *The Advocate,* November 16, 1977.

17. *ERA Illinois Newsletter,* Vol. 2, No. 2, November 1977, p. 1.

18. Source: ERAmerica.

19. From "Why Religious Groups Support the Equal Rights Amendment." Published by the Religious Committee for the ERA, an interfaith organization of more than 20 Catholic, Protestant and Jewish groups.

20. From "Catholics and the Equal Rights Amendment." Published by NETWORK, national organization of Catholic women.

21. Source: ERAmerica.

22. *Ibid.*

23. Based in part on the work of the Equal Rights Amendment Project, Anita Miller, Project Director, and data from NOW.

Chapter 11

1. *Majority Report of the Senate Judiciary Committee,* p. 15.

2. *Wyoming Constitution,* Article 1, Section 9 (1889) and *Utah Constitution,* Article IV, Section 1 (1895).

3. *To Form a More Perfect Union,* p. 29.

4. *Ibid.,* p. 27.

5. *DiFlorido v. DiFlorido,* 459 Pa. 641, 331 A.2d. 1974 (1975).

6. *To Form a More Perfect Union,* p. 27.

7. *Ibid.,* p. 28.

8. *Ibid.*

9. *Ibid.,* p. 27.

10. *Ibid.,* p. 28.

11. *Ibid.,* p. 29.

12. For a detailed analysis of the various state ERAs and how these have been interpreted, see Lujuana W. Treadwell and Nancy W. Page, *Equal Rights Revision: The Experience of the State Constitutions,* 65 California Law Review 1086.

13. See, e.g., *Darrin v. Gould*, 85 Wash.2d. 859, 540 P. 2d. 882 (1975) and *Commonwealth v. Pennsylvania Interscholastic Athletics Association*, 18 Pa. Commw.Ct. 45, 334 A.2d. 839 (1975).
14. *People v. Ellis*, 57 Ill.2d. 127, 311 N.E.2d 98 (1974).
15. *Ibid.*, pp. 132–133.

Chapter 12

1. *McGuire v. McGuire*, 157 Neb. 226, 59 N.W. 336 (1953).
2. *Ibid.*
3. *Ibid.*
4. *Majority Report of the Senate Judiciary Committee*, p. 17.
5. *Ibid.*
6. Section 36-102, *Revised Codes of Montana*, 1975.
7. For a good discussion of trial court decisions in this area, see *Twelfth Survey of Florida Law*, 30 U. Miami Law Review 107.
8. *Lash v. Lash*, 307 So.2d. 241 (1975).
9. *DiFlorido v. DiFlorido*, 459 Pa. 641, 331 A.2d 174 (1975).
10. *Ibid.*
11. *Cooper v. Cooper*, 513 S.W.2d. 22 (Ct. of Civil Appeals, 1974).
12. *Ibid.*
13. *Ibid.*
14. Market Opinion Research, Detroit, Michigan: Study done for IWY Commission in 1975, cited in *To Form a More Perfect Union*, p. 338.
15. *Female Family Heads*, U.S. Department of Commerce, Bureau of the Census, Washington, D.C., July 1974, p. 6.
16. *Statistical Abstract of the U.S.*, U.S. Department of Commerce, Bureau of the Census, 1974, p. 38.
17. *To Form a More Perfect Union*, pp. 13–14.
18. *Ibid.*
19. *Ibid.*
20. For the history of these changes, see Riane Tennenhaus Eisler, *Dissolution: No-Fault Divorce, Marriage, and the Future of Women*, New York: McGraw-Hill, 1977, p. 86.
21. Cited in *Proposed National Plan of Action*, p. 28.
22. *The Earnings Gap Between Women and Men*, Women's Bureau, U.S. Department of Labor, Washington, D.C., 1976, p. 1.
23. *Proposed National Plan of Action*, p. 3.
24. *To Form a More Perfect Union*, p. 305.
25. *Minorities and Women as Government Contractors*, U.S. Civil Rights Commission, May 1975, cited in *To Form a More Perfect Union*, p. 305.

26. *Ibid.*
27. *Ibid.*, p. 306.
28. *Ibid.*, pp. 183–184.
29. *Ibid.*, p. 49.
30. *Ibid.*, p. 170.
31. *Ibid.*
32. *Ibid.*, pp. 53, 54.
33. *Proposed National Plan of Action*, p. 9.
34. *To Form a More Perfect Union*, p. 253; for a comprehensive discussion of television and its effects, see George Comstock, *et al., Television and Human Behavior*, New York: Columbia University Press, in press as of S/78.
35. *Window Dressing: Women and Minorities in Television*, U.S. Commission on Civil Rights, August 1977, cited in *Proposed National Plan of Action*, p. 25.
36. *To Form a More Perfect Union*, p. 253.
37. George Gerbner, "Sociological Perspectives on Effects Research Needs," a paper presented during the symposium *Television Effects: Research Needs from an Action Perspective*, annual meeting of the American Psychological Association, San Francisco, Calif., August 27, 1977.
38. *Proposed National Plan of Action*, p. 25.
39. *Ibid.*, p. 10.
40. *To Form a More Perfect Union*, p. 187.
41. *Ibid.*, p. 344.
42. *Ibid.*, pp. 345–348.
43. 18 PSCA 3106, repealed.
44. *To Form a More Perfect Union*, p. 295.
45. *Proposed National Plan of Action*, p. 27.
46. *To Form a More Perfect Union*, p. 293.
47. *Ibid.*, p. 225.
48. *Proposed National Plan of Action*, p. 28.
49. *Ibid.*
50. *Georgia Code Ann.*, Section 53-501, 1974.
51. Flexner, *Century of Struggle*, p. 75.

Chapter 13

1. Judge Charles ("Carl") Muecke, as quoted in *Time*, February 24, 1975, p. 12.
2. Voir dire is the preliminary questioning by the attorneys for prosecution or plaintiff and defense (and also where necessary, the judge) of prospective jurors to try to weed out those who have prejudices that might affect their verdicts.
3. For an excellent discussion of this area, to which I am indebted for some of the analysis in the text, see Dale Rogers

Marshall and Janell Anderson, "Implementation and the Equal Rights Amendment," *Impact ERA*, pp. 46–57.

4. *Griffin v. Illinois*, 351 U.S. 12 (1956).

5. *Gideon v. Wainwright*, 372 U.S. 335 (1963).

6. Publications of the Citizens' Advisory Council on the Status of Women may be obtained by writing to the Citizens' Advisory Council on the Status of Women, Room 1336, Department of Labor Building, Washington, D.C. 20210.

7. Law reviews and law journals are usually available either at county law libraries or law school libraries.

8. Jane Trahey, *On Women and Power*, New York: Rawson Associates, Inc., 1977 (hereinafter cited as Trahey, *On Women and Power*).

9. Caroline Bird with Sara Welles Briller, *Born Female*, New York: Pocket Books, 1968.

10. Riane Tennenhaus Eisler, *Dissolution: No-Fault Divorce, Marriage, and the Future of Women*. New York: McGraw-Hill, 1977.

11. *Impact ERA*, Millbrae, Calif.: Les Femmes Publishing, 1976.

12. The Equal Rights Amendment Project, directed by Anita Miller, is a project of the California Commission on the Status of Women, Sacramento, California.

13. *To Form a More Perfect Union: Justice for American Women*, the Report of the National Commission on the Observance of International Women's Year, 1976, is available from the U.S. Government Printing Office, Washington, D.C. 20402.

Chapter 14

1. *The New York Times*, May 1, 1977, cited in Trahey, *On Women and Power*, p. 256.

2. Trahey, *On Women and Power*, pp. 242–243.

Index

Index

www.ingramcontent.com/pod-product-compliance
Lightning Source LLC
Chambersburg PA
CBHW030424290526
45786CB00001B/125